THE GOOD SEX BOOK

Recovering and Discovering Your Sexual Self

SHERRY SEDGWICK, M. Ed., AASECT, CADAC

CompCare®Publishers

2415 Annapolis Lane
Minneapolis, Minnesota 55441

Library of Congress Cataloging-in-Publication Data

Sedgwick, Sherry, 1941-
    The Good Sex Book: Recovering and Discovering Your Sexual Self / Sherry
    Sedgwick.
        p. cm.
    Includes bibliographical references and index.
    ISBN 0-89638-245-1:
    1. Sex therapy.   2. Compulsive behavior—Patients—Rehabilitation.
    3. Sex. I. Title.

RC5557.S37 1992
616.85'83—dc20
    91-6914
    CIP

Cover design by Susan Rinek

Inquiries, orders, and catalog requests should be addressed to:
CompCare Publishers
2415 Annapolis Lane
Minneapolis, Minnesota 55441
612-559-4800
Call toll free 1-800-328-3330

6   5   4   3   2   1
97 96 95 94 93 92

To Christopher Michael Johnson
November 19, 1990
my grandson
our future

Contents

PART TWO
Facing Sexual Challenges on the Path

PART THREE
The Journey of Sexual Recovery

Foreword

I believe I had to write this book. As a sex therapist and addictions counselor, I have adapted the Twelve Steps of Alcoholics Anonymous to recovery from sexual dysfunction and integrated them with other principles that help people discover and recover their sexual selves. I want to share the success of this combination therapy program and help quell and explain the shame, fear, and pain experienced by men and women whose addictive and sexual issues have disrupted their lives. I needed to write this book because so many of my clients requested it; because so many individuals have been and can be helped; because it addresses issues that haunt multitudes of people today.

Although much information has been written about addiction and sexual disorders, few people have recognized the critical association between them. This connection is the revelation of a lifetime, the "missing link" in addictions and sexual dysfunction recovery. The insight has changed my practice and benefitted my clients more than any other component of my education or experience.

Editor's Note

This book describes a program that treats the associated problems of sexual issues and addictions, not only dependence on chemicals, but other compulsive behaviors such as eating disorders and codependency. One of the plan's principal elements is the application of the Twelve Step model to intractable sexual problems. The other strand is the process developed by sex therapists, which re-educates clients in small increments, first introducing them to their own bodies' sensations and gradually enlarging clients' range of comfort to include emotional and then physical intimacy with partners. Because of the taboos of our culture, some of the author's suggestions may surprise readers. It is the client in Sherry Sedgwick's Good Sex Program, however, and the reader of her book, who ultimately decides which sexual activities are satisfying and compatible with personal values.

The sketches of clients and their problems have been reconstructed from actual cases in Sherry Sedgwick's clinical experience, the facts rearranged to make identification of actual people impossible.

Acknowledgments

Martha Gore, my literary agent, guided me when I had despaired that my plan would ever come to fruition. She recognized its value and provided the impetus and organization to make it possible.

This book could not have existed without Deborah Mitchell, my writer, whose perseverance and willingness to learn and trust in the process made the work possible.

During the past twelve years, my clients have been teaching me what they wanted me to share in this book. Their courage, openness, honesty, and willingness to recover at any cost have inspired me.

Jerry Burks carried me through this arduous project with consistent, loving energy when I could no longer continue. Ed Torrejon, my personal trainer, helped me through the tough times. Wendy Smith, my secretary, helped me with her cheerfulness and ability to handle the everyday details of my life. John Moritz's spiritual strength provided a source. June Kobriger's ability to organize the unorganizable freed me to write. The memory of Dr. Bill Routt and his spirit endure in me. My patient editor, Jane R. Thomas, knew from the beginning what it meant for a person who came from Battle Creek, Michigan to write this book.

Dr. Patrick Carnes, Sarah Sandburg, and the Advanced Study Group at the Institute for Behavioral Medicine have given me acceptance and support that helped me to spread my wings and discover how far I could stretch. Carole Thompson unfailingly provided me with nonjudgmental love, wit, and healthy recovery.

I especially appreciate Dr. Jennifer Schneider for her continuing encouragement and her prompt reading of the manuscript; Dr. Bernice Roberts and Jeannie Rigaud, who took time to read the first draft and make helpful suggestions; and Drs. W.H. Masters and V.E. Johnson, whose pioneering research built the foundations of sex therapy.

I give my personal thanks to my sons, Kirk Sedgwick Johnson, Erik Fielding Johnson, and Matthew Warfield, who have unfailingly and unconditionally loved and supported me through this project and so many before, no matter how audacious my aspirations or goals, often at great sacrifice.

Finally, I need to acknowledge the disease of alcoholism as I stand before it in awe, humility, and grudging gratitude. Without this disease, which is so prevalent in my family, I would have been either a suburban housewife or a boutique owner on Rodeo Drive. For better or worse, out of my recovery here is where the universe has taken me instead.

PART ONE

Preparing the Map

Making the Connection: Addiction and Sexual Dysfunction Are Often Associated

The most rewarding aspect of being a sex therapist and addictions counselor is the joy of helping people recover and discover their sexual selves. Every day new people arrive in my office, desperate for relief from addictive behaviors and sexual problems. They bring stories of deep sexual shame, anguish, abuse, and dysfunction. Millions carry these burdens, afraid they are alone and isolated with them. Believing they may be insane, they fear that no one can help or even understand them.

Among these people are adult children of alcoholics, cocaine users, pill abusers, overeaters, codependents, co-sex addicts, romance addicts, sex addicts, and alcoholics, as well as survivors of incest, child abuse, ritual abuse, and other trauma. They are mothers, fathers, neighbors, cousins, aunts, uncles, friends, and coworkers. They are all kinds of people, the walking wounded.

As I talked with my clients, I gradually understood that an intricate and logical connection exists between sexual dysfunction and addictions. I began to see that

- Alcoholism is one presenting issue of impotence

- A client treated repeatedly for cocaine addiction continued to relapse because his primary sex addiction had not been treated

- Adult children of alcoholics I was treating were unable to form healthy bonds in intimate relationships because they never saw them at home.

- Addictive substances were being used to mask sexual dysfunction and the enduring pain of past sexual trauma.

My growing understanding of such connections resulted in a unique therapeutic approach that integrates addictions therapy with sex therapy and raises clients' awareness of the interconnections. Once I applied this approach, treatment success increased tenfold. Men and women who had previously believed they would never heal were able to rebuild their lives.

The experience of one client demonstrates what happens in recovery. When Bob, the child of an alcoholic, first came to see me, he suffered from a common combination of addictions: cocaine and sex. He was a virgin and a compulsive masturbator. As we worked on the Twelve Steps for his cocaine addiction, I promised him that once his disease was in remission he would recover healthy sexual function.

"Recover?" he said. "You mean discover! I never had it in the first place!"

Bob was right; you can't *recover* what you never had, but you can *discover* it. Growing up in a dysfunctional family results in misinformation about normal sexual behavior and a lack of normal experiences. People who begin drinking and drugging early in their teens and those who survive incest or other trauma similarly lack the role models, guidelines, and other pictures of normality which they otherwise would have acquired in childhood.

The path to sexual fulfillment is recovery from a dysfunctional life, not a narrow treatment for a particular addiction or sexual issue. People who free themselves from the clutches of disease find that healthy sexuality and intimacy open up a new world. Leaving addictive behavior behind and working toward healthy sexuality, they may feel shy and embarrassed at first, blushing like a teenager exploring partners and themselves. As they recover, they become more comfortable. They become acquainted with their own spiritual hearts.

Sexual Secrets

The loss of sobriety months or years after treatment often results from an inability to deal with issues that remain hidden. As the saying goes, "We are as sick as our secrets." Considering how frantically many people guard and protect them, this statement applies especially to sexual secrets. Besides the shame of having grown up in a troubled family, difficulties and concerns about sexuality need to be dealt with because they undermine recovery.

Many men and women are tackling their fear and shame about the sexual skeletons in their closets. They come to me with all kinds of concerns: can't get it up, can't get it in, not coming at all, coming too soon, compulsive masturbation, cross-dressing, can't get enough, exhibitionism, and the ever-popular "Not to-night, I have a headache"—lack of sexual desire. They may be in recovery from one or more addictive diseases, and yet face another. Most of them can't understand why some sexual issues are still hanging around, disrupting their lives, when they had expected healing and recovery from the Twelve Steps of AA. To stay sober, or to overcome bulimia, codependency, or compulsive exercising, addicts need to confront their sexual issues.

The Good Sex Program

The serenity described in this book is attainable by anyone, regardless of the severity of the problem. Using the Good Sex Program, men and women, gay and straight, become happier than they ever thought possible. They discover all they have been, are, want to be, and can be.

The process begins with the realization that our society forbids discussion of sex. Therefore, people have a very hard time getting in touch with authentic feelings about their sexuality. The connection between sexual trouble and addictive behaviors clearly shows the importance of sexual discovery to overall recovery from addictions. But the Twelve Step program of AA is only half the picture.

No one can solve sexual and addictive problems separately, because their relationship is interwoven. The Good Sex Program takes account of that critical interconnection. It also recognizes that **sexual recovery is possible only if the other existing addictive behaviors are in remission**. (These addictive issues are so crucial that they are discussed separately in later chapters.) Once the addiction is checked, my clients can begin to use the Good Sex Program, which incorporates the Twelve Steps of AA adapted for sexual recovery. It lovingly combines various therapeutic techniques and tools that allow them to discover their unique sexual selves. This form of behavioral sex therapy is a valuable addition to the Twelve Steps of AA and is based on the work of traditional behavior therapists.[1]

Women and men need not be afraid to learn about themselves. Self-knowledge permits sexual enjoyment, free from preconceived notions of what love and sex "should be." People willing to learn, feel, and express their own personal sexuality begin healing and building themselves. The Good Sex Program is a gradual journey.

I currently consult at treatment centers and with clinicians across the country about integrating sexual recovery with addictions recovery. My message to them and to my readers is plain: if someone is having sexual problems, look at possible addictive causes; if someone is recovering from alcoholism or other addictions, do not neglect the essential sexual healing. Because people with sexual issues live in shame, fear, and pain, they feel isolated and often believe they will be ostracized and ridiculed if others know the truth about them. But the conjunction of addiction and sexual dysfunction is very common.

Discovering Spirituality

This book opens up the subject of sexuality so that people can safely identify and learn about their issues and discover they are not alone. Indeed, they are far from being alone: 83 percent of the American population have been members of alcoholic, addictive, codependent, or otherwise dysfunctional families.[2] Many who feel unique in their isolation are in fact among the majority.

The discovery process begins with finding the singular being that exists in each person. An inherent element of recovery from any issue is the connection made between inner self and others. This link acknowledges each individual's spirituality, which concerns unconditional love and self-worth. The opening of spirituality uncovers the inner light everyone possesses, and then manifests that light to the world. When individuals allow themselves to feel the joy that comes as they find their unique selves,

---

1. Helen Singer Kaplan, *The New Sex Therapy* (New York: Brunner/Mazel, 1974), 181-82.

2. Patrick Carnes, *Don't Call It Love: Recovery from Sexual Addiction* (New York: Bantam, 1991), 35.

they begin to experience their spiritual and sexual energy. As they identify and put aside the preconceived notions, fears, expectations, performance anxieties, and other obstructions between themselves and experience, they become fully themselves. Then they learn to connect with others who are on that spiritual path of healthy sexual recovery.

No matter how much anyone has suffered, every person's positive desire for health can win over addictive disease. People need to get in touch with that kernel of health and let it grow. Once the process begins, separation of sexual identity from identity itself is impossible. True identity transcends all the pictures of who people "should be," when they connect with another person in a healthy sexual way.

Sex: Problem, Symptom, or Both?

When clients first come to me with sexual issues, they are usually unaware that one or more underlying issues could be associated with their sexual symptoms. They want to deal with their impotence, lack of sexual desire, or unmanageable affairs. Because I am a sex therapist as well as a certified addictions counselor, I can address both addiction issues and sexual issues; and that is the vital connection that needs to be made. **Before any recovery program begins, I need to determine which issue is the most life-threatening.**

One of the first things my clients do is tell me what they are doing in all areas—not only in their sex lives, but also at work, play, and home—in order to see what issues they have. If a man tells me he has little or no sexual desire, could it be from a cocaine or heroin habit? Is it from sexual trauma he is not aware of, or is he an adult child of an alcoholic who has trust issues? When a woman tells me that she never has an orgasm, is she hiding an eating disorder? Does her partner have an alcohol or drug problem? Any one or all of these basic underlying problems can masquerade as inhibited sexual desire or the inability to have an orgasm, so I ask many questions to determine what we are facing.

When Addiction Is the Primary Issue

Couples often complain about inhibited sexual desire. When Pat and Bob came to see me, they had been married for seven years and had consulted several therapists. Both partners told me together and separately that they loved one another and wanted to make their marriage work, but they fought constantly.

After our third session, it was apparent that Bob was an addict. During a vicious argument they had in our session, Pat stormed out of the room. Bob stayed behind and screamed, "I'm in total despair. It's hopeless." When I encouraged him to continue, he revealed that he had been stockpiling pills and was prepared to kill himself if their sexual relationship did not improve.

Bob had been abusing prescription drugs daily for years "to cope with this unforgiving woman." Clearly, his drug addiction was life-threatening; therefore, we addressed it immediately. Bob's chemical dependency and Pat's codependency were brought into remission. Then they began using sex therapy and addictions therapy together to begin a sexual recovery.

On the surface, Pat and Bob believed they had only a sexual problem, Pat's lack of desire, that they wanted "fixed." Like many other couples, they discovered during therapy that the obvious sexual issue was interconnected with addiction. Which issue is the primary problem depends on the people involved and must be individually determined. Once clients begin to explore their issues and discuss them, the priorities become evident.

When the Sexual Issue Is Primary

Sometimes the sexual problem is the primary or most life-threatening issue. Luke, a handsome and nervous young man, had consulted the best treatment centers for his cocaine addiction before he came to me, but none had been able to help him stay sober. I discovered that Luke's cocaine use was connected to his compulsive masturbation, which he engaged in six to twenty hours every day.

Until Luke dealt with his sexual addiction, he continued to relapse with cocaine. He had spent enormous time and money feeling more and more hopeless and desperate. Now Luke and I are working together on his sex addiction and cocaine addiction, and he has remained chemically free for more than one year.

The Road to Healthy Sexuality

The path to healthy sexuality is clear. First, men and women need remission of their addictions. Then they can begin the Good Sex Program, which incorporates the Twelve Steps of AA adapted for sexual recovery. As people work through the Twelve Steps for sexual recovery, they lay the foundation for the rest of their journey through the program. The benefit of this process is its adaptability to the unique needs of each individual who uses it, as will be demonstrated in the following pages.

Starting with the Twelve-Step Program

For decades, members of Alcoholics Anonymous have used the Twelve Steps to address their addiction. As a starting point, the Twelve Steps of AA are ideal for addictive behaviors—alcohol, sex, drugs, eating, spending, work, exercise, volunteerism. When only alcoholics were in these programs, and trying to keep them sober was all anyone did, the Steps worked very well. But about two-and-a-half to five years after starting their programs, people began to relapse when their unaddressed core issues (such as codependency or consequences of trauma or having been children of alcoholics) finally surfaced. Some were victims of rape or child molestation. Others had a biologic mood disorder: this condition occurs in one of ten men and one of four women in recovery. Still others had sex addictions, such as compulsive masturbation, which these men and women could not stop even when they were in recovery from their chemical dependency.

After someone has achieved years of recovery, statements like, "You need more meetings," or "You're not turning it over to your Higher Power," or "You need to do another Fourth Step" are not adequate explanations of relapse. Clearly, other issues needed to be addressed that previously had not been identified.

Determining the Core Issue

Not every client comes in with a life-threatening issue. But the most important factor must be faced first. Some people are best helped when the Twelve Steps of AA and the Good Sex Program are used simultaneously. Others start with the Twelve Steps and integrate sexual discovery after working through the first few Steps for their addiction. Because every man and woman is unique, with different issues, each program must be approached as a new adventure on the road. Often clients practice two or more addictive behaviors—alcohol dependency and an eating disorder,

THE TWELVE STEPS OF ALCOHOLICS ANONYMOUS

1. We admitted we were powerless over alcohol—that our lives had become unmanageable.

2. Came to believe that a Power greater than ourselves could restore us to sanity.

3. Made a decision to turn our will and our lives over to the care of God, as we understood Him.

4. Made a searching and fearless moral inventory of ourselves.

5. Admitted to God, to ourselves, and to another human being the exact nature of our wrongs.

6. Were entirely ready to have God remove all these defects of character.

7. Humbly asked Him to remove our shortcomings.

8. Made a list of all persons we had harmed, and became willing to make amends to them all.

9. Made direct amends to such people wherever possible, except when to do so would injure them or others.

10. Continued to take personal inventory and when we werewrong, promptly admitted it.

11. Sought through prayer and meditation to improve ourconscious contact with God, as we understood Him, praying only for knowledge of His will for us and the power to carry that out.

12. Having had a spiritual awakening as the result of these steps, we tried to carry this message to alcoholics, and to practice these principles in all our affairs.

say, or codependency and compulsive spending. Finding these addictive issues is like peeling away the leaves of an artichoke one at a time to reveal the heart.

Much of what I saw during my development as a therapist were sexual symptoms—impotence, inability to have an orgasm, gender identity issues, lack of sexual desire, fear of sex. A therapist must determine what the sexual issue is and whether it is the symptom or the core issue. If it is the symptom, what does it symptomize, and what is its source?

For example, if a woman comes in complaining of painful intercourse, I first need to determine whether this problem is a symptom or the core issue. If she fears sex because her mother told her as a child that it was a filthy, disgusting act, then her pain is a symptom of her core issue, which may be sexual aversion, low self-esteem, or gender shame. No addictive behavior lies at the root of her sexual dysfunction. As she works the Twelve Steps of AA for sexual recovery, she discovers herself first—surrendering to her issue so she can work on it.

However, her painful intercourse may be the result of a codependency issue. She may be unconsciously controlling her vaginal contractions as a way to say, "I won't have sex while my husband is drunk," or she may be so ashamed about an abortion that she unconsciously denies herself sexual pleasure. If any of these situations exists, then her sexual dysfunction might symptomize a larger issue—sexual trauma, co-sex addiction, or chemical dependency. She then needs to bring the addiction into remission first, or while simultaneously addressing the sexual issues.

Who Needs the Good Sex Program?

An imaginary couple, a typical composite of the couples who have worked with me, helps to show how the link between addiction and sexual dysfunction works. This fictitious couple also portrays the ordinary characteristics of the diseases that afflict my clients. Gustave and Geneviere are not freaks. They are like our friends, our employers, or the people next door; they are like ourselves.

Gustave and Geneviere are in their mid-forties and have been married for twenty years. Their three children are fifteen, twelve, and eight years old. Gustave, a professor at a state university, is a child of upper-middle-class parents. He is also a codependent and a co-sex addict. His father was an alcoholic, a workaholic, and a well-known business leader in his community. His mother was a codependent, a compulsive overeater, and an incest survivor. Gustave is the eldest, with two sisters.

Gustave soon learned to take the place of his father in his mother's life, a covert sort of incest. During his father's frequent business trips, Gustave's mother often took him to bed with her. Gustave also helped her raise his two sisters, playing the role of father. He grew up with the characteristics of adult children of alcoholics, such as feeling responsible for others' happiness. At an early age, he learned to medicate painful feelings with food.

Gustave was a superachiever, especially in school. He earned a bachelor's degree at a state university and completed a doctorate at a prestigious eastern university, where he fell in love with Geneviere. Because he had concentrated most of his energy on his career aspirations, Geneviere was only his second girlfriend.

She had all the attributes Gustave desired in a woman: she was spontaneous, sexually experienced, outgoing, socially adept, accommodating; she also adored him. They married when Gustave found his first teaching job, and he established his academic reputation while Geneviere raised their children. When their youngest child was born, he had achieved a full professorship. He slowly became aware, however, that he was eating too much and working too hard. Going home was not as pleasant as it once had been because he never knew what the emotional climate would be. He started finding ways to stay away, immersing himself in his work and his life at the university.

Seven years ago, Gustave's friends confronted him about his wife's alcoholism. He arranged for her to enter inpatient treatment, which she completed successfully in a month, for her alcoholism and prescription drug abuse. At the same time, Gustave began addressing his own codependency. Attending Al-Anon, Overeaters Anonymous (OA), Adult Children of Alcoholics (ACoA) meetings, he began to glimpse what forces drove him. He realized that he had been using work and compulsive overeating to reduce his stress, and he had dealt well with those issues two years before coming to see me.

Gustave was not the first client who told me that he and his wife had had a great sexual relationship in the past. Although it had been "pretty crazy" in her using days, he said, since she had gotten clean and sober, it had "tapered off to nothing during the last two years." He felt that, at forty-five, he was too young to throw in the towel; he wanted a way to be sexual with his wife.

"So many issues cleared up in recovery, both individually and for our whole family," he said. He had watched the emotional climate of the family improve, and his and Geneviere's recovery programs were working well. He felt their family was emotionally closer than ever. Everything was perfect except the lack of sex.

Geneviere told me another story. She had grown up in a midwestern middle-class household. Her father was a salesman, her mother a homemaker. She was the middle child, with an older brother and a younger sister. Her father was a binge alcoholic who drank during business trips. Her mother was an untreated compulsive overeater, a codependent, and an incest survivor.

For as long as Geneviere could remember, she said, "I lived in fear and shame." She discovered at an early age that eating and masturbating were two ways to relieve that stress. When she was ten or eleven, Geneviere also discovered alcohol and pills in her parents' medicine cabinet. Their use relieved stress and enabled her to feel whole and proud for the first time. She had her first blackout at thirteen. She became a different person while using, a person she liked instead of one who was fearful or ashamed. "I was the life of the party," she told me.

Whereas Gustave had been a late bloomer sexually, Geneviere began socializing with boys at thirteen; she first had intercourse during a blackout at fifteen. When she discovered she had been sexual but couldn't remember anything about it, she felt that she had been a "'bad girl.' But now that it was done, I might as well continue." By the time she met Gustave, she had "probably been sexual with more than twenty-five men." Gustave attracted Geneviere with his stability, responsibility, caretaking, and professional aspirations. For a woman of her era, he represented success.

Geneviere and Gustave had the dream wedding. She worked as a nurse for a few years and then became a mother, in the role of professor's wife. When situations were too stressful, she turned to alcohol. Then she asked many different doctors for pills "for my nerves." In the meantime, Gustave was too busy to see what was happening to Geneviere. On the surface everything looked fine, but inside trouble was brewing.

Ten years into the marriage, Geneviere launched an intensely lustful affair, seemingly out of resentment that Gustave was gone so much. Soon she lost control. Her drinking and pill abuse escalated until Gustave and the children did not want to be home with her. She went to treatment after concerned people intervened.

In early recovery, Geneviere worked a seven-day-per-week program. She restored her professional status and began nursing again. She began to work on her eating disorder and had three years of recovery from anorexia and bulimia. Many of her issues as an adult child, and other codependency characteristics were addressed. She felt that in her drinking days she had been a sex addict. She had not believed it was a problem for her in recovery, so she had not attended any meetings for sex addicts.

When she came to see me, she was hurt, angry, and frustrated. After having worked so hard in the Twelve Step program of AA, the sexual component of her relationship with Gustave remained elusive. She said Gustave was "too demanding" and that this conflict might propel a slip back into drinking. Although the affair had ended many years prior, she still thought about the man. She wanted to get on with life and not make sex a big deal.

By the time I saw them, Geneviere was not able to have orgasms and she had no sexual desire. Gustave was experiencing premature ejaculation when he felt any sexual desire at all. The Good Sex Program provided a framework for sorting out this complex tangle of interconnected issues in which Geneviere and Gustave were individually ensnared, and for strengthening the ties that bound their relationship. Issues that had resisted treatment and made their marriage untenable gradually gave way to a new mutual understanding and appreciation.

Men and Women Facing Their Sexual Selves Today

How do individuals like Gustave and Geneviere begin to recover their sexual selves? How can they get help from the insanity of their drinking and drugging, addictive sex, and eating disorders? How can they break through their sexual dysfunctions to achieve healthy sexuality?

First I look at the concomitant issues. Gustave had been a

codependent, a co-sex addict, a compulsive overeater, and an adult child of an alcoholic. In addition to the effects of having grown up in an alcoholic household, Geneviere had several chemical dependencies and a sex addiction to compulsive masturbation which dated from childhood. They came to me with these issues in recovery, but not all of my clients do. This couple's stories clearly show how recovery from various addictive issues can leave individuals sober but not sexually healthy. The story of Gustave and Geneviere's recovery process begins in chapter 11, and we follow their progress throughout the book.

One crucial lesson of their experience bears repeating: individuals need to recover from their addictions before they can work with the Good Sex Program. Chapters 3 through 9 and their appendices describe these addictive behaviors in detail. This information is offered for several reasons. For women and men who have brought their addictions into remission, the facts can provide an understanding that their sexual secrets are shared by many others. Knowing they are not alone gives people hope and strength while they proceed with the Good Sex Program. The chapters which describe addictions are also intended to help readers who have not brought their addictions into remission or who want to identify themselves or someone else who may be living with these concerns.

The Solution: The Good Sex Program

Some therapists call the disease of chemical dependency an intimacy disorder or a dissociative state, because individuals often abuse alcohol and other drugs as a way to deal with their feelings of shame, anger, and fear about intimacy and sexuality. The same can be said for those who abuse sex, food, other people, money, and exercise.

Where Are the Heroes?

Many people lack the role models or heroes who help men and women with addictive behaviors learn to be healthy in their sexuality. Some addicts may remember an alcoholic father's abuses, or a mother who warned them about the horrors of sex. Others may feel a great deal of shame about sexual trauma or hold very rigid beliefs about good and bad or right and wrong. They buy into the mass media's stereotyped myths of sexuality: the cocky swaggering of John Wayne, the cool self-assured stare of the Marlboro man, the seductive pout of Madonna. None of these figures is the most functional model of healthy sexual expression.

Many men and women have dealt with childhood trauma, shame, or rigid morality partly by wearing masks—false selves behind which they could hide and feel safe. Often, they medicated their pain with addiction. What they believed to be true about a certain idea or situation, such as the normal behavior of a father or the appearance of healthy sexuality, became fixed in their memories and they carried those misconceptions into adulthood.

Beginning the Program

After clients start working the Twelve Steps of AA and their

addiction is checked, they can begin to use the Good Sex Program. This plan helps them learn what healthy sexuality is and how to feel good about themselves as sexual men and women. Clients progress by gradual stages, beginning with a second passage through the Twelve Steps, this time adapting them to sexual recovery. (In order to avoid confusion, especially since both the stages and the Steps which they incorporate are numbered, this book will refer to parts of the Good Sex Program as "Stage 1" and so on; the Twelve Steps will be called "Step One" and so on.) The Good Sex Program comprises the following stages:

1. Giving the Problems and Symptoms a Name

2. What Sexual Wellness Looks Like

3. To Be versus To Do: Discovering Sexual Identity by Nurturing the Self

4. Awakening the Senses and Discovering Self-Sensuality

5. Discovering Sexual Identity through Masturbation

6. Fore-Foreplay: Discovering Sexual Potential by Nurturing Partners

7. The Scenic Route: Discovering Sexual Potential by Sharing Sensuality with a Partner

8. Closed for Repairs: Discovering Sexual Potential by Sharing Sexuality without Intercourse

9. Going All the Way: Discovering Sexual Potential through Genital Sex with a Partner

10. The Ultimate Orgasm: Discovering Sexual Potential When Spirituality and Sexuality Merge

The various stages will be summarized here to provide the reader with a foothold; a detailed description of both the Good Sex Stages and the adapted Twelve Steps begins in chapter 11.

Stage 1
Giving the Problems and Symptoms a Name

Here and in Stage 2, men and women become acquainted with themselves and their problems and work through the Twelve Steps of AA once again, this time adapting them for sexual recovery. The therapy that clients do now is crucial, because they need to know and understand what they are dealing with before they can act.

As people realize what is wrong sexually and integrate that knowledge, they come to understand that sex and sexuality are not the same. I offer them the definition of healthy sexuality so they know where to begin their discovery process. Sex is a behavior, the manifestation of sexual feelings, while sexuality is a total state of being. *Healthy* sexuality is the positive energy of a person's basic nature, from birth through death, as a male or female, gay or straight. It is interwoven in a person's intellectual, emotional, physical, spiritual, and interpersonal functioning. It is a positive statement of self. Both men and women have many choices about how they wish to direct this energy throughout their life cycle.

Stage 2
What Sexual Wellness Looks Like

In the second stage of the program, clients assess their own attitudes and consider what constitutes healthy sexuality. They explore the influences of socially ingrained assumptions in their lives as they review their maturation. At this stage, people strive to see clearly where they stand today, and where they want to be.

Although Stages 1 and 2 have been divided here for the sake of clarity, working them in practice is an integrated and very fluid process that varies from client to client. Thus, conversations about sexual wellness occur not only in Stage 2, but throughout Stage 1 and thereafter. Both stages incorporate the adapted Twelve Steps, summarized briefly below, but these Steps remain vital to the program throughout.

The Twelve Steps for Sexual Recovery

1. **We admitted we were powerless over our sex issue(s)—that our lives had become unmanageable.**

My clients surrender, acknowledging their powerlessness over their sexual addiction, romance addiction, incest, ritual abuse, nonorgasmia, premature ejaculation, or inhibited sexual desire. This First Step is also called the "honesty step." Here people acknowledge *what is*: "That's who I am today."

2. **Came to believe that a Power greater than ourselves could restore us to sanity**.

Step Two involves sexual issues a great deal because it says "restore us to sanity," and most Americans truly are insane about sexuality. The greater power that people turn to may be God, clergy, nature, spouse, therapist, sponsor, confidant, a Twelve Step group, or the universe. People need to look outside of themselves for encouragement, understanding, and support because alone they have not been capable of restoring themselves to sanity.

3. **Made a decision to turn our will and our lives over to the care of God, as we understood Him**.

The first three Steps are often summarized as "We can't, He can, so let Him." The Third Step is also a surrender step—where individuals turn their will and lives over to the care of their higher power, as they understand it. These men and women seek their higher power's energy in beginning to heal because they have depleted their own.

4. **Made a searching and fearless inventory of ourselves**.

This Step is crucial to sexual recovery. Most men and women are always telling me what's wrong with other persons—too fat, too passive, too inhibited, too smelly, and so on. Here clients learn to stop pointing the finger at others, take a look at themselves, and begin to realize they can change only themselves.

5. **Admitted to God, to ourselves, and to another human being the exact nature of our wrongs**.

Honestly confronting themselves and admitting what they find to their higher power, therapist, sponsor, and themselves relieves clients of terrible burdens. Although facing the facts can be frightening, it also is a freeing growth process that allows them to separate themselves from the pain and go beyond it.

6. **Were entirely ready to have God remove all these defects of character**.

When they have finally listed all the actions and attitudes that have hindered their sexuality, many people want an instant fix. They need to be *ready* for these character defects to be removed; faults are not necessarily removed when people think they should be. Gradually these women and men build humility, serenity, and a sense of unity with the universe.

7. **Humbly asked Him to remove our shortcomings**.

The Seventh Step simply means that, in all humility, simplicity, and surrender, women and men ask that their faults be removed. When God removes them is His business, not theirs, much as they may protest.

8. **Made a list of all persons we had harmed, and became willing to make amends to them all**.

The Eighth Step cleanses people with sexual issues. Some people make amends by firmly committing themselves not to repeat their past mistakes. Others feel so much guilt and shame about their actions that they need to make amends mostly to themselves; although other people have forgiven them, they themselves have not been able to do so.

9. **Made direct amends to such people whenever possible, except when to do so would injure them or others**.

Men and women need to be honest enough about what they've done, if they are to make amends for their having hurt their spouses, parents, children, and others. People need to be humble and honest to make amends. Those who have been victims need to make amends to themselves for not having spoken up or gone to the authorities, for having kept the secret of child abuse or molestation, for staying isolated, or for not trusting anyone since the incidents. These are wrongs that require amends, because they perpetuate the condition of victim.

10. **Continued to take personal inventory and when we were wrong, promptly admitted it**.

No one is perfect after the first time through the Steps or ever. A daily moral inventory identifies repeated old errors, which are just part of being human. When people own their humanity, then they can let mistakes pass. Aiming for an 80 percent "success rate"— getting it right 80 percent of the time—is a realistic working goal.

11. **Sought through prayer and meditation to improve our conscious contact with God, as we understood Him, praying only for knowledge of His will for us and the power to carry that out.**

    Spiritual healing is the only kind of healing that is effective in healing sexual issues. Men and women need to know that somehow things in the universe are fine the way they are. They need to surrender to the way life is, including their own. Finding the strength, support, and understanding to accept this reality, however, involves praying for the courage to follow the path of a higher power's will.

12. **Having had a spiritual awakening as the result of these Steps, we tried to carry this message to others and to practice these principles in all our affairs.**

    Those who are in recovery from sex addiction, incest, cross dressing, nonorgasmia, impotency, and other issues have been truly insane about sexuality. The Twelfth Step is about carrying the message of recovery to others. Recovering people can practice these principles in their daily activities, not only in the sexual dimension but also the other areas of their lives.

The Rest of the Program: A Brief Look

After clients have established a foundation by completing this initial part of the program, they progress to the next stages. The program can be tailored for individual needs, wants, and desires. Therefore, Part 3 of this book presents a detailed explanation of each stage, including examples of how Gustave and Geneviere used some of the tools, and ways men and women can develop their own programs. The following brief summary of the rest of the program completes the overview.

Stage 3
To Be versus To Do: Discovering Sexual Identity by Nurturing the Self

When clients reach Stage 3, they are ready to begin exploring, accepting, and celebrating their core. Using various techniques and affirmations, they learn how to nurture themselves and how to accept their sexuality.

Stage 4
Awakening the Senses and Discovering Self-Sensuality

If people allowed themselves fully to experience their five senses, they would live more exciting and fulfilling lives. The tools and techniques offered in Stage 4 help people make the connection with their senses and become comfortable with themselves as they experience these senses in new ways.

Stage 5
Discovering Sexual Identity through Masturbation

As I've worked with individuals and couples over the years, one thing has remained constant: the intense energy from fear, shame, and embarrassment about the "M" word—masturbation. Learning to be comfortable with masturbation is critical for most people because it is the area that many lie about or deny. During this stage, individuals learn how to masturbate without shame and how to use masturbation as a sexual alternative and a way to experience their bodies.

Stage 6
Fore-Foreplay: Discovering Sexual Potential by Nurturing Partners

In Stage 6, men and women, gay or straight, learn how to share with a partner the good feelings they have discovered in the previous stages. Communication is an integral part of this segment of the program. Here partners learn and practice skills involved in conflict resolution, processing past hurts and resentments, and relinquishing power struggles. This one is the "no sex" stage: a time-out for couples to get away from the cycle of failure they have been experiencing, a chance to learn how to be affectionate and have fun together without its leading to sexual intercourse.

Stage 7
The Scenic Route: Discovering Sexual Potential by Sharing Sensuality with a Partner

Starting from the time-out stage, couples need to progress slowly. Often they are in such a hurry to reach the Big O that they forget to appreciate the scenery along the way. In Stage 7, people learn how to share the sensuality they have learned. They discover what foreplay is, what it is not, and how to use all their senses in this sharing process.

Stage 8
Closed for Repairs: Discovering Sexual Potential by Sharing Sexuality without Intercourse

Our society tells us that if the penis or vagina does not work, there can be no sexuality. The truth is that men and women manifest their sexual energy in many ways. Stage 8 teaches the means by which everybody can be sexual without intercourse. Techniques are explored for achieving orgasm through the senses, including mutual masturbation, visual stimulation, and oral sex.

Stage 9
Going All the Way: Discovering Sexual Potential through Genital Sex with a Partner

Because sexual expression is a personal statement, I never ask my clients to do anything they are not comfortable doing or that would violate their beliefs. In Stage 9, men and women find, define, and redefine their comfort zones as they slowly incorporate new experiences, ideas, and behaviors into their sexuality. Genital sexuality—both penis-vagina intercourse and oral-genital activity—are explored as a joyous celebration of self.

Stage 10
The Ultimate Orgasm: Discovering Sexual Potential When Spirituality and Sexuality Merge

Many people equate spirituality with religion, but they are two different concepts. When clients first reach this stage and ask what spiritual sexuality is, I tell them it's when their higher power is with them in the bedroom.

Stage 10 encompasses the deep belief that sexuality and spirituality are intertwined. Spiritual and sexual energy are identical, originating in the center of every man and woman, a force people can use to affirm, celebrate, and transform themselves. The guidelines in this final stage enable men and women to discover the power at their core.

Looking at the Map

Now that the scenario has been presented and a destination has been chosen, it's time to look at the map of the journey. Once people familiarize themselves with the names of places they've been and where they're going, the path to healthy sexuality is clearer.

Giving the Symptoms and Problems a Name: Stage One

3

The terms *sexual dysfunction, sex addiction, co-sex addiction, sexual trauma*, and *intimacy issues* are phrases many people have heard. Like the implications of many other well-worn words, their true meanings are often confused or misunderstood. Many words and phrases associated with sexual dysfunction and sexuality appear repeatedly throughout this book. Later chapters explain in detail the association between specific addictive behaviors and sexual issues. This chapter introduces and explains these terms generally as a foundation of understanding and familiarity.

Sexual Dysfunction: A Look at the Symptoms

Sexual dysfunction is the condition in which sexual functioning, for physical or psychological reasons, does not operate in a healthy and optimal way. Complaints of sexual dysfunction range widely and vary in intensity. They come from every age, socioeconomic and religious group, regardless of sexual orientation, race, or gender. Symptoms may result from ignorance or misinformation; they might be caused by an underlying physiological condition; or they may be related to addictive or psychological behaviors or states.

Take It or Leave It: Inhibited Sexual Desire

Inhibited sexual desire is probably the most common symptom and complaint. For both men and women, it is an awareness that at one time they were more sexual and felt more sexual desire than they experience now, and they do not know why it has faded. Many people never had a sex drive in the first place and feel they are missing something. Psychological reasons for inhibited sexual desire often center in sexual trauma, anger, workaholism, power and control issues, poor communication or conflict resolution skills, or past hurts and resentments. Physiological causes include food or lack of it, alcohol, cocaine, heroin, and amphetamines.

Paula's story is typical. The attractive twenty-eight-year-old nurse had not been interested in sex during the entire five years of her marriage. For three years, she had been in recovery from alcoholism, but her sexual desire had not returned with sobriety as she had hoped.

The first thing I discovered was that Paula was an untreated manic-depressive. Prescription drug treatment eventually regulated her depression, but sexual desire did not return as it sometimes does. Paula revealed that, when she was a young child, her mother had pressured her into an endless stream of beauty pageants, but she could not remember much else about her childhood. I suspected sexual trauma. We worked together until some flashbacks and memories came back and we uncovered a history of sexual abuse by agents and pageant officials. At the same time, Paula asked her doctor to run a hormone level test. She was not producing testosterone, which is unusual in women her age except those who have undergone much trauma and stress. Paula began hormone therapy, and together we have been resolving her sexual trauma issues. She has recovered her sexual feelings and desires.

Virginity

More men and women are virgins than people realize. This misconception exists because many virgins do not want to admit they have not had intercourse for fear they will be ridiculed or labeled "gay." Often they have avoided sexual intercourse out of fear, shame, or anger. Or perhaps they were caught in an addictive behavior, and sex was not part of their lives.

I extend the concept of virginity to include two categories. True virginity is the state of men and women who have not had an intimate experience leading to sexual intercourse. Secondary virginity exists when they have stopped practicing an addiction like alcoholism and have not yet been sexual in sobriety. After they stop behaving as they did when their disease was active, they are suddenly faced with new identities. They are starting over, redefining their sexuality as well as other elements of self, and they don't know where to begin.

Some chemical dependents, codependents, romance addicts, sex addicts, and co-sex addicts have never been sexual or had sexual intercourse while in recovery. Once their sexual recovery begins, some of my clients report that they feel like teenagers or little kids again. Suddenly they are shy and don't know how to act, even though they had many lovers while under the influence of their addictions.

Mike turned his embarrassment into joy. When this healthy, single, thirty-five-year-old mechanic came to see me several years ago complaining that he was impotent, he had been sober for three years. I asked him to tell me what made him think he was impotent. "During my drinking days," he said, "whenever I picked up women, I could never perform." After recovery from his disease, he never tried again because he "couldn't stand the shame or humiliation while sober." But he insisted he was impotent and wanted to correct his condition so he could start socializing and find a wife.

At first Mike looked shocked and confused when I told him that he wasn't impotent—he was a virgin. He had started drinking at age thirteen and had never had sex. Through the miracle of recovery, today he is married and has discovered a healthy sexual relationship.

When the Thought of Sex Turns the Stomach: Sexual Aversion

Individuals who are repulsed by the thought of sex or seeing or hearing about it have the symptom called sexual aversion. Their lives revolve around avoiding anything sexual, which may include jobs, people, places, and even certain clothing. They may react by feeling nauseated, afraid, ashamed, and dirty. This reaction is usually consciously or unconsciously associated with sexual trauma.

Sarah was able to resolve a lifetime of sexual aversion. During her nine-year relationship with Paul, she had been completely turned off by the thought of sex. She also had been in recovery from alcoholism for eight years. Paul was unable to cope with the situation any longer and urged Sarah to seek help.

Her father had been an alcoholic and a sex addict. When she was about eight years old, Sarah had discovered his child pornography collection, which included sadomasochistic photographs. Whenever she had a sexual feeling, these images returned to haunt her, filling her with disgust. With Paul's support, we worked together to address her revulsion and discover her sexuality. Sarah and Paul have a stronger bond now because they addressed these issues together.

Can't Get It In: Vaginismus

Vaginismus is a condition in women who are not able to allow the penis or outside objects to penetrate the vagina, for whatever reason. Physiologically, the pubococcygeal muscles (those in the area of the vagina, clitoris, and anus) go into spasm and make entry impossible. Some unconscious psychological reasons include a desire to avoid a partner; fear of becoming pregnant; fear of growing up; stress; lack of sex education; or a preference for virginity until marriage. Other women fear remembering past sexual trauma. Vaginismus is the first sign many codependent women notice that indicates something is wrong for them.

Painful Intercourse (Dyspareunia)

Among the physical causes of painful intercourse for women are vaginal infections or genital injuries, such as tears, lacerations, bruises, or scar tissue from an episiotomy or an abortion. During menopause, the vagina's mucous membrane becomes fragile and thin and less lubricated from lack of estrogen, which may make penetration painful.

Some women and men have an allergic reaction to the plastic or rubber in condoms or diaphragms, or react to vaginal creams, foams, jellies, or suppositories. Serious medical causes for dyspareunia include a displaced or prolapsed uterus, endometriosis, polyps, cysts, or tumors in the reproductive system.

Psychological causes are common in women who are in addictive situations. Fear of sex, fear of a partner, anger, or unresolved abuse issues can make intercourse painful.

Lack of Orgasm (Nonorgasmia)

Nonorgasmia is seen mainly in women; it is said that between 30 percent and 50 percent of women are nonorgasmic at some point in their sexual lifecycle.[3] Some psychological reasons for lack of orgasm include fear of losing control, the belief that they don't deserve it, poor self-image, lack of assertive or communication skills, fear of intimacy, or lack of trust. Often people simply lack information about what orgasm is and what is necessary to achieve it. Nonorgasmia occurs in many women in addictive populations. It may be a primary condition in itself or the symptom of some other condition.

Limited Orgasmic Response

Some women may become sexually aroused but fail to lubricate, or they may lubricate but fail to experience orgasm. (See Appendix 3-1 for sexual response cycle.) Many women need more foreplay than their partners realize, and many men need more foreplay than women give them. Some women can have an orgasm when they use a vibrator, through masturbation, or with some partners and not others. Women with limited orgasmic response cannot consistently predict an orgasm in response to sexual stimulation.

Impotence

Impotence may result from both physiological and psychological causes. Whether it is itself a condition, or merely the symptom of some other problem, impotence is the inability to attain or maintain an erection that allows a man to masturbate to orgasm or to penetrate his partner. Erectile dysfunction, which is closely related to impotence, occurs when a man's penis can become erect but unexpectedly loses its rigidity. Physical causes of impotence which may originate in birth or childhood include polio or juvenile diabetes. Others that can occur at any age include spinal cord injury, renal disease, hypothyroidism, urinary and prostate disorders, high blood pressure and its medication, cirrhosis, or testicular atrophy (wasting away or degeneration of tissue) from

---

3. Lonnie Barbach, *For Each Other: Sharing Sexual Intimacy* (New York: New American Library, 1984), 13.

alcohol. Because alcohol kills liver and testicular cells, men may become permanently impotent from alcohol abuse.

Some men are afraid they will not perform well, talk themselves into thinking they can't, and therefore do not. This circular thinking is commonly called performance anxiety. Others have had a series of failures and are so afraid of failing again they will not even try. Some men may not make another attempt because they are angry or lack trust. Perhaps they cannot be honest about their lack of interest in their partner. In some relationships with a woman whose chemical dependency is active, a man may become impotent if she demands sex in drinking situations and he doesn't want to "prove" himself or condone her drinking.

Premature and Retarded Ejaculation

Premature and retarded ejaculation are two symptoms that need clarification. I define premature ejaculation as one which comes sooner than a man wishes *most of the time*. There is much disagreement over the exact length of time a man should be able to control his ejaculation before it is judged "premature." Some even gauge it by the number of thrusts. It is best to say that premature ejaculation is absence or loss of voluntary control over the orgasm and ejaculation, regardless of the time or number of thrusts.

Some men think they have premature ejaculation because they or their partners want them to stay hard for an hour, and they can do it for only forty-five minutes. They need to understand that perhaps these expectations are unrealistic.

Psychological causes of premature ejaculation include lack of education, as occurs when men have their first sexual experiences or use women as masturbatory objects. Stress, anger, anxiety, fatigue, sex after a long abstinence, and lack of self-confidence are also common causes. Premature ejaculation is common among alcoholics. They lose control over every facet in their lives, including their penises.

Retarded ejaculation occurs when a man wants to ejaculate and cannot, or when he keeps his erection far beyond the time when he chooses to ejaculate. This experience is common among marijuana users and adult children of alcoholics. Although such prolonged erection is the "dream" of many men and women, it can be a nightmare, because excess blood that remains in the penis for twenty-four hours or longer can cause permanent damage. Psychological reasons for retarded ejaculation include some men's inability to be vulnerable, fear of women, need to be perfect, and lack of trust in their partner.

"I-Hate-Who-I-Am" Homosexuality

Gay individuals who cannot accept that same-sex attraction is their true sexual preference are said to be "egodystonic." Many men and women deal with this self-hatred by becoming chemically dependent, hoping the feelings might go away. Sexual recovery depends on accepting who they are.

Gender Identity Issues

Men and women with this symptom know they are male or female, but they don't know how people of their gender behave. Gender identity issues may occur when children have had no adequate role models or have been told that their gender is somehow bad. I had a client named Maria, for example, whose mother, Olivia, was abused by her alcoholic husband. Olivia impressed upon her daughter that womanhood was a curse and predicted that Maria would end up in a situation similar to her own. Subsequently, Marie had talked herself into not being a woman, but she knew she was not a man. Although she hated her gender, she didn't know how else to be in the world.

When Sex Is the Problem

Some sexual dysfunctions have the potential to become addictive behaviors. I present them briefly here, because when they appear in the diagnostic history of a client, I determine whether they are addictive or life-threatening, or simply dysfunctions. A deeper explanation of these behaviors as addictions is in chapter 6 on sex and romance addicts.

Masturbation

Masturbation is a natural behavior that is observed even in infants. Teenagers typically masturbate as often as once or twice a day. Most adults masturbate consistently throughout their lives. When this normal behavior becomes unmanageable or is the focus of a person's life and a trigger for other uncontrollable behavior, however, it is a sex addiction.

Fantasy

Most people engage in some sexual fantasy or obsessive thinking about other persons, sometimes while masturbating. Fantasy can enrich sexual relationships and every individual's own sexuality. If it becomes the driving force in a person's life, then it is a sex addiction.

Pornography/Erotica

Written and pictorial material, videos, dial-a-porn, and computer sex designed specifically to elicit sexual responses can be classified as either pornography or erotica. Although the line between the two is controversial and defined by the eye of the beholder, this material is generally considered pornographic when it is degrading and dehumanizing. Erotica is sexually oriented material that has artistic or literary value. Some men and women use pornography or erotica while masturbating, to enhance solitary sex. Men seem to use and collect pornography more than women. It is a common element of sexually addictive behavior.

Prostitutes

Going to strip bars or peep shows and using prostitutes for sexual stimulation is common among straight, married men and is less common among gay men and heterosexual women. In many states, such behavior is a misdemeanor. It can become highly addictive and is one path of sex addiction.

Paraphilias

Paraphilias are sexually oriented activities engaged in by men and women who need to focus on or use unusual imagery or stimuli to experience sexual arousal. These behaviors include cross-dressing, indecent liberties, exhibitionism, voyeurism, fetishism, masochism and sadism, bestiality, self-mutilation, and pedophilia. These activities also have the potential to become addictive behaviors and are explained briefly below.

Cross-Dressing (Transvestism). Most cross-dressers are men who wear women's clothes to achieve sexual excitement, gratification, or a sense of well-being. Contrary to what many people believe, cross-dressers are usually heterosexual, married men. Women who cross-dress as men are rare. Because this behavior usually does not involve a partner, it is often undetected and easier to hide than other behaviors. It is somewhat common among active alcoholics and amphetamine users.

Peeping-Tom Compulsion (Voyeurism). This behavior (most common among men) involves secretly watching women and teenagers dress and undress, in showers or bathrooms, as well as observing sexual activity. It is a common sex addiction.

Exhibitionism. The traditional idea of the flasher as a man standing in the park dressed only in a raincoat comes to mind. Exhibitionism is the exposure of the body's private parts to unwilling and unsuspecting observers in an effort to achieve a sexual high. This behavior is another common sex addiction.

Indecent Liberties. Indecent liberties usually involves a man's violating another person's boundaries, usually a woman's, by touching her private parts without her consent. This aggression often occurs in crowds, at malls or ball games, and in crowded elevators, where it is easy to brush against the breast or thigh of unsuspecting victims.

Women's actions, however, go unnoticed in this area. Without asking, women touch, caress, or hug another adult or child. Men who "feel up" women are often accused of pawing and lechery, while such women are called loving, nurturing earth mothers. Generally, it is best for both men and women to get permission before physically touching another person.

Fetishism. Fetishism is a paraphilia in which sexual arousal is achieved by the substitution of a symbolic sexual object (rather than an activity, like most other paraphilias) for a love partner. More men than women engage in fetishism. The objects used include women's clothing (especially high-heeled shoes, nylons, panties, bras, vinyl clothes, and gloves), doorknobs, animals, diapers, or articles made of leather and rubber. Another fetish is practiced by people who are aroused by watching or participating in defecation and urination rituals.

Bestiality. Having sexual relationships with animals, behavior including masturbation of them, is called bestiality. Alfred Kinsey and his associates reported that 65 percent or more of teenage boys living in rural areas have had sex with animals (the statistics vary by region). Such behavior is not necessarily abnormal.[4] Sex with pets sometimes occurs among children and

---

4. Alfred C. Kinsey, Wardell B. Pomeroy, and Clyde E. Martin, *Sexual Behavior in the Human Male* (Philadelphia: WB Saunders, 1984), 671.

teenagers in alcoholic families because the family pet is the only source of nurturing and love. This activity may be itself a problem or a symptom of some other condition. Bestiality can become part of an addictive pattern.

Bondage, Sexual Masochism, and Sadism. Both men and women practice these behaviors. Masochists receive sexual pleasure from being hurt, either physically or mentally, by their partners. On the other hand, sadists derive sexual gratification from inflicting physical or psychological pain on their partners.

Sadistic and masochistic rituals often include bondage; individuals render partners helpless or they themselves prefer to be bound to achieve sexual gratification. All of these behaviors can become addictive.

Self-Mutilation. To achieve sexual highs, some men and women cut and puncture their skin, pull their hair out, put knives into the vagina, burn their skin with cigarettes, place objects in the rectum, pierce erotic areas such as the labia, or use asphyxiation. Carried to extremes, these behaviors obviously can cause permanent damage or death.

Pedophilia. Pedophilia is adults' use of children for sexual arousal. They may expose their genitals to children, masturbate in their presence, sexually fondle them, or engage in intercourse with them. (Incest as an addiction is described in chapter 5.)

Transsexuals: A Class by Themselves

Men and women who believe they are caught in the body of the opposite sex are called transsexuals. Often they wear the clothing typical of their preferred sex. They are so revolted by their own gender that they are willing to undergo extensive counseling, hormone treatment, and surgery to alter their sex.

Sexual Trauma

The survivors of any sexual abuse are among some of the most injured individuals I work with in therapy. These include survivors of incest (both covert and overt), child molestation, and rape. Adult victims of child molestation are seen in both sexes and in every category: alcoholics, chemically dependent individuals, codependents, and adult children of alcoholics.

Incest is sexual activity that occurs when there is a power imbalance between family members who are closely related by blood or affinity. In covert incest, the parent or family member does not touch or fondle the child. Other children are exposed to sexual acts or behaviors. Children who are fondled sexually or forced to have sexual intercourse with a family member are victims of overt incest.

Rape is a crime of violence. The prime motivation of rapists is rage against their victims and a desire to dominate, hurt, and humiliate. Various forms include marital, acquaintance, date, and stranger rape.

Co-sex Addiction

A sex addiction is characterized by the use of sex as a drug, when a person's sexual desires are out of control and have made life unmanageable. Co-sex addicts see sex as love. They are codependents who may or may not become aroused sexually. They do whatever their partners want to get sex or to feel loved. Many times they control or conceal their partners' sexual actions and give in to demands, only to feel empty, degraded, ashamed, angry, and disgusted afterward. Their relationships with their partners often lack intimacy, trust, and commitment.

It is often difficult to determine whether someone is a sex addict, a co-sex addict, a romance addict, or a combination. Some people are all three.

Sexual Preference Confusion

This sexual problem occurs when men and women do not know whether they are gay or straight. Many people in early recovery are confused, especially if they also have an addictive disease that began early in adolescence when they had not worked out their sexual identity. They remain uncertain about their sexual preference in sobriety, even thirty years later.

For Charles, it was more than forty years. He was a married Catholic grandfather, fifty-seven years old, who came to see me after he had been sober for one year. He called me one day, saying, "I can't go on living with the fear that I'm gay." He was afraid he was attracted to young boys.

When we met, I discovered that he had begun drinking at age thirteen, the age when same-sex thoughts and feelings commonly emerge in normal adolescents. He was emotionally and sexually frozen at age thirteen. We worked through these issues until he was aware that he had simply missed going through many of the psychosexual stages in his life because of his drinking.

Fear of Being Gay: Homophobia

Excessive fear of being gay is a syndrome that occurs in some recovering men and women. They may have had same-sex thoughts, feelings, or behaviors while actively in their disease, and may not be aware that many straight people have had such experiences. Homophobia is common among alcoholics and appears in both straight and gay individuals.

Romance Addicts

Individuals who seek the euphoria of falling in love are romance addicts. When people fall in love, a chemical change occurs that creates a high. Romance addicts are addicted to the euphoria of falling in love: it is their drug. Later the high fades, and they need to find a different person or an object to get the high back.

Amy, an attractive college senior, kept searching for that high. When she came to me seeking help for her romance addiction, she made a contract with me agreeing that she would have no contact with attractive, available men for a given period of time. Because Amy needed her fix and had agreed not to pursue men, she decided she was a lesbian and began to seek out women. We changed the contract so that attractive, available women also were excluded. Unfortunately, Amy so needed the fix that she then focused her attention on animals and considered involving herself in bestiality. At that point, she could see her disease and realized that she had hit bottom.

Multitudes of other people like Amy suffer from the conditions summarized in this chapter. This basic terminology of sexuality and sexual dysfunction provides a foundation for what follows. These terms appear repeatedly in subsequent discussions of specific addictive behaviors and the sexual issues that often appear with them.

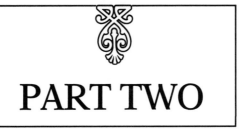

PART TWO

Facing Sexual Challenges on the Path

I've Got to Be the Only One: Chemically Dependent Men and Women

4

"I'm here because my wife insisted that we needed help," admitted Thomas, a successful thirty-four-year-old land developer. He had earned a million dollars a year for four years and was a recovering cocaine addict and alcoholic. His wife, Clara, wanted children. Although she had accepted her husband's lack of sexual interest during his cocaine days, now that he had been sober for two years, she was becoming disturbed because their sex life had not resumed.

As I interviewed Thomas alone, it became clear that his substance abuse and workaholism days were, in part, an attempt to run away from the fact that he had date-raped two women while under the influence and that he had sexually abused two young girls when he was a teenager. The intense shame, guilt, and worthlessness he felt now, in recovery, prevented a healthy sexual relationship. Every time he had sexual feelings, incredible shame came up; Thomas had used his drugs to medicate this feeling. Now in sobriety, his inhibited sexual desire was the presenting "problem to be fixed."

Dealing with the Shame

"I can't stand the unbearable shame of it all," Thomas often repeated as his sexual feelings emerged during our sessions together. This overwhelming feeling, called "toxic shame" by John Bradshaw in *Healing the Shame That Binds You*, can be life-destroying. Natural shame, in contrast, is a healthy emotion that lets people know they are human and therefore not perfect; this knowledge enables them to accept their unavoidable mistakes. Healthy shame helps men and women keep their feet firmly planted and set their boundaries. Thomas, however, was experiencing the shame that hides in an individual's deep dark recesses. The hopeful part of Thomas's story is that he gradually realized as he progressed through sexual recovery that he could break through the shame. He could expect recovery from his inhibited sexual desire and could experience the joy of sexual wholeness as he and Clara worked toward a healthy sexual relationship.

The Sexual Dysfunction Tells Me What People Are Using

Like many of my clients who have substance abuse issues, Thomas's drug of choice was easy to pinpoint, a hypothesis based on the sexual dysfunction he and Clara asked me to "fix." Many cocaine users tell me that when they started using cocaine, their sex lives improved. They had "incredible, all-night sex," they could last longer, they were intensely sexual, and cocaine was "the best aphrodisiac" imaginable. During the middle and late stages of abuse, however, sexual desire and activity had diminished and usually disappeared. Far from the hot-and-heavy sex, continued abuse interrupts sexual desire and eventually turns it off.

The Altered State of Chemical Dependency

When men and women are actively using chemicals, they are in an altered state, psychologically and physiologically. (See Appendices 4-1 and 4-2 for characteristics of chemical dependency and ways to recognize it.) Many men can accept that, during their drug-dependent days, this altered state affected their lives as they became more unbalanced about their jobs, finances, physical health, relationships, and other life circumstances. But when they find that their sex lives also are dysfunctional, they do not recognize that this distortion is also part of their disease.

It is natural for chemically addicted women and men to feel their sexuality is askew. They may not know whether they are gay or straight. They may use prostitutes, masturbate in public, molest a child, feel no sexual desire, or be unable to become erect or ejaculate. The good news is that this behavior does not necessarily indicate what sobriety will be like.

What You See Is Not What You'll Get

Men and women in recovery need to know that they are not alone with their issues. Every recovering person I have met has questions about what sobriety will be like. If sexual interest does not return after a period of sobriety, or if a recovering person becomes too sexual or feels fear or aversion about sex, it is time to ask for an evaluation by a therapist trained to determine physical or psychological causes for the dysfunction. People can get broken here, too, and sometimes they need some outside help to fix themselves. When they consult with a sex therapist who understands the interrelationship between addiction issues and sexual issues, recovering individuals can work through a sexual recovery program to reach a level of sexual wholeness and wellness that was never possible while they abused chemicals.

A Look at the Drugs of Choice

The common drugs men and women are using are described below. Some of the effects of these substances apply to both genders; others affect men and not women, or vice versa. (Also see Appendix 4-3, "Effects of Drugs on Sexual Function.")

Depressants

Depressant drugs, also known as downers, include barbiturates and methaqualone. In low doses, their effects are similar to those of alcohol: inhibitions are lowered, and users experience a mild high. As the dosage increases, the depressant effect increases, while sexual desire and activity rapidly decrease.

Alcohol: The Great Culprit of Sexual Dysfunction.

One of the depressants, alcohol, has for centuries been reported to be the greatest inhibitor of healthy sexuality. Alcohol has a great depressing effect because it is almost completely metabolized in the body, and that process takes a long time. Its effects are long-lasting and generally uncontrollable. "That drink went right to my head" is not just a flippant remark. Alcohol affects the ability to think clearly, lowers the level of blood flow to the brain, dulls the senses, and turns motor abilities into disabilities, including slowed reflexes, staggering, and loss of balance and consciousness. (See Appendix 4-4, "Progression and Recovery of the Alcoholic and the Disease of Alcoholism.")

The behavior changes are caused by alcohol's ability to impair the areas of the brain responsible for these functions. The effects, which vary among individuals, range from drowsiness to aggressiveness, or even belligerence. Alcohol can make people feel they are Don Juan or Lolita, and "anything goes." However, although many alcoholics *feel* increased sexual desire, wishing does not make it so; sexual performance actually decreases.

Ralph certainly related to the frustration this combination of decreased performance and increased desire can bring. He is a fifty-five-year-old military officer and widower who, since his wife's death, had relied increasingly on alcohol to deal with his grief. During the few years preceding her death from cancer, they had not had sex.

When Ralph started dating again, he discovered that, although his sexual desire was strong, his ability to perform was weak; he was impotent. Convinced that this condition was permanent, he became suicidal. He told me over the phone that if I couldn't "fix" his erection, he had nothing to live for. I reassured him that in most cases of impotence caused by alcohol, men completely recover.

Ralph believed he could not stop drinking because he could not deal with his pain and the shame of being impotent. He wanted to deny that he needed to stop drinking for his potency to return. Eventually he admitted that his way was not working and agreed to try something different. After six weeks of sobriety, he noticed his first early morning erections; within four months he could function fully with his new girlfriend.

Stimulants: Cocaine

When I ask a cocaine addict who is still actively using, "How's your sex life?" he usually replies, "What sex life? My sex life is my drug." Perhaps that's why they call cocaine "the lady." During the early stages of the disease process, cocaine users experience an increased interest in sex; some have multiple and spontaneous orgasms and prolonged endurance. Those who abuse amphetamines, another stimulant, report similar effects. These "benefits" are short-lived, however. After prolonged use, cocaine reduces production of the brain's chemicals that are responsible for normal sexual functioning. These hormone changes result in depression and a loss of sexual desire.

Words of encouragement are important here if permanent damage has not been done. Cocaine addicts usually see an improvement in sexual functioning after two to three weeks of complete cocaine abstinence. Abstaining from cocaine means eventually leaving behind all the other effects of abuse as well: loss of appetite, paranoia, hypertension, irregular heart beat, irritability, and insomnia.

Psychedelics: Marijuana

There are more than ninety types of marijuana, each containing varying amounts of active ingredients. It is no wonder that the effects on smokers vary as well. Some users report decreased sexual desire and performance, while others claim it improves both desire and performance. Most marijuana smokers do agree, however, that it enhances the sensation of touch.

When a man tells me that he has retarded ejaculation or little interest in sex, the next question I ask him is, "How much do you smoke?" and he knows I'm referring to marijuana. Like cocaine, marijuana enhances sex in the beginning, but loss of erection, loss of sexual desire, and inability to achieve an orgasm occur in later stages of use.

A few marijuana users mistakenly still believe that marijuana is not addicting. In addition to its damaging effects on sexual desire and performance, the benzopyrene present in the drug also causes depression and apathy, contributes to infertility, damages sperm cells, increases the incidence of miscarriages and birth defects, and imbalances hormones during women's premenstrual period.

Narcotics

Narcotics, such as heroin, morphine, and methadone have the same effects as cocaine. In the beginning, users report increased sexual activity, which in later stages diminishes to a minimum.

This effect is likely caused by reduction of the testosterone level, which dampens sexual desire and causes impotence or delayed orgasm. In women, heroin can eliminate menstrual periods and interest in sex, and prevent pregnancy.

Inhalants: Amyl Nitrite

This substance has been used to treat heart pain for more than one hundred years, although nitroglycerin has essentially replaced it. On the street, amyl nitrite is known as "poppers." Inhaled, it rapidly decreases blood pressure. Although it reportedly increases sexual desire when ingested, this effect is believed to be caused by the dizziness that results from the rapid fall in blood pressure after its use. Use of amyl nitrite is risky in those with a heart or respiratory condition.

Hallucinogens

LSD (lysergic acid), PCP (phencyclidine hydrochloride), and "magic mushrooms" are among the drugs that cause hallucinations. Reports of their effects on sexual function vary, with some users reporting increased desire and others claiming desire is reduced. The effects of these drugs include dizziness, weakness, nausea, blurred vision, rapid mood changes, body distortions, visual hallucinations, and difficulty in thinking. Hallucinogens can also harm a fetus: the association between LSD use and damage to chromosomes, leading to birth defects and a high incidence of miscarriages, has been noted since the late '60s.

Common Sexual Issues among the Chemically Dependent

Chemically dependent men and women seek help for a variety of sexual issues. Some of the most common sexual difficulties are explained below. Both addicts and their partners can benefit from understanding these issues.

Cross-Dressing and Chemically Dependent Men

"I must talk to you or I'll kill myself" was my introduction to Stewart, a chemically dependent married man in his twenties who called me one day at about ten in the morning. He had awakened from a drunken stupor in a man's apartment, dressed as a woman. He had no idea how he had gotten there. After seeing himself in the mirror, he looked in the telephone book under sex therapist, removed the dress and makeup, and took a cab to my office. Stewart didn't realize he was an alcoholic, but he had been so shocked that he realized his life was unmanageable. He decided to enter treatment.

Stewart is not alone. Cross-dressing occurs among chemically dependent men, especially those addicted to speed and alcohol, but not exclusively those drugs. Another cross-dresser, Joshua, was a twenty-six-year-old man who had just become sober after thirteen years of marijuana abuse. The secrets related to his cross-dressing became too much for him to bear. He came to me fearful that he would never have a healthy relationship and that he was doomed to a life of isolation in sobriety. As Joshua grew stronger in his drug recovery, he also developed skills in forming relationships with women, including sexual skills, and the sexual excitement associated with cross-dressing diminished greatly.

Premature Ejaculation and Impotency

Along with increased sexual desire among alcoholics often comes frustration from the inability to satisfy that desire. Premature ejaculation and impotence are the primary sexual dysfunctions that actively drinking alcoholic men experience. These men go to their meetings and tell how their lives were out of control in every way, but they are too afraid to share the secret of what happened (or didn't happen) sexually. They think they are alone and that nobody would understand. They tell me about their shame and sense of isolation.

Most men experience an impotency cycle during their drinking days that makes them fear they will not be able to "get it up." This worry prompts them to fortify themselves with a couple of extra drinks, which further hinders their attempts, which in turn further lowers self-confidence and raises anxiety. Then they drink even more to medicate those feelings. Some men continue in this impotency cycle for many years. By the time they get sober, some have been impotent for five to ten years or more. Even if physiologic damage has not caused impotence, they have built up so much anxiety about their sexual ability and have lost so much self-esteem that they have convinced themselves they must remain impotent. A psychological cycle has firmly been established.

"Not Tonight—I Have a Headache": Inhibited Sexual Desire in Men

Small amounts of alcohol have a sedative effect, which reduces inhibitions and increases libido. But during the later stages of disease, the excessive drinking done by alcoholics causes the opposite effect. Diminished sexual drive or its complete absence may result from damage to the hormonal system that occurs during alcohol and other drug use. Heavy drinking kills brain, liver, and testicular cells. When these cells die, the testicles shrink and shut down production of the male hormone, testosterone. The liver filters the female hormone estrogen, which all men have in small amounts. Liver damage results in improper filtration and consequently increases the estrogen levels. These hormonal changes lead to a loss of sex drive and the appearance of feminine signs, such as enlarged breasts and loss of facial and body hair. Alcoholics also often have nutritional deficiencies and experience fatigue and depression.

"Not Tonight—I Have a Headache": Inhibited Sexual Desire inWomen

Contrary to the myth that promiscuity, sex, and drugs go hand in hand in alcoholic women, the reverse seems to be true just as often. Inhibited sexual desire is probably the biggest presenting issue for women in recovery. Women alcoholics commonly report that they started using alcohol and other drugs in response to feelings about having been molested as children, to deal with date rape, to cope with shyness and inhibitions, or to "forget I'm female."

This statement came from Darlene, a recovering alcoholic housewife: "Being a woman was never a very safe or joyful state for my mother, my older sisters, or myself, because my father put us through so much abuse. But what could I do about it? Physically I'm a woman, but I didn't want what came with it."

Marguerite, on the other hand, had been promiscuous in her drinking and drugging days. When she came to see me, this nurse was thirty-two years old and three years into recovery from alcohol. She said, "I feel like I am in a sexual wasteland."

46

She had not been sexual with anyone since she got sober. In the later stages of her drinking, she had become a prostitute to pay for her drugs. As occurs with many women in recovery, when Marguerite became sober, her sexual thoughts, feelings, and behaviors came to a halt.

"There was a time when I never thought I could be a sober, sexual, recovering woman," she said. But recovery was within reach. Marguerite gradually revealed her fear that, if she experienced her sexuality, it would be out of control and trigger her return to substance abuse. She associated sexuality with drug abuse, and sobriety with abstinence from sex. As we worked together, she realized she could be both sober and sexual. She had suffered so much from the self-imposed stigma of being "a druggy and a slut" that she completely reversed herself to be sober and sexless.

Marguerite also had to deal with her feelings of shame, low self-esteem, and belief that she was not entitled to any elements of a good life, including sexual pleasure. She felt she deserved such a punishment because of what she had done during her addict days. Like men, many women can accept that their jobs, finances, relationships, parents, and the physical damage associated with their alcoholism were out of control. But when it comes to their sexuality, they see their behavior as an indictment of their very souls. Recovering women deserve and can have healthy sexuality in sobriety.

Alcoholic women believe that "a few drinks" will relax them and make them appear normal. When they become sober, their inhibitions and feelings of pain, shame, fear, and anger about their sexuality return because these feelings were present before the drug abuse began.

Physiological changes also occur. Estrogen production increases among actively alcoholic women. After drinking stops, estrogen levels—and therefore sex drive—decrease. If hormone test results show low estrogen levels, hormone replacement therapy successfully treats this condition.

Lack of Orgasms and Other Related Conditions

"I don't even know how to have an orgasm." "Do I deserve to have an orgasm?" "How could I even ask?" Among recovering alcoholic women who are physiologically capable, the lack of orgasms occurs as frequently as does the absence of sexual desire. Like Marguerite, these women tell me that they don't know where to begin or what feels good. They don't believe they have a right to experience an orgasm and to have that need met.

Some women say they feel pain during intercourse, especially once they get sober. During their drinking days, the muscle spasms causing this pain may have been present, but the women were medicating it with chemicals. In sobriety, these physical complaints "reappear." The cause of the pain, whether it is physical or psychological, needs to be determined by the woman and her therapist and physician.

Other Physiological Effects of Alcohol in Women

Women alcoholics suffer from a multitude of effects from alcohol. Intoxication increases in women who take oral contraceptives because their bodies metabolize alcohol more slowly. It seems to affect women differently at different times in their monthly cycle, and their tolerance and reaction can change from one menstrual cycle to the next. Women alcoholics often have suppressed immune systems, so they seem more prone to gynecological problems than the general population.

Unrecovered female alcoholics lose fifteen years of their lives: their mortality rate is four times that of nonalcoholic women. Common consequences of alcoholism are miscarriages, hysterectomies, difficulties in conceiving, fetal alcohol syndrome, and alcohol-induced diseases like hypertension, obesity, malnutrition, liver disease, and higher risk of pneumonia.

For Women Mostly: Alcohol, Depression, and Emotional Issues

According to the National Institute on Alcohol Abuse and Alcoholism, one in thirty women in the United States is an active alcoholic. Some therapists observe that the problems of male alcoholics are so distinct that their disease might be thought of as a different illness from that of alcoholic women. Much of this difference is associated with the fact that the onset of women's alcoholism corresponds closely with depression or other emotional problems. Some of these women have a biologic mood disorder which, according to Nathan S. Kline, M.D., in *From Sad to Glad*,

48

affects about one in four recovering alcoholic women (and one in ten recovering alcoholic men).[5]

What are women medicating? They use alcohol to medicate their shame, anger, pain from divorce, feelings of desertion, fear of death, neglect or abuse of children, financial difficulties, gynecologic problems, and difficulty accepting their role as women. Some are dealing with shame about the fetal alcohol syndrome of their infants, unplanned or unwanted pregnancies or abortions, or sexual relationships with men they never would have dreamed of associating with if they had been sober. Sobriety may bring the realization that they have contracted herpes, which is common among alcoholic and recovering women, as well as other sexually transmitted diseases. All of these psychological issues are difficult barriers to serenity for recovering alcoholic women. Jeannette came to me with some of these issues. Her face bore fifteen years of grief when her husband and three children insisted that she get help. She was forty-three years old and had been drinking alcoholically since the age of twelve. Fifteen years earlier, one of her children had died of fetal alcohol syndrome. Frozen in the grief of that death, Jeannette had shut down sexually. It was important as she became sober that she deal with her grief about the child's death. Otherwise, she could not have begun to maintain sobriety.

Another married woman with similar issues, Bonnie was in her early thirties and had two children. "I just can't believe I did such a horrible thing!" she said over and over as we sat together. She was referred to me because she had suicidal feelings about an abortion that followed a lost weekend of drinking. Her values and love for her husband were so contrary to that behavior that she could hardly believe she had done such a thing.

I helped Bonnie see that she was definitely in the progression of her alcoholism; her drinking as well as her sexuality was out of control. As she began to understand the disease process, she knew that it affected her sexual behavior. She had been subjected as a child in an alcoholic family to covert and overt incest, an issue she needed to face. Now she was in a marriage with a distant and controlling partner who constantly implied he would abandon her.

Bonnie had never acknowledged to herself or to her hus-

---

5. Nathan Kline, M.D., *From Sad to Glad* (New York: Ballantine, 1983), 186.

band what her wants, needs, thoughts, and values were because she believed she would appear too demanding. She drank silently so she would not feel. She feared that, if she became a whole woman, her partner would leave her. The safest way was to stay quiet and submissive and to drink secretly. Bonnie had low self-esteem, which is very common among women alcoholics.

The Need for Self-Esteem

Although low self-esteem is an important issue among male alcoholics, it's the biggest issue I see in women alcoholics who are in the process of sexual recovery. Many are physiologically capable of being sexual in healthy ways, yet they punish themselves or feel society is punishing them for their chemical abuse. They lack the self-esteem that would enable them to ask for what they want and need, so they feel lucky to get "the crumbs."

One such woman was Patricia, who, at age thirty-eight, had been sober seventeen years when she came to see me. She had just divorced her third husband, and was once again mired in a failing relationship. She told me that she had yet to find a relationship that was not abusive to her. The major factor for Patricia seemed to be her conflict about her role as a woman in society and in relationships. "I was raised in the South," she told me, "and was taught that 'good girls' and 'good wives' showed only positive feelings and were passive, nurturing, compliant, and nonassertive." She was stating her setup for the abusive relationships that were part of her adulthood. Her beliefs about women's role conflicted with what she had learned in recovery: she wanted to set boundaries, to voice her desires, and to find her own path in the world.

Patricia knew her goal was to discover her identity as a whole, sexual woman in today's society. To reach that goal, we integrated what seemed like polar opposites so she could effectively take care of herself, ask for what she needed, learn how to communicate with her partner, and deal more openly with her bad feelings. As the pieces came together, she began to see a picture of sobriety she had not envisioned before.

The Promise of Sexual Healing

"We believed that one of the promises of the program was that there would be healing and wholeness," said Bob and Elizabeth, a couple in their mid-thirties. These childhood sweethearts had three children. He was an alcoholic, she a codependent. They came to see me when they were three years into recovery. Over the years, they had become asexual. As Bob's alcohol consumption had increased, Elizabeth's desire for him had decreased. His ability to become erect diminished more and more until he had avoided sex entirely for the previous two to three years.

They said they were too young not to have a sex life. They had expected both physical and sexual healing from the Twelve Step program, but their expectations were not materializing. They felt frustration.

Although Bob had suffered no physical damage, he was hurt psychologically; he was so convinced he could not be sexual that he had stopped trying and was afraid to make any more attempts. He started using the Good Sex Program by integrating the Twelve Steps of AA adapted for sexual recovery and moving through each stage. I attended a party celebrating their eight-year sobriety, where Bob and Elizabeth renewed their wedding vows. Clearly their sexual recovery along with the Twelve Steps of AA had been successful.

It's So Good When It's Bad: Sex and Romance Addicts

5

Harry had been in AA recovery for eight years when his wife, Bea, insisted he come in to see me. She was ready to leave the marriage because their sexual relationship, which had been poor when Harry was drinking, had not improved since his recovery from alcoholism. When Harry talked with me alone, he said that he was disappointed and confused because his exhibitionism had not gone away in recovery. The thrill of being an exhibitionist had started when he was a young boy. His father had "instructed him" on how to expose himself in the neighborhood, as other fathers teach their sons to "drink like a man."

Harry's flashing had continued during his drinking days and into his recovery, and now it was unmanageable. He was spending eight hours a day driving the streets and mall parking lots fantasizing about exposing himself. His wife threatened to leave him, and his job was in jeopardy. He had denied his exhibitionism until he began an affair with his secretary, which for him was bottom-line behavior. Only then did he begin to see that his life was truly out of control because of his sex addiction.

Harry is an excellent example of the question, which came first—the chicken or the egg? His sexual addiction was his core issue, and it had deep roots in his childhood. When he stopped drinking, the sexual insanity remained.

What Are Sex and Romance Addictions?

Sometimes people kid each other, saying so-and-so is "addicted to sex," or "has to have it," or seems to "be in love with being in love." These jests are a normal part of the way some individuals handle their feelings or insecurities about sex and love. Others use sex or love as their drug, their addiction. One definition of addiction is "a pathological love and trust relationship with an object or event such as alcohol, sex, money, drugs, exercise, volunteering, food, or anything used to medicate feelings." A sexual behavior, relationship, or another person can be the object of an addiction. (See Appendix 5-1, "Sex Addicts Anonymous Self-diagnostic Evaluations for Sex and Romance Addicts.")

Sex Addiction

Misinformation obstructs understanding of sexual behaviors and effective treatment for sexual issues. For example, normal sexual behavior for a teenage boy may be masturbating once or twice a day. He and others may label him a sex addict, even though daily masturbation is common for adolescent boys. That label may hinder his future sexual behavior. Many sexual behaviors, such as having multiple partners, using pornography, or visiting prostitutes, are considered normal for men in parts of American society. Some who engage in these activities may be told by therapists that they merely have a high sex drive.[6] Men and women can avoid such misinformation by tapping into the wealth of written materials and services that can help them find appropriate treatment.

The Roots of Sex Addiction: Childhood Abuse

The previous chapter presented the sexual issues that are symptoms of addictions to substances like alcohol, cocaine, and prescription medications. But sometimes sex and romance addiction is the core problem, as it was for Harry. Often, the roots of the core issue are in childhood abuse.

Shame is one result of the abuse many sex addicts experienced as children, regardless of what the abuse was. Children who have not been abused usually grow up believing that, even if they do something wrong occasionally, they are still good people. Abused children often believe that they are bad down to their core.

---

6. Charlotte Davis Kasl, *Women, Sex, and Addiction* (New York: Ticknor and Fields, 1989), 227.

The feelings of badness are so overwhelming in these individuals that they medicate to relieve the pain. According to Patrick Carnes, 87 percent of the sex addicts he surveyed in a national study reported that they were victims of childhood sex abuse. The misguided signals and lessons from childhood remain damaging to adults.

Taking a Closer Look at Sexual Addictions

Sexual dysfunctions have the potential to become addictive. However, individuals who simply think about or act on some of these behaviors at some point in their lives are not necessarily sex addicts. Only if behavior becomes compulsive and diminishes a person's quality of life or that of others is it an addiction.

Patrick Carnes, in his pioneering work about sex addiction, *Out of the Shadows*, conveniently categorizes sex addictions into three levels of behavior. These are not stages that people progress through; they are merely an effective organizational tool that makes this concept easier to understand. Each way in which sex addiction manifests itself can become lethal, regardless of the level. It is also not unusual for people to exhibit three to five of these sexual behaviors at the same time.

Level One

Although these behaviors can be life-threatening, they are not against the law. They include compulsive masturbation; obsessive use of pornography, including literature and videos; strip shows; engaging in or watching anonymous sex in book stores; multiple partners; fantasy; cruising bars for anonymous sexual contact; same-sex encounters by heterosexuals; and opposite-sex encounters by homosexuals.

Masturbation. When masturbation becomes unmanageable and also triggers other sexual activities, it is an addiction. Although this condition is seen more often in men, it also occurs in women and can threaten the addict's life, as Sylvia demonstrated to me.

The phone rang one day, and the woman on the other end said that her name was Sylvia, and I was her last call. She told me she was masturbating about forty times a day with her vibrator and that killing herself was the only way she knew how to stop. She had a gun beside her. If I could not give her an answer, she was going to shoot herself.

Compulsive masturbation was the focus of Sylvia's life. I told her that she was not alone; I knew others who had suffered the same compulsion, who in recovery were living happy lives. She consented to come in for treatment, and we uncovered her alcoholism. We brought her chemical addiction and her sex addiction into remission, and her obsession with masturbation began to moderate. Sylvia has been sober for six years. She has worked on her incest issues and has a healthy intimate sexual relationship today.

Pornography. Some men and women risk their reputations, jobs, and businesses by spending thousands of dollars to amass huge pornography collections. Individuals who masturbate compulsively often do so with pornography. Although men collect pornography and frequent strip shows and peep shows in adult bookstores more than women do, some women use romance novels, fantasy, and soap operas in much the same way.

Fantasy. Some people spend more than 90 percent of their lives living in a fantasy they create about love affairs or sexual activities. They lose touch with reality, and the distortion adversely affects their daily functioning and relationships.

Excessive fantasizing is the triggering mechanism that starts about 90 percent of sex addicts in their disease (see "Fantasy: Where It All Begins" later in this chapter). This obsessive thinking can threaten one's life. It threatened Barbara's. She was so caught up in fantasy about her sexual relationship with her boyfriend, Eddie, that she became anorexic, lost her job, and became terrified to leave her house (agoraphobia). One day she needed groceries. As Barbara drove to the store she became so involved in her fantasy of Eddie that she lost control of her car and nearly died as a result. In recovery she discovered serenity in the Twelve Step program of Sex and Love Addicts Anonymous (SLAA).

Extramarital Affairs. This category includes men and women who continuously engage in extramarital affairs solely because they are looking for the high that comes with doing something forbidden. The sex within their committed relationship is usually satisfactory. In their disease, however, they need to take more and more chances with their extramarital sexual encounters. At first, they may restrict their extra-marital meetings to dis-

56

tant locations, gradually becoming more daring until they risk having sex in their own homes while their spouses are at work or out visiting.

Multiple Partners. Many sex addicts have multiple partners, often engaging in continual one-night stands, threesomes, or serial affairs outside their committed relationships.

For people who engage in extramarital affairs or who have multiple partners, sex is a drug that they abuse. It is not an expression of love; rather, it is marked by an absence of love and intimacy. They can't control it, and they go to any lengths to get it, as Roberta did. She was a prominent community leader until her life became unmanageable because of her multiple affairs. Roberta's first marriage had been physically abusive, and she rationalized her sexual liaisons as a consequence of the bad relationship. After her marriage "to the man of my dreams," however, she continued the affairs, uncontrolled fantasizing, and compulsive masturbation. She had had affairs with more than one hundred men and could not stop despite the fear of AIDS and her worry that her husband would discover her activities.

Cruising. This activity is the search by either straight or gay men and women for a sexual high among the crowds in bars, bookstores, bathhouses, streets, and social gatherings. In women, it is called the Mr. Goodbar syndrome, after the movie. Addicted women and men may cruise seven nights a week.

Opposite Sex Preference. Some sexually addicted men and women have encounters with partners whose gender is the opposite of their usual preference. This experience makes them feel confused, ashamed, isolated, and afraid. They medicate these feelings by repeating the behavior. Once these individuals enter therapy, they can distinguish genuine sexual preference issues from manifestations of sexual and chemical addiction.

Level Two

Level Two behaviors usually involve a victim and are classified as misdemeanors in some states. These activities generally focus on or use imagery, stimuli, or both, which sexually arouse the participants. Some of these behaviors include exhibitionism (flashing), voyeurism (peeping-Tom behavior), fetishism, bondage, masochism and sadism, bestiality, cruising in search of anonymous sex, going to prostitutes, and making obscene phone calls.

When one or more of these activities dominates the lives of men and women, it has become an addiction.

Prostitutes. Compulsively using prostitutes can lead individuals to financial, emotional, and spiritual bankruptcy. They often risk losing their families, homes, businesses, and lives, as John discovered he was doing.

When he came to see me, John was a high school teacher in his middle twenties. He had six years of alcohol recovery, but he was unable to stop cruising for prostitutes. This activity had left him penniless and terrified that the school board would find out what he was doing. After he started the Good Sex Program for his recovery, he stopped these behaviors.

Voyeurism. Many men combine their voyeuristic—"peeping Tom"—activity with compulsive masturbation and pornography. When men need to increase the frequency and risk to get the same sexual high, voyeurism becomes unmanageable.

Marvin felt out of control when he came to see me. Despite his recovery from alcoholism, he said he could not stop his voyeurism. He was a successful broker in a large city; at night he was a peeping Tom in wealthy neighborhoods. As his tolerance increased, he became more daring. He trespassed and hid on the properties of famous people for hours. Eventually, the fear of being arrested overcame him, and he sought help.

Exhibitionism. Although both men and women expose their sexual parts to unsuspecting victims, exhibitionism is condemned in men more often, because our society more willingly accepts women as sexual objects. Décolletage in women's dresses and revealing bikinis, for example, are considered chic fashion. As with voyeurism, exhibitionists often need to increase the frequency and risk in their activity to reach the same high.

Obscene Phone Callers. Most obscene phone calls are made by straight or gay men while they are masturbating. These men are usually angry, feel socially isolated, and have low self-esteem. The telephone provides a means for channeling their hostility and revenge. Some men spend most of their spare time in this behavior. They may even call from work and risk losing their jobs.

Fetishism. Substituting one or more sexual symbols for a love partner can be addictive. Men and women with fetishes become sexually aroused by inanimate objects, such as high-heeled shoes or nylons. Another kind of fetish involves men and women seeking arousal by watching or participating in defecation and urination rituals, or focusing their attention on a body part of the opposite sex, like feet, breasts, or the labia.

Bestiality. Sexual relations with animals is a means of arousal for some people. In this case it is a fetish. When people have sex with animals compulsively, they have become addicted to the behavior.

Bondage, Sexual Masochism, and Sadism. Women and men who participate in these rituals often develop an increased tolerance for them. As they find more and different ways to achieve a sexual high, they may pierce nipples, scrotum, and labia. Some people even practice asphyxiation. Often one or more of these activities occurs with other addictive behaviors.

Cross-Dressing (Transvestism). Some men use cross-dressing to arouse themselves sexually. In this case, the practice is a fetish. For men who cross-dress compulsively, the high comes from doing the forbidden and risking discovery by family, friends, or co-workers.

Level Three

Sexual addiction acted out in rape, child molestation, incest, or sexual violence is classified as Level Three activity. (Consequences to victims are described in "Sexual Trauma," in chapter 9.) The three classes of Level Three sex offenders—pedophiles, sociopaths, and sex addicts—differ and require different treatments.

Most pedophiles are men who are attracted to, fondle, and engage in sex with young children. Pedophiles account for about 30 percent of sex offenders. Treatment success rates with this group are low.

Most sexual sociopaths are men who commit incest or rape, molest children, or are violent sexually with their partners. These individuals have no shame, guilt, or remorse about their activities. They use sex as a tool for aggression and continue their behavior unless they are stopped by the law and other intervention.

Other sex addicts at Level Three, however, are filled with self-loathing and remorse. Often they are suicidal, because they are powerless to control their behavior. They do not wish to harm their victims. They are out of control.

Sex addicts come from all walks of life. Carl, a married businessman with two children, had a loving wife and a good reputation in the community. When he drank, however, Carl cruised playgrounds for young children and sexually fondled them. Eventually he was arrested and sentenced to twenty years in prison. Without proper therapy, his alcoholism and sex addiction will not be cured, and he will repeat his behavior when released.

Child Molestation. Approximately 50 percent of child molestation cases are committed by a family friend, relative, or acquaintance of the victim.[7] Paul, a camp counselor, was a typical child molester.

"Every time I quit a camp counseling position, I swore to myself that I would never touch another child," Paul insisted during our first session. At age twenty-six, he was referred to me from a treatment center after he had been caught molesting six- and seven-year-old boys at the last camp where he had worked. Because he had moved around the country a lot and worked in small camps and daycare facilities, he had repeated this behavior for eight years without being discovered.

When Paul began discussing his childhood memories and fantasies, he revealed that his parents had had frequent drinking binges. During those times, they had locked him in a dark closet for hours without food, water, or any way to reach the bathroom. Unlike many sex addicts, Paul did not have a substance abuse problem. Before molesting each child, however, he spent hours fantasizing, using child pornography and compulsive masturbation. Immediately before he was arrested for the last incident, he had contemplated suicide, because "it's the only way I know to stop."

Incest. Covert or overt incest and alcoholism frequently occur in the same household. In covert incest, parents or family members do not touch or fondle the child. Instead, they expose the child to explicit sexual behavior, such as continually bringing lovers into the home, allowing the child to witness sexual acts or pornography, or routinely sleeping with the child. Dirty jokes or blatant sexual remarks made around children also can be covert incest. Overt incest is sexual fondling and intercourse between a family member and child.

Rape. The various types of this criminal offense are rape by a spouse, acquaintance, date, or stranger. Some men and women

---

7. Carnes, *Don't Call It Love*, 115-16.

have been conditioned to believe sex is rape. They cannot discern the difference.

For an addicted rapist, rape is part of a pattern of addictive sexual behaviors. This pattern begins with the man's masturbating and fantasizing compulsively. He then cruises for a woman, follows her home, and—believing that the woman wants him—rapes her.

Some rapists feel no remorse or guilt about raping their victims. Known as sociopathic rapists, these individuals are impulsive, unstable, and callous; and they have a limited ability to feel the anxiety that normally results from wrongdoing.

The Cycle of Addiction and Isolation

Sex addicts believe sex is their greatest need. Their definition of nurturing and love is sex and lust. They become increasingly frustrated and full of rage when their sexual behaviors do not fulfill them. Their fear of discovery while acting out their addiction isolates them from others. That risk also adds to the thrill of doing something forbidden, like smoking their first cigarette or having their first sexual encounter.

To mask their shame and their desperate need to fill that empty hole in themselves, sex addicts often go out of their way to convince others that they are "scoring" or "making it." These claims are attempts to medicate their shame and lack of self-esteem. They may create elaborate stories about out-of-town trips or fictitious meetings in order to act out their sexual behaviors far from home. The lying isolates addicts from their families and friends. Their lives become a cycle of deceit, shame, obsession, and frustration. The main factor fueling this cycle, illustrated in Appendix 5-1, is fantasy.

Fantasy: Where It All Begins

Fantasy is a major component of sexual addiction. Used to enhance sexual encounters, either during masturbation or with a partner, it can be healthy. But many sex addicts' cycle of compulsive sexual behavior starts with fantasy. After it becomes compulsive, people's lives have become unmanageable and the other behaviors follow.

Fantasy can trigger a relapse for sex addicts who are working to keep their disease in remission. These men and women need to recognize when they may safely shift from the here-and-now to fantasy and learn how to control that transition.

Some experts suggest that sex addiction, co-sex addiction, and sex offending are expressions of post-traumatic stress disorder. Eighty-seven percent of sex addicts and co-sex addicts have been sexually abused.[8] These individuals use fantasy to dissociate from the shame, anger, and pain associated with abuse. Some addicts describe their fantasy cycle as a trancelike state in which they are powerless over what they envision.

More Than One Is the Norm: Multiple Addictions

It is common for sex addicts to be addicted to alcohol or other drugs or both, as well as to have more than one sexual addiction. These multiple addictions reinforce each other. Patrick Carnes, author of *Don't Call It Love* reports that 94 percent of sex and romance addicts have other addictions. He notes that 42 percent of sex addicts are also chemically dependent, 38 percent have eating disorders, 28 percent are workaholics, 26 percent are addicted to nicotine, 26 percent engage in compulsive spending, and 5 percent are compulsive gamblers. Codependency tops the list at 57 percent.[9]

The therapist sorts out the multiple, simultaneous addictions in order to determine which are primary or life-threatening. If two addictive behaviors are equal endangerments, which was true in Christopher's case, both need to be addressed simultaneously.

"I feel like the world's oldest virgin," Christopher said bitterly when he walked into my office. At thirty-six, he was very depressed after losing his job as a manager at an automobile dealership. His parents were helping him pay for his apartment, and he couldn't afford to drive his car.

Christopher's spiral to the bottom involved his cocaine addiction and his compulsive masturbation. He had started using cocaine while he worked at the dealership, to help him get

---

8. Carnes, *Don't Call It Love,* 109.

9. Carnes, *Don't Call It Love*, 35.

through the sixteen-hour days. He also began drinking excessively after work. Then he discovered that he could get a bigger high by mixing cocaine with masturbation. Soon he also needed to watch pornographic videos to become aroused while masturbating.

Both addictions had become life-threatening. Christopher was masturbating and doing cocaine eight to sixteen hours a day when he could, and several times he had gone to the emergency room because he had injured his penis and scrotum from excessive and overly vigorous masturbation. I learned that Christopher had been involved in his addictions for more than eight years. Behind it all was an intense intimacy disorder, a great fear of being close to other people or intimate with them. Christopher had never been intimate sexually with another person. Although he was terrified that his suffering would continue for the rest of his life or that he would die, he didn't know how to break the addictive cycle. He needed to address his substance abuse and sexual addiction simultaneously.

Another common situation occurs among sex addicts who are in recovery from substance abuse but have not yet faced their sexual addiction. Bob, a thirty-eight-year-old self-employed office cleaner, was one such person. After six years of recovery from alcohol, he still had not lost his compulsion to expose himself; he centered his life in his exhibitionism. Bob cleaned offices from five until eleven at night. After work, he habitually stripped from the waist down and rode through the neighborhood on his bike, displaying an erection. Someone would call the police and he would be arrested. After sleeping in jail, he'd appear in court in the morning and then go to his office job.

After more than three hundred arrests, Bob finally accepted that his addiction was unmanageable and causing him uncontrollable shame, pain, and loneliness. Taking control of his alcohol addiction had been only half the battle. Only after he was willing to seek help for his exhibitionism could we begin to work toward sexual recovery.

Sex Addiction and Related Addictions

Bob's achieving sobriety took him only halfway to recovery; his sexual dysfunction did not stop when the drinking did. The correlation between sex or romance addiction and substance abuse is high. In about 30 percent of my clients who have both sexual and chemical issues, a sexual issue is at the core. Achieving sobriety does not eliminate the dysfunctional sexual behavior if the core issue is not resolved. On the other hand, about 70 percent of my clients need to address their chemical issue first. Once they are sober, they work through their sexual problems in the Good Sex Program.

Which came first, the chicken or the egg? The need to medicate the sexual insanity with drugs, or the need to medicate the drug insanity with compulsive sexual behavior? This question is the reason it is imperative that, in determining the core issue, therapists look closely at a person's history prior to substance abuse.

Coping with the Shame and Guilt

By working the adapted Twelve Steps within the Good Sex Program, many sex addicts have been able to achieve sexual recovery. During that process, feelings of shame, anger, and loneliness often emerge that need to be addressed.

Like all addicts, sex addicts often experience intense mood swings as part of the disease process. They spend a great deal of time in the throes of their disease, like Christopher. To cope with the shame and isolation of their behavior, many medicate their feelings with drugs. Because addicts are often secretive and deceitful in order to continue their behaviors, their family, work, and personal relationships suffer. They divorce, lose their jobs, lose custody of their children, and cannot maintain a close relationship with themselves or others.

Secrecy and deceit eventually caught up with George, a prominent attorney who told me that he had had sex with his clients, his sister, and other relatives. His attitude was, "If Jimmy Bakker can do it, so can I. Boys will be boys." This grandiose attitude, typical of sex addicts, is part of their denial. George's arrogance, did not save him from being brought up before the ethics board and the bar association, which ruined him professionally. His wife divorced him, and he went bankrupt. Despite these disasters, George could not accept that his addiction was uncontrollable. He exemplifies how far some individuals go before they can admit that their behavior is unmanageable.

Women Sex Addicts in Our Society

It has been difficult to accommodate the idea of women sex addicts in our society. The stereotypical sex addict is the disheveled man wearing a raincoat who flashes in the park, the "dirty old man" who lures children into his car with candy, or the man who masturbates compulsively while watching triple-X movies in adult bookstores. But women are also dealing with sex addiction.

Thirty-five-year-old Georgianne was a teacher who had divorced her husband three years earlier. Originally, the courts had awarded her custody of their two children. When her children moved back with their father to avoid seeing her bring home nameless men every night, she realized her life was out of control. Georgianne spent every night cruising the bars seeking any kind of sexual contact. She was not interested in forming relationships or falling in love; all she wanted was the sexual connection. Her colleagues were questioning her behavior, and she worried about contracting AIDS or being abused.

Like Georgianne, Felicia came to see me because she was powerless over her lust. Felicia was a physician who had been divorced for twelve years. During that time, all her relationships were based exclusively on sex. To ensure that she would keep meeting all her sexual needs, she kept several relationships going at the same time, all with men whose company she did not enjoy.

She finally realized the severity of her addiction when her fifteen-year-old daughter called her one night from a high school dance and asked her mother to pick her up. On the way to the school, Felicia stopped at a lover's home for three hours while her daughter sat alone on the curb outside the deserted school, waiting for her. Knowing that she had jeopardized her child's safety prompted her to seek help.

Romance Addiction

Falling in love can be an exciting, euphoric experience. Most people realize that the ecstasy does not stay at a high level of intensity.

For those who are "in love" with being in love and who are totally seduced by the euphoria, that feeling of ecstasy is their drug. When people fall in love, their bodies release endorphins that produce a high similar to an amphetamine high. Romance addicts need to feel that euphoria more and more, as alcoholics need more drinks while their tolerance increases. Romance addicts seek situations and people that help them get this sexual high.

Most romance addicts have more than one addiction. Excessive exercising, eating disorders, workaholism, compulsive spending, and chemical dependency are common accompanying issues.

Fantasy

Romance addicts become obsessed with love either in their own lives or in the lives of fictitious characters in romance novels and soap operas. People in the latter category get caught up in the drama of the stories as a way to medicate their pain about what is happening in their own lives.

Other romance addicts go to extremes, trying to be worthy of love from another person. Like Doris, a professional woman in her late twenties who had been married briefly, they believe they cannot live without being loved and adored. Doris wanted me to tell her what was wrong with her, because she could not maintain a long-lasting intimate relationship. She was anorexic and deeply in debt from extensive cosmetic surgery procedures (breast enlargement, tummy tuck, nose job, and dental work), and from constantly adding to her extensive wardrobe. She admitted that she did these things to make herself a more desirable sex object. Love was her drug, and it controlled her.

Living for the Fairy Tale

Distinguishing between love and infatuation and between romance and real love is impossible for romance addicts. This fuzzy understanding was an issue for Laurie, a petite woman in her middle forties. She was six years into her third marriage when she came to see me. Laurie was always looking for the euphoria of falling in love. She used that feeling to validate her self-worth. Believing in the fairy tale, she fantasized that her partner should be Prince Charming and sweep her off her feet.

As we worked together, she began to understand that sex is not love, intensity is not love, and her need for the continual high of a love affair was her addiction. She realized that her perception was not based on reality. After she learned what healthy intimate relationships are about, she looked closely at her behavior and decided to stay married.

Laurie began to understand that healthy relationships involve sharing and a communicative commitment to another person based on mutual trust and concern. Relationships built solely on sex and the desire to control the other person, especially sexually, are destructive. Laurie's expectation that the relationship with her partner would always be smooth was unrealistic. Disagreements and differences of opinion are part of the growing process between partners. (Compare the checklists for healthy and addictive relationships in Appendix 5-2 and 5-3.)

Not for Women Only

I have worked with both men and women romance addicts, gay and straight. Like women, men often have an accompanying addiction. For Mario, it was alcohol. A self-proclaimed "king of three-month relationships," he was an unmarried recovering alcoholic in his mid-thirties. He had been sober for five years when he came to me feeling suicidal and fearful that he would never marry and have children. As he explained his relationships, his romance addiction cycle became apparent. He would fall in love with good, beautiful, honest women (Madonnas) whom he could "take home to mother." The minute they stepped out of his fantasy and he saw that they were people with opinions and sexual desires, he withdrew. He believed that women who were sexual were bad (whores), and he broke off the relationships. Because he was addicted to the feelings of falling in love, he would pursue another Madonna. He kept thinking his dream woman was around the corner.

As he untangled the Madonna/whore issue, Mario established an understanding that women are real people, not objects of adoration or disgust. From that point he began recovery toward healthy sexual intimacy using the Good Sex Program.

Bringing Sex and Romance Addiction into Remission

Much is written about the process of recovery from alcoholism, but little such material is available about sex and romance addictions. No one who is actively abusing alcohol or other drugs can benefit from a program of sexual recovery. It is also impossible to implement the program for someone whose life is unmanageable because of compulsive behavior concerning sex and romance. Using the Twelve Steps of recovery for sex or romance addiction is the first and most important step.

Treatment Is a Family Affair

For sex and romance addicts who have partners, therapy usually involves both parties. As Jennifer Schneider says in a 1989 article in *Family Relations*, "Because sexual compulsivity, like chemical dependency, is a family disease, the spouse of the sexual addict needs treatment for...excessive dependency on the addict. The couple can be viewed as enmeshed in an addictive family system in which the co-addict supports the addict's addiction."[10] Therefore, couples counseling—utilizing the Twelve Steps of SLAA and the Good Sex Program—is recommended treatment for sex addicts, romance addicts, and their partners.

Abstinence: Working toward Healthy Sexuality

Recovery begins with Steps One through Three, where addicts accept that they are powerless. At this point, therapists, treatment centers, and many Twelve-Step groups of Sex Addicts Anonymous (SAA) and SLAA ask participants to observe a period of celibacy.

Abstinence is an important transition to healthy sexuality; if old sexual behaviors are not in remission, new, healthy behaviors have no room to grow. A celibacy contract (see Appendix 4) is made between sex addicts and their sponsors, therapists, or group leaders. Both parties mutually agree on its length, usually from thirty to 120 days. An abstinence contract is analogous to compulsive overeaters' abstention from addictive eating in order to experience normal eating. They do not, however, abstain from eating. Similarly, sex addicts abstain from their dysfunctional sexual behavior, but they do not abstain from their sexuality. Every man and woman is a sexual being; sexuality is a state of being. Once sex addicts understand that they need to abstain from their uncontrollable sexual behavior—but not from who they are sexually—they can begin to discover healthy sexuality.

While under the abstinence contract, recovering people work the Twelve Steps of recovery for sex and romance addiction

---

10. Jennifer Schneider, in *Family Relations* (July 1989): 289.

and the Good Sex Program. They also need to attend meetings, be in an inpatient program if their behavior is really out of control, and have a sponsor whose story closely resembles their own and who has progressed further in recovery. As recovering addicts become empowered by their celibacy, they work on an abstinence contract of bottom-line behavior that they agree to follow with the help of their sponsors, significant others, or higher power. This contract provides the behavioral guidelines they need.

Discovering Personal Boundaries

When sex and romance addicts are working their adapted AA Twelve Step program, they explore the issue of personal boundaries—their own and others'. Boundaries are the edges of comfort zones: they define who people are and where they start and stop. For example, some people feel comfortable when their friends greet them with a hug; others prefer a handshake or a verbal greeting. Learning to respect and appreciate their own and others' boundaries and values is important for sex addicts who are recovering and discovering healthy sexuality.

Becoming Aware of the Triggers

Part of the recovery process aims to reduce the risk of relapse. Sex addicts identify the triggers, such as fantasy, pornography, certain movies, videos, or magazines, that could cause them to return to compulsive behavior. Specific social situations are triggers, like meeting people in night clubs or going to particular parks or shopping malls. Addicts work Step Four at this point. As they take a searching and fearless moral inventory, they identify and honestly evaluate these triggers. In this part of the healing process, recovering persons grow in awareness of their addictive and recovering personalities. They begin to notice when the addict within is talking and when the healthy part of them is in charge. They avoid relapse by learning coping skills to deal with stress and feelings of shame, guilt, and anger.

Breaking Out of Isolation

Sex and romance addicts are one of the most isolated groups of addicted individuals. They find support and develop social skills by attending Sex Anonymous (SA), SAA, and SLAA meetings. Bringing their other addictions into remission is necessary for romance and sex addicts because addictive behaviors may trigger the sexually addictive activities.

Management of leisure is another issue that faces many recovering addicts. Suddenly, the time they used to spend in addictive behavior hangs before them. Boredom and indecision may trigger relapse. Attending support groups and developing new hobbies, friendships, and activities to fill that time are essential. Only after a period of recovery can these individuals begin to explore their healthy sexuality.

A Word of Caution to Sex and Romance Addicts

Information about restoring healthy sexuality in the later chapters in this book include engaging in certain behaviors, like fantasy, masturbation, and viewing erotica. Some of these behaviors may not be feasible for recovering sex and romance addicts.

In individuals whose sex addiction is fantasy, pornography, or compulsive masturbation, these behaviors may activate their disease. Occasional use of masturbation, fantasy, and sexually explicit literature or movies can enhance the sexual experience for many sex partners. However, sex and romance addicts may need to eliminate some sexual activities that were part of their addiction in order to maintain their bottom-line abstinence.

These prohibitions can be decided only as the recovery process unfolds under the guidance of sponsors, other recovering people, or therapists trained in sexual addiction. Eliminating these few behaviors from the sexual recovery program for sex and romance addicts, however, does not diminish chances for healthy sexual recovery.

Society's Views of Sex and Romance Addiction

Like substance addictions, sex and romance addictions are fueled by childhood issues. Many men and women with these diseases have a background of sexual, spiritual, or emotional abuse and neglect, or other compulsive behaviors that affected them. Some people still view sex and romance addictions as moral issues because of our taboos and secrets about sex in general. Notwithstanding these attitudes, sexual compulsions do occur which can be brought into remission.

Was It Good for Me Too? Codependent and Co-Sex Dependent Men and Women

6

"Everyone said Preston and I were the most loving couple they had ever seen," said Rachael, a thirty-five-year-old housewife. In public, she was always attentive to her husband. Behind closed doors, Rachael was even more submissive. She had agreed not to return to work after the birth of their second child, who was now eight, because "Preston didn't want me to," even though she had held a responsible administrative position in social welfare before their nine-year marriage. Preston, a thirty-eight-year-old attorney, dictated how Rachael was to dress for the many social affairs he was required to attend, and told her whom she could speak to and how to behave. He always referred to her at these functions as "my little wife," never as Rachael. But Rachael also had another name: codependent.

Codependency Is Nothing New

Although some people think *codependent* is a flashy, modern label, the concept has a long history. In the Greek myth about Narcissus and Echo, Narcissus was the youth who was so in love with his image that he was incapable of loving anyone else. When Echo came along and fell madly in love with him, she could not tell him so because she could only repeat what others said to her. During her continuous pursuit of Narcissus, he finally said to her, "I will die before I give you power over me." "I give you power over me," she echoed. Thus an excellent example of codependency's roots exists from antiquity.

Most people have heard the classic story about how to identify a codependent: he's the fellow who, after being struck by a car, is slowly dying on the side of the road—and watching someone else's life pass before his eyes. Not even their own sexual lives have priority in codependents' minds.

How Do Codependents Act?

Experts have compiled more than one hundred characteristics to identify codependents. Most people possess some of these traits, but they are not necessarily codependents. (See Appendix 6-1, "Diagnostic Criteria for CoDependency.") Briefly, these individuals echo the likes, dislikes, desires, ambitions, strengths, and weaknesses of another person or persons to the point of obsession. Codependents try to control other people's behavior or situations. The belief that they can do so has been perpetuated by society, which, according to Anne Wilson Schaef, was founded on the illusion of control.[11] Codependents are emotionally, spiritually, intellectually, and even physically unaware of their own wishes and needs. Their relationships often fail because they try so hard to control other people. They do not focus on their own identities, because they define themselves using the identity of another person or thing. Rachael was the "little wife" Preston wanted and acted according to his desires.

In *Lost in the Shuffle*, Robert Subby offers a concise but comprehensive summary of codependents' traits.[12] Because these characteristics are not as clearcut as the signs of physical diseases like diabetes, people need to judge for themselves whether their own traits have reached the point of obsession.

An overdeveloped sense of responsibility. Codependents have difficulty distinguishing between responsibility *to* others and responsibility *for* others. Glenda always gave in to her husband's sexual demands at one in the morning, when he arrived home from his part-time job. These sessions left her resentful, unable to sleep, and tired the next day. Zach insisted that he needed his "nightcap" to help him unwind for his full-time day job, so

---

11. Anne Wilson Schaef, *When Society Becomes an Addict* (New York: Harper and Row, 1987), 105.

12. Robert Subby, *Lost in the Shuffle* (Pompano Beach, Fla.: Health Communications, 1987), 16-17.

Glenda felt she had to comply or be responsible for his inadequacy the next day.

Difficulty identifying and expressing feelings. A good example of this characteristic occurred between Gustave and Geneviere. When Gustave started losing interest in sex with Geneviere, he didn't know how to explain these feelings to her. Although he loved her very much, he wasn't "really sure what I'm feeling or why." Instead he chose to work harder at the university so he could avoid being at home as much as possible.

Fear of abandonment that results in maintaining dysfunctional relationships, to avoid the pain of being alone. Some individuals stay in dysfunctional relationships because the thought of being alone is worse than what they are experiencing in their current situation. This inertia can be dangerous, as it was for Priscilla. After she endured four years of her husband's sadomasochistic sexual behaviors, he nearly asphyxiated her one night during a sexual session. Only then did she seek treatment for her codependency.

Perfectionism. The ebb and flow of life does not allow for perfectionism; it allows for growth and change. Having unrealistic goals for themselves and others is a common trait of codependents. Men and women need to know who they are and what they can achieve realistically in their relationships, work, families, and selves. Sometimes they make mistakes. Sometimes they feel like having sex, and other times they don't.

Repeated relationships with people who are dependent on food, work, drugs, or alcohol. "A codependent keeps dating the same alcoholic again and again," SueEllen said. She was attracted to men who were alcoholics or drug abusers and who abused her emotionally if not physically. Linked with this trait was the commonly held belief that she could "change them," and thus take responsibility for them. This trait is associated with another characteristic of codependents, explained below.

React to situations and other people rather than risk responsible action on their own behalf. Iris repeatedly blamed her partner for her lack of sexual desire. "He's an alcoholic, so how can I be turned on by that?" Yet she refused to acknowledge her cocaine addiction, saying she used the drug only "to lift my spirits." Like Iris, some people live off the reactions of others rather than being empowered by their environment.

Another codependent, Rodney, always seemed to be the "shoulder everyone could cry on." His friends called him at all hours to ask favors and unburden their sorrows. He allowed their dependency to continue because it supported his other codependent traits: he felt like a martyr because his "helping others" took most of his time. His behavior served a purpose, however, keeping him so busy with others' problems, he could avoid his own.

Pervasive sense of failure and low self-esteem. When people don't feel good about themselves, they don't do good things for themselves. SueEllen is a good example of this pattern. She repeatedly dated abusive men because she did not feel that she deserved better. She surrounded herself with people who hurt her. Rodney did the same thing. Both excluded people who could have been beneficial to them.

As the above examples show, when individuals live others' lives with little or no regard for their own, they are codependents. Recovering their own identities is possible using the Twelve Steps of AA through Al-Anon and ACoA. When they have sorted out their codependency, these recovering men and women can deal with their sexual issues by using the Good Sex Program.

Recovery from Codependency

A clear definition of healthy sexuality (see the beginning of chapter 2) helps men and women understand what they can achieve. Because codependents experience others' feelings, thoughts, and actions rather than their own, they need to understand what the internal experience feels like so they can refer to it as they heal. They need recovery from codependency before sexual recovery can occur, because connection with their own feelings precedes healthy sexuality. It is unrealistic for codependents to expect healthy sexuality if they do not have a sense of identity.

How Did They Get This Way?

Addicts and Narcissus are similar, as are codependents and Echo. Rather than owning their own hearts, souls, and opinions, they hide behind a false self. Masks protect codependents from the trauma or dysfunction they experienced at an early age. These facades are survival mechanisms that they adopted as protection against someone or some traumatic event they've repressed. They become people pleasers to maintain the mask that helped them survive.

When they were children, many individuals experienced abuse from their caretakers. In response to these situations, they felt rage, physical pain, depression, grief, isolation, betrayal, and shame. As adult survivors, they medicated these feelings and tried to "lose the memories." In the process they lost fragments of themselves, the inner children who live inside them. Masks (false selves) are inner children's ways of coping with feelings that remain in adulthood. These men and women do not consciously remember why they have these feelings. They only know they feel angry, betrayed, depressed, isolated, or ashamed. They also may need to resolve sexual issues.

Much has been written about the development of children who are traumatized. To deal with the bad feelings associated with the trauma, the inner children in these adults die or stay immature. Then the adults assume a mask. Drew is an example of this process.

His father was an alcoholic and rageaholic who often was unemployed. Because Drew's mother could not handle her husband's outbursts, she often turned to her only son for support and comfort. He became the "little man of the house," his mother's caretaker in place of his terrifying father. Rather than let the child inside of him grow and be nurtured, Drew put on a mask and became what his mother needed. Like Drew, some men and women become caretakers or scapegoats. They do whatever it takes to cope with their world.

Removing the Mask to See Who Lives Underneath

Part of the therapy for codependents involves dismantling the mask to release the authentic person behind it. Getting in touch with the inner child, as John Bradshaw explains in *Homecoming: Reclaiming and Championing Your Inner Child*, is an essential part of the journey toward healthy sexuality. When a traumatic event occurs, a mask defends against the pain. The inner children who were buried at that point in their development can be reached. Adults can relive the trauma in a safe way, pick up the pieces they lost, and continue on their path.

The journey involves filling the black hole that many addicts describe in various ways. Some say it's the undefined, lost inner child inside them, while others call it the light or the god within that needs a chance to grow.

How Codependents Medicate Their Pain

Codependents medicate by using people, things, or places as insanely as addicts use food, drugs, or sex. They are obsessive about work, volunteerism, fantasy, exercise, cleaning, thinking, their kids, or their parents. Their obsession makes their lives totally unmanageable, but this fact is difficult for them to see because their focus is directed outward. They blame others for the way things are. A codependent says, "I'm fine; what's wrong with you?"

I'm Okay, What's YOUR Problem?

As a therapist, I help codependents realize that each person in a dependent/codependent relationship contributes to the dysfunction. Often I hear, "If he stopped drinking, then I would be interested in sex," or "If she lost twenty pounds, then I would take her to my business functions." When people use "If...then" statements, they are focusing their identities outside of themselves. After codependents understand they are giving others responsibility for their own thoughts, feelings, and actions, they can begin to eliminate that behavior.

Alicia and Frank

Frank's alcoholism was at such a severe level and Alicia's denial abilities were so strong that only when their sexual issue arose could she acknowledge the condition of their relationship. They were in their early forties and had been married for eight years when I met them. Alicia had been married before and came from a religious family in which divorce was not allowed. After living with her alcoholic and physically abusive first husband for eleven years, Alicia left him and went to a shelter. She met Frank one year later.

Alicia had been attending Al-Anon meetings for about two years because both her first husband and her father had been alcoholics. When she had first met Frank, he said he had had a drinking problem but that he didn't drink anymore. Rather than join AA, he had involved himself deeply in church activities. Alicia started to suspect that Frank might be having problems. She returned home from an Al-Anon meeting one night and found

Frank dressed in her clothes. At first, she believed it was a sex problem and not an alcohol problem. She was so filled with rage and revulsion that she reached out to me as a sex therapist.

As we worked together, I saw that, while Frank possibly had a sexual problem, his drinking—which was again out of control—made it difficult to tell. He had been drinking on his part-time job. After Frank finished treatment, he and Alicia began couples counseling. Alicia had shut down sexually since childhood. When they began applying the Good Sex Program, she realized that, in order to be sexual, she needed to share equal responsibility for their sexual situation. Working Steps Eight and Nine of the Twelve Steps would enable her to let go of her resentment and forgive Frank for his insanity during his drinking days. Because she was totally in charge and Frank had become passive, the power struggle between them also needed realignment.

As Alicia worked the Twelve Steps for her sexual issues, she remembered that, when she was six years old, she had been sexually molested by a church member. To help develop a connection with their adult sexuality, Alicia and Frank abstained from sex for a while. Instead, they focused on their senses by giving one another massages, planning romantic dinners, showering together, and using touching exercises to learn what sexually pleased each of them. As Alicia started to trust that Frank's cross-dressing might be a result of his drinking and not necessarily an underlying sexual problem, she began to accept him as a potent, sexual man.

The Dangers of Codependency

The compulsive behaviors and feelings of codependency are progressive. They can cause hypertension, ulcers, psychosomatic illnesses, depression, and even death. They also can drive people to other addictive behaviors. Codependents feel pain, shame, rage, and depression, because they are powerless over their environment; these feelings lead them to their drug of choice—control.

Codependents are master manipulators. They never feel that they have enough. Compulsive behavior is similar to what happens when most people eat one potato chip and then want more. The addiction to control, combined with codependents' low self-esteem and fear that they may not get enough (of whatever "it" is), drives them continuously to seek more and more control.

I have known codependents whose need to retain control was so extreme that they felt justified in killing their alcoholic partners just to save them from booze. That is the degree of insanity that can arise from codependency.

Marylou and Roger

"Sex with Marylou is like sex with a dead fish," complained Roger. He and Marylou had been married for twenty-two years and had a sixteen-year-old daughter and a twelve-year-old son. Marylou had a degree in education. She was an adult child of an alcoholic and an anorexic, but her most severe issue was her codependency. Roger was a stockbroker, and his business was in financial trouble. He had been an alcoholic when they married, and then he switched to pills and became a rageaholic.

Marylou told me, "I can't imagine living without Roger or the kids; they're everything to me." She was convinced that her life would end without them.

Roger said everything about Marylou was okay—"the kids are fine, the house looks great"—except that, when it came to sex, she was only a receptacle. Although she never denied him sex, he wanted a woman who was orgasmic, who was sexually creative, and who would seduce him occasionally. He had tried candlelight dinners and buying flowers and sexy nighties for her, but "nothing sparked her flame."

One night he went into a rage and raped her. Then he sent her to me to "get fixed sexually." It was clear to me that Marylou had shut down her feelings, including her sexual ones, to cope with this difficult man. She was afraid that if she allowed herself to feel, she would want to kill him.

"If I show him how I feel," she said, "he'll leave me." Although he verbally abused her and the kids, she felt so inferior and flawed that she could not live without him. Her thought disorder focused on her sense of worthlessness. She would not spend money on a haircut or therapy for herself, but she made sure her kids went to private schools, had their own horses, and wore the best clothes.

Marylou's worst fear came true one day when Roger beat her, and she could no longer pretend they had a wonderful marriage. As she removed the mask of denial, she entered a treatment center for her adult child and codependency issues, against Roger's wishes. It was the first stand she had taken for herself.

In treatment, she began to identify her despair; she felt like a doormat. She attended meetings after she completed treatment, and began individual therapy. I suggested a workup by a gynecologist and a biologic psychiatrist. A low testosterone level, discovered by the gynecologist, and a biologic depression, diagnosed by the psychiatrist, were two reasons for her lack of sex drive. I tried to persuade her to take a trial of medication for her biologic depression, but she said she could not pay for it.

Marylou had spent her entire life as a victim, living in fear. Although a path before her led away from that life, she was too afraid to try it. She insisted, "If I feel sexual feelings or any feelings, I'll be vulnerable and get hurt again." She chose to live in depression and asexuality rather than risk being beaten down again. Even her sacrifice of self, however, could not protect her. Roger then confirmed Marylou's worst fear by leaving her. Not until that point could she begin getting her own life back together as she pursued a real estate career and began a long, slow road toward recovery.

Codependent Women and Their Sexual Issues

Codependent women often shut down all or most of their feelings "to stay in the game." That mechanism explains why lack of sexual desire is common among these women. Although they cannot explain their feelings, desires, and needs, they know what their partners want. When asked what turns them on sexually, they parrot whatever their partners like and never get in touch with their inner selves.

Secondary virginity also is common. In recovery, men and women codependents need to reach their sexual selves for the first time. I try to find where in their childhoods they stopped, donned their masks, and put up walls that allowed them to survive. Once they see where they stopped sexually, they can go behind the mask and allow their inner children and sexual selves to emerge.

Two big issues among codependent women are painful intercourse (dyspareunia), and muscle spasms that prevent the penis or other objects from penetrating the vagina (vaginismus). Although these women shut off their feelings, their bodies react. If women get vaginal spasms at the thought of intercourse, usually this reaction is their bodies' way of saying that something other than sex needs to be addressed. The body continues to respond to feelings that the mind has suppressed.

Codependent women's inability to have an orgasm usually is associated with relinquishing control, with plunging into that black hole and being lost forever. That anxiety is so overwhelming that some women shut down and do not allow themselves to have orgasms. The recovery issue here is letting go enough to experience orgasm.

Fear or aversion to sex is another common issue among these women. The severity of the emotional, physical, or sexual trauma they experienced as children sends them running away from sexual encounters. As they work through the Good Sex Program they learn how to nurture their inner children and how to grow into healthy sexual adults.

Harvey and Jolette

"Looking back, I realize that it felt like I was at the wheel of an out-of-control race car," said Jolette. "I always assumed the wheel was connected to the car, but it wasn't. I didn't know what was happening." Harvey and Jolette, both thirty-five, had been married for fourteen years and had two sons. They had met when she was in law school, but she had dropped out of school to ride motorcycles with him.

When they came to see me, Harvey was in his third year of sobriety and was attending three to five AA meetings each week. His business was in good shape, but the situation at home was not. They were having sex every six months. Jolette was nagging continuously and was suicidal. Confused, Harvey said, "I don't want a divorce because I love my family."

During my discussions with Jolette, she revealed that she was a compulsive overeater and bulimic. First we worked on her eating disorders and then we addressed her codependency issues. Jolette used sex as a tool to control Harvey's drinking. As long as she had known him, she felt she "had some power over his drinking" by deciding whether or not she would be sexual. The illusion of control, including sexual control, can be very strong in codependency, especially when it is reinforced intermittently. If Jolette agreed to sex with Harvey one night and he didn't drink, then she risked sex on another night based on her previous apparent power to control him, hoping the ploy would work again. But there was no "sure thing." For Jolette, sex was manipulation, her power over Harvey's alcoholism.

When I asked Jolette what pleased her sexually and what she perceived as her sexual identity, she became apprehensive. During therapy, she became aware that she had been sexually traumatized at age nine. To cope with the shame, she believed that whatever control she had over her sexual energy was inadequate. As she worked through her shame and despair, she realized she had exerted increasing control as a survival mechanism, using herself as a tool that she hoped would govern Harvey's alcoholism.

Jolette began to relinquish her belief in control. She went to Al-Anon and began to know her own thoughts, feelings, and actions. For the first time she had sexual feelings and was experiencing secondary virginity. One night she called me at midnight to tell me she had had an orgasm. Harvey and Jolette put together a healthy sexual relationship as she worked her recovery program.

Codependent Men and Their Sexual Issues

Codependent men can be more difficult to treat, because society gives them more permission than it does to women to act out codependent behaviors. They are supposed to take care of the "little women" and children and be their knights in shining armor. If their wives drink, the husbands' "job" is to control them. So it is easy to understand why the common sexual issues for these men codependents center in control.

Psychological impotence is a big concern for them. Because they are trying so hard to be everything—caretakers, parents, money earners—their healthiest parts, their penises, shut down and refuse to work. Retarded ejaculation is more common than premature ejaculation among male codependents. Some of them try to keep it up or hold out longer for their partners, but when they decide it is okay to let go, they don't know how.

Fear of sex also occurs among codependent men. Because many of them also grew up in alcoholic or otherwise dysfunctional families, their fear arises from the way they have or have not seen sex used and abused in their childhoods. Lack of sexual desire occurs more frequently among male codependents because they feel that sex is a task or a job.

Garrett and Maggie

Garrett was a forty-three-year-old physical therapist who had "married the same alcoholic" in his second marriage. He had been in therapy intermittently for six years. He finally returned because he and his second wife, thirty-four-year-old Maggie, had not had intercourse for more than a year. Garrett had a son by his previous marriage, to Lorie, and he and Maggie had a daughter together. Lorie, who was five years his senior, had been a compulsive overeater. Garrett's father was alcoholic, his mother anorexic, and his sister anorexic, alcoholic, and a compulsive spender. The main reason Garrett's first marriage had ended was his total loss of interest in sex. Lorie had always been the initiator, but Garrett complained that she hadn't done "a very good job, and I wasn't interested." Now the same pattern was developing with Maggie, who was very depressed and had an uncontrolled eating disorder. Maggie told me that she thought Garrett didn't love her. She felt unattractive and undesirable. As her self-esteem faded, her feelings of worthlessness increased.

Garrett and Maggie began working the Twelve Steps of AA for sexual recovery. He defined sex as something to do, a performance. He was always acting as the caretaker in his physical therapy work, and he applied that mentality to his sex life. Sex was something he did to keep his wife happy. Sex with Maggie was like a job, and the paycheck was her orgasm.

As he worked through the self-nurturing, self-sensuality, and self-sexuality stages of the Good Sex Program, he learned the concept of "going skin in." He discovered literally how to get in touch with his skin and then go beyond that: how his body felt, what he found pleasurable, and what his preferences were. He began to see that sexuality springs from inside, and that it is not a task to be performed.

Garrett is a classic example of a sexual codependent. He could not see that sexual behavior is only part of the total picture of sexuality. Because he believed that sex is task-oriented, with no connection to his internal state, he lost interest.

This focus on task and performance also defines sex for women who are called upon every night to service their husbands. Darlene came to me with that complaint. She said that she had to perform oral sex with her husband every night during their four-year marriage. This task was his definition of her sexuality. Like a good codependent, she had adopted it as her own. She reacted to her environment instead of her own inner needs and desires. Coming to see me was her first step toward reaching the inner self she had been repressing.

Co-Sex Addiction

Co-sex addicts are men and women who need sex to feel loved. They usually have no sexual identity of their own and believe the only legitimate way to receive love is through sex. To get this love, they give in to their partners' sexual demands, regardless of whether these demands cause them shame, fear, and pain, or conflict with their own values or ethics. Their partners' sexual needs are the only ones that matter to them because they focus their entire world on their partners.

Who Are Co-Sex Addicts?

Co-sex addicts usually have sex addicts as partners. Trying to please them, co-sex addicts often participate in their partners' sexually addictive activities, such as incest, exhibitionism, sadomasochistic behaviors, voyeurism, and use of pornography. Sex addiction and romance addiction are common among co-sex addicts as well. (See Appendix 6-2 for the characteristics of co-sex addicts.)

Sexual Dysfunctions and Co-Sex Addicts

Co-sex addicts and codependents have similar sexual dysfunctions. I treat them in a similar way, but with a few variations. Like sex addicts, co-sex addicts make an abstinence contract in the early stages of the Good Sex Program, agreeing not to engage in sexual activity for a period of time, usually 30 to 120 days. This time-out allows them to explore life without their drug.

Identifying the triggers for relapse and preventing them is important for both co-sex addicts and sex addicts. These triggers include fantasy as well as certain situations and places, pornography, or anything that sparks a return to active addictive behavior. Although eliminating these few behaviors may be necessary for sexual recovery, sex addicts' and co-sex addicts' chances for full healthy recovery are the same as for other recovering individuals. (See chapter 5, "Becoming Aware of the Triggers.")

"I'll Do Anything You Want Me to Do"

Co-sex addiction, carried to its extreme, is almost the way American women are expected to act. However, co-sex addiction is not reserved for women only. Fearing that their partners will leave them, some men or women, gay or straight, do anything a partner wants. Such compliance is part of the definition of a co-sex addict. Not only are they "perfect" sex companions, they also are completely submissive and pleasing. Like Echo, they give up their power and sense of self. Some co-sex addicts come to me asking for some "new ways" to sexually satisfy their partners. Others, like Kathy, go to extremes before realizing that they have given up their identities to their partners.

Kathy was forty-six and had been married for twenty-seven years to a salesman. She said she wanted a divorce, but she felt "stuck." Her husband, Jerrold, had been her first sex partner. He was very involved with sadomasochism and had had a special whip made for her. Kathy's nipples and labia had been pierced, and Jerrold had insisted that she wear leather and vinyl clothing around the house. As his cruelty became increasingly frequent, she became afraid for her life.

About two years earlier, Kathy stopped using alcohol to mask her fear. In sobriety, she learned to take care of herself and began to deal with her inability to ask for what she wanted and needed. She had been neglected and physically abused as a child, and her older sister had put her through ritual abuse. Kathy had carried her obedience and compliance into adulthood. Once she was sober, she lifted the mask and regained her identity. Kathy left Jerrold and began her own sexual recovery.

Jody

Jody was a twenty-three-year-old co-sex addict, anorexic, and compulsive overeater with seven years of recovery from alcohol. As a child, she had been abused by her parents. By age thirteen, she was drinking and having sexual experiences with groups and her older brothers' friends, pleasing men however she could. She had been sober for two years, when, at nineteen, she became involved with Vic, who abused her physically and sexually. When she refused to bring home another man so Vic could watch her and the stranger have sex, Vic beat her up badly. This prompted her to seek treatment for her co-sex addiction.

Several years after she completed treatment, Jody met Wendell in the program, and they became engaged. While Wendell thought he had found the best lover on earth, Jody finally could admit to herself and me that she had no sexual feelings and that she was faking all responses. Jody worked gradually through the Good Sex Program, including touching and nurturing techniques to get her in touch with her sexual likes and dislikes. Eventually she realized her sexual identity and was able to have orgasms.

Codependency and co-sex addiction are both forms of intimacy disorder. Like the people whose experiences this chapter describes, other men and women who seek help with recovery can find it in the Good Sex Program.

I'm Hungry, Not Horny: Men and Women with Eating Disorders

7

"Everything I did revolved around what I was going to eat or not eat, when I was going to exercise, and how much. My body size ran my life and nearly ruined it." Wendy, a twenty-eight-year-old divorced woman with a six-month-old baby, was attending Overeaters Anonymous and had been in recovery from her anorexia for one year. The question she wanted me to help her answer was why did she lack sexual desire.

During our first session, Wendy told me she had had an eating disorder since she was a young child. As we explored her childhood memories, Wendy discovered that she had much pain and rage associated with the sexual abuse she had received from her grandfather, father, and two older brothers. She felt worthless and realized she also had adult child issues to address.

With her anorexia in remission, we explored the consequences of her abuse by her alcoholic father. A physician checked Wendy's hormone levels and discovered that she had low estrogen and testosterone as a result of her anorexia. Because these hormones are essential for maintaining sex drive, Wendy began replacement therapy. This treatment, along with the progress she made dealing with her trauma, revived her sexual desire. Soon she was looking forward to starting a relationship with a man.

Fortunately, Wendy's story had a happy ending, but Wendy is just one of millions who are affected to some degree by eating disorders.[13] The definition of pathological eating has broadened to include more than skin-and-bones anorexics or bulimics who

---

13. Carole Thompson, personal communication, 1992.

compulsively binge and vomit. (See Appendices 7-1 and 7-2.) The spectrum includes other distorted relationships with food, such as compulsive and obsessive exercising and dieting, as well as compulsive eating. The faddish and unrealistic obsession with being thin is endangering the physical and emotional health of many men and women.

Stuffers, Starvers, and Skippers

Terms like *anorexic, bulimic*, and *overeater* evoke negative mental pictures that force people into denial. In *The Callaway Diet*, C. Wayne Callaway refers to individuals with these behaviors as "starvers," "stuffers," and "skippers." These terms are more appropriate because eating disorders are not about people's appearance to others, but rather their relationship to food. "Normal-looking" people also obsessively starve, purge, or overeat. Not all starvers are underweight; not all skippers (so-called because of overeaters' tendency to skip meals) weigh more than their ideal weight.

All three eating disorders commonly occur in the same person simultaneously, especially anorexia and bulimia. Individuals therefore cannot be labeled as strictly one type or another. Many starvers and stuffers begin in their eating disorder with one behavior or the other and then alternate between the two. (See Appendices 7-3 and 7-4.)

Men and women in all three categories share traits. Their self-esteem depends on their weight and looks. They are constantly preoccupied with eating and food. Like codependents, they feel a need to control everything in their environment, especially food. In many cases, at the core of these behaviors and characteristics is a history of covert or overt sexual abuse as well as other kinds of trauma.

Sexual Dysfunction and Eating Disorders: Common Origins

When individuals with eating disorders bring their disease into remission, whatever they are medicating comes to the surface. The origins of their issues about sex and food are usually the same.

Below the Surface: Sexual Abuse

According to Carole Thompson, an eating disorders specialist and president of the Addiction Consulting Corporation in Boston, approximately 85 percent of individuals with eating disorders have been sexually abused (given the phrase's broad definition to include overt or covert abuse).[14] This fact suggests that there are many more sex addicts with eating disorders than are known. The phenomenon is especially hidden among men, who are less likely than women to acknowledge their eating disorders. Covert sexual abuse includes incestuous behaviors, like use of sexual language in the house concerning body shape or sexual organs, parents who dress improperly around their children, or children bathing with their parents until puberty or beyond. Even if no sexual activity occurred, these children were not provided any guidelines or boundaries by which to gauge their future actions. At an early age, they found comfort in eating or not eating food.

Once these women and men address their eating disorders, their sexual dysfunction becomes apparent. The precipitating factor behind these issues is post-traumatic stress disorder (see chapter 9). Gender identity issues and sexual preference issues are common.

Men with this disorder often have a history of neglect, sibling incest, or parental incest. Arnie, a forty-three-year-old engineer, had three years of recovery from alcohol and was heavily into starving behavior. At five-feet, ten inches, he weighed 137 pounds, and he used compulsive and excessive bicycling to maintain that weight. He also maintained an unrealistically low caloric intake. Arnie has yet to understand that his anorexia medicates the pain about his emotional and physical abuse from his mother and the sexual abuse his father inflicted upon him. Until Arnie lets these memories into his conscious awareness, he will continue to misuse food dangerously.

Releasing Past Sexual Abuse

One of the dynamics behind eating disorders—past sexual abuse or sexual overstimulation—is similar in both men and women. Men don't remember abuse as often as women or are less likely to

---

14. Thompson, personal communication, 1992.

believe that remembered behavior was actually abuse. Whereas women almost expect to be abused in today's society, men believe it is the worst thing that could happen to them. They equate abuse with being gay or being a "wimp." Many men cannot accept that their mothers slept with them to keep their husbands away. Others refuse to acknowledge that their fathers, older brothers, or friends fondled or molested them. As men learn that these actions were abusive and not their fault, perhaps more will seek therapy.

Little or No Sexual Desire and "Don't Touch Me"

In the '50s, sex was forbidden. In the 1980s and 1990s, food is forbidden. Because society focuses on appearances—how much individuals weigh, how they dress, how much fat shows—people deprive themselves of healthy eating. The most prevalent sexual issue among people with eating disorders is lack of sexual desire. The distorted body image and sense of self hinders a positive, healthy vision of the self as a sexual being.

"I Never Have an Orgasm"

Lack of orgasm is common among stuffers, reports eating disorder specialist Carole Thompson. People with eating disorders characteristically have low self-esteem and believe they don't deserve anything, including the right to experience orgasm. Therefore, starvers tend to retreat from sexual encounters, denying themselves any sexual pleasure. Stuffers, on the other hand, have little or no sexual desire. They sometimes engage in various romantic and sexual fantasies, but they do not like themselves or their bodies enough to act on these thoughts.

People recovering from eating disorders need to learn to love their bodies and to be comfortable with them. Self-massage, self-exploration of body parts, and leisurely bubble baths help in the process of learning to be orgasmic.

Painful Intercourse (Dyspareunia)

Along with a lack of orgasm, painful intercourse is common among women with eating disorders. Many have such low self-esteem that even women capable of orgasms do not believe they deserve them. They view sexual deprivation as punishment for their failure to be good girls and maintain their weight "where it should be." Their anxieties and fears may result in spasms of the vaginal and pubococcygeal muscles and consequent painful sexual intercourse.

Relationship with Food: Friend or Foe?

What people eat, how they eat it, and how they believe their bodies look are important issues, but how they think about food is more injurious. (See Appendix 7-5 for an eating disorders assessment that poses questions about how people relate to food.) When people consider food to be their best friend or their enemy, it has taken over their lives. When their higher power is the bathroom scale, when they weigh themselves every morning and let that weight determine whether their day will be good or bad, food controls them. Those who organize their lives around eating and exercise have an eating disorder.

The first question in the eating assessment questionnaire is, "Do you ever think of food as bad or good?" Many people say, "I'm eating well; why haven't I lost weight?" Lacking accurate information about nutrition or following fad diets and eating patterns, they get into ritualized eating behaviors. (See Appendices 7-1 and 7-2.)

When Food Is the Relationship

Elliott complained to me that although he wanted very much to share his life, he "could not maintain a relationship with a woman." He was forty-three years old and single, and he had six years of recovery from cocaine. After several sessions it became apparent that Elliott was anorexic and bulimic. I pointed out that he already had a relationship—his obsession with food and his body. As we worked to bring his behavior into remission, he started purging compulsively to offset any weight gain, and he began starving himself.

Eventually Elliott realized that his desire to "look and feel good" could be achieved without his compulsive behavior, which had included four hours daily at the gym after he stuffed. He also realized that, as he turned his focus away from food and exercise, he could concentrate on establishing a healthy relationship with himself and others.

Education about Food and Nutrition

Elliott and others like him lack general information about metabolism, body composition, and nutrition. They need this basic education as part of their recovery process; once they understand good nutrition, they can make different food choices. Elliott did not realize that starving himself and exercising more and more to control his weight had disrupted his metabolism. His body needed fewer calories because it had adjusted to starvation. Elliott needed to take back the power food had over him.

The Power of Food

Many Americans permit food to govern them. I hear all kinds of excuses: "If I eat that cookie, I'll have to exercise an extra ten minutes," or "I eat only once a day so I can keep my weight down, but I'm tired all the time," or "I have to throw up everything I eat or I'll get too fat." Americans spend more than $32 billion a year on dieting. They waste much of that money on useless products and false information.[15] Physicians, nutritionists, and dieticians who are knowledgeable about nutrition and eating disorders are reliable sources.

Food Fight: Society's Role in Distorting Self-Image

"Mom always said to me, 'Gayle, a woman can never be too thin and a man can never be too rich.' I guess I believed her." Gayle was lying in a hospital bed with intravenous feeding tubes running into her stick arms. "Everyone thinks that way, right?"

Apparently more and more people are thinking like Gayle. Starving and stuffing behaviors used to occur mainly among teenage girls; experts attribute their aberrance to emotional disturbances arising from dysfunctional family situations, including sexual abuse. But today, 2 percent of women older than thirty, more than one million, have anorexia, and 6 percent have bulimia.[16] The number of overeaters is harder to determine, but it is estimated to be more than 5.5 million. These figures do not include the increasing number of men who have been caught in the "thin-is-in" mentality.

Feeling Guilty about Feeling Good

It is almost unacceptable in American culture to say, "I feel good

---

15. *U.S. News and World Press*, 14 May 1990, 56.

16. American Anorexia and Bulimia Association, 418 East 76th Street, New York, NY 10021.

about how I feel," or "I like what I weigh." People who make these statements sometimes get comments from others who tell them how they should look or feel. "How can she eat that and stay so thin?" and "If you keep eating that, you'll look like a blimp" are the remarks of individuals with distorted self-images. They need to understand the essential role of food and healthy eating habits. These mixed messages are destructive; those who receive them believe they will be rejected and unloved if they do not look a certain way.

Melody, a recovering starver, found herself challenging similar comments made by her friends. "I used to meet my girlfriends for lunch, and all they talked about was how much they weighed, how much they did not eat, how they purged and hid food from their families," she reported. "They didn't even say hello to each other first; all they wanted to know was 'Did you lose any weight?' or 'Did you work out yet today?' As I went through recovery, I began feeling good about myself and my sexual relationship with my husband, but they didn't understand that. They made me feel guilty about feeling good." Melody gradually removed herself from that crowd and developed new healthy relationships.

The messages from every quarter of society imply that men and women need to look thin to be loved, to get a promotion, to be hired for a job, to be liked, or to turn on their partners. Tara, a starver, believed these myths. "I always thought that if I could be a little thinner, my husband would be more attentive," she said. This distorted thinking eventually led to Tara's hospitalization after she starved herself to a dangerous weight.

Starvers, stuffers, and skippers have overstepped the boundaries of logical thinking about food or exercise. Moderation is the answer, but obsessive behavior has taken over.

"When I'm Thinner, Then I'll...."

People with eating disorders are good at putting their lives on hold. "When I get thin enough I will...." "When I get my implants I will...." "When I am 160 pounds with a body fat of 12 percent, then I'll...." Healthy sexuality is the positive energy of a person's basic character. People choose how to direct that energy. Sexuality does not depend on a perfect body size or some ideal weight, or looks like Tom Selleck's or Julia Roberts's. Healthy sexuality has little if anything to do with ideal weight or appearance.

Society stresses that women's talent is to be beautiful and thin—sex objects in a male-dominated culture. Men, on the other hand, are objectified for money. Now that women are earning more money, men are also falling prey to the distorted thinking of never being too thin or exercising enough.

This twisted perspective brings with it the terrifying tradeoffs of unrealistic expectations and damage to people's physical, emotional, and spiritual health. Diets that severely limit caloric intake or types of food, such as liquid protein or grapefruit diets, cause countless ailments—including mood swings, malnutrition, dehydration, gallstones, constipation, and in extreme cases, death. Why people with these conditions lack sexual desire is easy to understand.

Viola had suffered so much emotional damage that she wanted to kill herself. "If you don't help me, I swear I'm going to die," she told me over the phone. This fifty-year-old woman had been battling compulsive eating for fifteen years. Although she faithfully attended Overeaters Anonymous, she still was overwhelmed by her compulsive eating and found it "impossible to maintain a relationship with any man."

As we worked to stabilize her weight and compulsive eating, memories of her childhood sexual abuse came up. Although they horrified her, she was relieved that "now I know why I am the way I am." Her suicidal thoughts ended, and she now is realizing better self-esteem and a sense of herself as a sexual woman.

"Fat" Isn't Where It's At

Some clients tell me that they were as young as four or five when their parents told them that they were getting too fat. Other children were told, "No one will love you if you're fat." These messages led many men and women to believe themselves unworthy of love and affection unless they stayed thin. When these same clients bring in childhood photographs of themselves, they can see that they were not fat. Yet the words stayed with them into adulthood, and society constantly reinforces those messages.

Daddy's Little Girl

Many women intentionally keep themselves thin or small, almost incestuously, as a way to please their fathers. They were always "Daddy's little girl," or "Daddy's little princess," or the "little wom-

94

an" of the house where the mother often was an alcoholic or was absent. These women still hear those messages in their minds and are vying for their fathers' love by keeping a prepubescent image. Their behavior is kept alive by their strong drive to feel loved and their low self-esteem.

Sex Addiction, Co-Sex Addiction, Romance Addiction, and Food

According to Patrick Carnes, author of *Out of the Shadows*, the groundbreaking book about sex addiction, 38 percent of sex addicts, co-sex addicts, or romance addicts also admit they have an eating disorder.[17] It is understandable why these addictive behaviors often appear in the same individuals, because both addictions can involve body image. Individuals with both addictive behaviors have uncontrollable feelings that they try to medicate by actively involving their bodies in some way. For example, they engage in stuffing, starving, or skipping as well as masturbating, prostituting, cruising, or voyeurizing.

Life in the Fast Lane

Compulsive spending, workaholism, and compulsive exercising are common among individuals with eating disorders. When their therapists say, "Do something good for yourselves that is not food related," the first thing these clients think of is buying something.

For some people, like Leslie, compulsive buying takes the place of the food they no longer are using to fill their void. "To the casual observer, I was the classic 'before and after' photo subject to prove the success of a diet," said Leslie, a twenty-nine-year-old social worker. After shedding more than one hundred pounds as a member of Overeaters Anonymous, she had gradually eliminated her dysfunctional eating habits. As she stopped these behaviors, however, she began to feel uncomfortable with her body and to experience nervousness and anxiety. These feelings intensified as the pain she had suppressed concerning her childhood incest issues arose in her.

To deal with these new feelings, she began spending money

17. Carnes, *Don't Call It Love*, 35.

recklessly. Although she earned only $16,000 a year, she bought a $13,000 car and spent to the limit on all six of her credit cards. As soon as she started on the program of Debtors Anonymous, she began entering sexual relationships compulsively. While in recovery from her eating disorder, she had promised not to get into a relationship, but she started dating a man who abused her as her father had done. She ended the relationship when she realized it was destructive, but she returned to compulsive overeating, which lasted three years. Leslie then saw that her fasting, sexual abuse, destructive relationships, and compulsive spending were related problems, which she determined to address.

Leslie needed to learn how to live by established boundaries and to moderate her behavior, something she had never done. Her initial reaction was rebellion. She insisted that she felt confined, saying, "This is not fair. Why do I have to do this?" She had no idea that other people lived moderate lives by choice.

She began attending Incest Survivors Anonymous meetings. After each session, she either spent compulsively, overate, or thought about starting a relationship. Her emerging incest issues triggered these other behaviors. Because we knew that sexual abuse was her core issue, we addressed her eating disorder and compulsive spending first and stabilized her behavior before working on her incest issues.

Fantasy and the Mind/Body Connection

People with eating disorders have the ability to slip into their own fantasy worlds. When Carole Thompson asks skippers whether they feel sexual, they usually respond, "I'm hungry." Compulsive overeaters are excellent fantasizers. Although they've lost their sexual desire, they fabricate fantasies about being in love and don't act on them. These fantasies temporarily satisfy their sexual desires so they can avoid being sexually active in a physical way.

Among stuffers and skippers, fear of sex or aversion to it goes hand in hand with fantasy. As Ferdinand revealed to me, food is a safe "sex" partner. "I don't have to answer to it, perform for it, or be anyone except myself with food," he said. "I can hide in my apartment and eat all night, knowing no one will judge me." In just such ways, stuffers use food to keep out sexual feelings they don't want to confront. Food is their relationship and comfort; it places no sexual demands on them.

96

Compulsive overeaters who are obese take fantasy one step further. They refuse to look at themselves in the mirror below the shoulders, thus detaching themselves from their bodies (being "out of their bodies") and living in their heads. Many of these men and women also watch television compulsively. They escape into the fantasy of soap operas and live their lives through the characters. Some compulsive overeaters let television serve the function of masturbation without having any physical connection. The same effect can be achieved by obsessive readers of romance novels.

Starvers have a different perspective on fantasy. Because they see elephants where there are skeletons, they fantasize about food. They image elaborate dinners or worry constantly about what they will or will not eat.

Neurochemicals and the Mind/Brain Connection

When starvers are asked which drugs they would prefer to take, they ask for stimulants. Skippers, however, prefer downers. This choice is also characteristic of overeaters, who use food as a sedative. They eat bread or pasta until they fall asleep.

The erratic and compulsive eating and exercise that individuals with eating disorders engage in affect the neurochemicals in their bodies. These substances affect people's moods. Production of neurochemicals works like a computer, with the brain acting like hardware and the mind like software. When people think about food or exercise or sex to medicate whatever they need to deal with at that moment, the mind says "It's okay," and the brain sends neurochemicals into their systems. These chemicals, such as endorphins, numb pain and change moods. People over-exercise or stuff themselves with food until they feel intoxicated. Their judgment is impaired because the influx of neurochemicals disrupts their systems.

Men and Eating Disorders

Eating disorders are conventionally associated with women, but men are affected as well. Today's society strongly emphasizes the belief that the leaner people are, the more they care about "health." The focus on body shape, style, and the body-builder look also has increased the use of steroids among athletes.

Compulsive behavior concerning body image used to be prevalent among gay men, because the younger and leaner they were, the more likely their success in attracting other men. During the '80s, these beliefs infiltrated straight society among men.

Men with eating disorders often are workaholics as well. In one common pattern, men who lose their jobs also lose their self-esteem and sense of self. One of the first ways they react to this situation is to eat, diet, or exercise compulsively.

Winning the Battle with Food

"I can stop at any time; it's no problem" is a common comeback of many individuals with eating disorders. Eating disorders are diseases, like chemical addictions, and not just a matter of will power. Surrendering to the fact that they need help is the first step for starvers, stuffers, and skippers. Once they begin working the Twelve Steps and get into remission for their eating disorder, they can learn how to live as sexual women and men.

Where's the Instruction Manual? Adult Children of Alcoholics

8

"I love Judy very much and want to marry her and have children, but I can't bring myself to have sex with her." Vince, a thirty-two-year-old astronomer, had not been sexual with Judy during their two-year relationship. In frustration, she had broken off their engagement.

Vince's father had been an alcoholic who had shamed Vince about being a man. "My dad's idea of sex was what he called 'banging the old lady' every night," Vince admitted to me. "I could hear everything through the thin walls." So Vince denied his sexual feelings and the role his father projected, trying instead to be the kind of man he thought his mother would want. This gave Vince two choices: he could have his mother's approval and not be sexual, or he could be sexual and risk losing his mother.

Obviously Vince had chosen the first way. He also had the Madonna/whore idea from his father that women were either saints or sluts, but they should not and could not have sexual feelings. Women who did were "only good for one thing," while decent, moral women were Madonnas. Vince believed he was trapped in a dilemma: he had no idea what a normal relationship with a woman was like, and he had no adequate male role model.

It took Vince two years to work through the damage associated with this issue. Eventually, a relationship developed with Gladys, a woman five years his senior with whom he began the painfully slow process of building a healthy and intimate sexual relationship using the Good Sex Program.

They Are Not Alone

As noted in chapter one, 83 percent of the population have been members of alcoholic, addictive, codependent, or other addictive families. A large percentage of this group are adult children of alcoholics or of dysfunctional families. They come from all economic and social classes, all races and religions. They have issues they need to acknowledge, understand, and resolve so they can live complete lives.

Understanding Why They Are the Way They Are

Adult children share many characteristics, most of which they developed as survival mechanisms. These behaviors helped them to cope with an alcoholic family environment. (Appendix 8-1 lists some of these traits.) Although the coping behaviors are familiar to many people, this book explores the way they relate to sexual issues that adult children need to address. Not all of these traits apply to every individual, and the degree to which any one of them does apply varies for each person. These traits provide a good point of reference for our purposes.

Hope and joy are audible in the voices of adult children who learn about the close connection between their sexual issues and the characteristics typical of people who grew up in alcoholic families. Recognizing this connection is the beginning of recovery. "My God," clients often say, "now I understand why I've been acting this way all these years. I thought I was crazy." They hadn't realized that their upbringing could have such an impact on sexual development. The feelings of isolation and fear they suppressed seriously affected all their relationships. Applying the Twelve Steps of AA adapted for sexual recovery, adult children can address the trauma associated with living in an alcoholic environment. Therapeutic approaches vary, depending on the individual.

This chapter explores the relationship between adult sexual behavior and the emotional and spiritual baggage carried from childhood. It shows how various persons have benefited from the Good Sex Program. All references in this chapter to therapeutic methods and exercises are offered as a guide. Details of the program appear in section 3 of this book.

Classic Traits

Two characteristics of adult children stand out. First, these people feel that they are different from others, which makes them feel isolated. They are convinced that everyone else has a better life than they do, that other people are sexier or more attractive or can perform better in bed than they can. "She got the good-looking man because she's sexier than I am," or "I don't feel I can satisfy my girlfriend as well as her last boyfriend could." Such self-defeating and often unrealistic attitudes cause discomfort in social settings. They distance people and make it difficult to form relationships, especially sexual ones. Interestingly enough, adult children often feel this isolation even in ACoA groups.

The second trait is even more significant: children of alcoholics guess at what normal is. Without a clear picture of what normal, healthy behavior is and what is expected in certain situations, they can only guess at how to act or what to say. They lack a starting point from which to begin a relationship with themselves and others. Therapy for chemically dependent and codependent men and women generally focuses on returning individuals to the relationships they had before they started using chemicals. But adult children do not have standards of normal behavior or knowledge of how normal families function.

"I often wish I could have a 'before' picture to go with the 'after' shot of what normal and healthy relationships look like," remarked Joslyn, a recovering adult child and sex addict. "Those before-and-after diet photos in magazines show you what those people had to work with and what they've achieved. At best I had a blank picture for a 'before' shot." When alcoholics' children guess at what normal looks and sounds like, they do not guess very well. Because they lack a script to show them how to behave, they improvise. This characteristic is the point from which they begin their recovery.

What Some Characteristics Mean

Thousands of people like Vince and Joslyn have found answers to their questions about the past and their feelings of rage, anger, shame, and guilt; why they feel isolated and afraid of people; why they lack sexual desire or have premature ejaculation or painful intercourse. Understanding common traits enabled them to bloom as healthy, active, sexual men and women.

For example, the tendency to excessive loyalty even when it is not warranted translates into fear and insecurity. Many individuals stay in relationships because they believe that being alone in an uncertain future is worse than their present situation.

Excusing other people's behavior or taking the blame for anything that goes wrong in a relationship is another characteristic of adult children. "Maybe I deserved to be raped," one may say. "I must be doing something wrong to make her not find me sexually attractive," says another. Some adult children excuse their partners' behavior and belittle themselves with such rationalizations. Others believe they are responsible for their partners' inorgasmia or premature ejaculation, but they will not acknowledge their own issues and needs.

Many of these traits overlap and work together. Overreaction to changes in their lives is a survival mechanism adult children developed against powerlessness as children. When they take charge as adults, they are often accused of being controlling and rigid. This trait may combine with another behavior, personalizing situations. When people are used to having sex three times a week and suddenly their partners try to change the routine, they immediately think they did something wrong that turned their partners off. They take responsibility for something they may not have influenced at all.

It is difficult for adult children to nurture and maintain fulfilling relationships until they follow the Twelve Steps of AA adapted for adult children. Many go through years of therapy for their sexual issues without ever addressing their prior issues first. Integrating the Twelve Steps with the Good Sex Program leads to recovery and joy.

Intimacy Disorders

Intimacy disorders are common among adult children because these men and women have no healthy role models from their family environment on which to base intimate behavior. Healthy sexuality involves being spiritually, emotionally, intellectually, and sexually intimate. Part of intimacy is the ability to have fun sexually. Sex often comes out of spontaneity, joyfulness, and fun-loving feelings. People who have trouble letting loose and having fun often have intimacy disorders.

Lack of Sexual Desire

Inhibited sexual desire is another characteristic which many adult children share. Everyone is born with sexual feelings. When adult children try to act on those feelings, they behave as they saw their parents act in their dysfunction. This imitation of dysfunction results in hurt and confusion; to avoid their pain, adult children shut down sexually. They believe that, if they don't talk, don't feel, and don't trust, they won't get hurt.

Lack of desire often results from a history of sexual trauma. Rape, sexual overstimulation, incest, child molestation, or witnessing violent sex can cause people to turn off their sexual feelings.

Mindy recalled years of sexual, physical, and spiritual abuse. "I was called a whore and a slut since the age of five," she said. "I see now that my father had a very low opinion of women, and that he was a seriously ill man. But naturally I didn't realize his condition until I began recovery." Mindy was thirty-six years old and anorexic when she came in to see me. Her father had been a rageaholic, and her mother, a pill addict. When she caught Mindy masturbating one day at age seven, she put clothespins on Mindy's labia in front of her brothers and sisters as shaming punishment. The constant abuse throughout her childhood caused her to shut down her sexual feelings. She believed she could gain some control over her life by controlling her eating, and she became anorexic. Now she is in recovery for her adult child issues and eating disorder, and she is working on her sexual trauma issues.

Never Again Is Too Soon: Fear of or Aversion to Sex

Human behavior is a complex intertwining of the effects from past events which individuals often have forgotten. When Ruth-Ann called me, she was forty and had been married for eight years. It had been an asexual relationship, and eventually her husband told her he was gay. Ruth-Ann completed treatment for her adult child issues, met Calvin, and married him three months later. Calvin, who was contending with premature ejaculation, became impotent.

Ruth-Ann revealed that she had had an incestuous relationship with her older brother, and a history of sexual and physical abuse from her alcoholic mother. After several sessions, it seemed that Ruth-Ann was unconsciously picking sexually unavailable men so she would not have to repeat the abuse of her past.

Virginity

Both primary and secondary virginity are common among adult children. Primary virginity describes the situation of a person who has never had sexual intercourse. Secondary virginity, however, occurs when men and women who had intercourse during their disease are afraid to resume sexual behavior. Because they were caught in the dysfunction and lacked sufficient role models, or because all of their sexual experiences were compliant ones, they have no idea how to be authentic sexual beings. In treatment, they newly discover themselves.

Rhonda, a twenty-six-year-old single woman, was uncertain whether she was "technically" a virgin. Her alcoholic father had forced her to have sex with him several times when she was ten. He also had continually physically and sexually abused her mother. Now Rhonda was in a relationship with Lucas, who was very religious, and he wanted to know whether she was a virgin. None of Rhonda's past relationships had been sexual; she was sexually inhibited and had preferred remaining platonic with men. She believed she was a virgin, but the incestuous relationship with her father haunted her. When Lucas learned about Rhonda's past, he had difficulty accepting it. He underwent counseling to help him understand and accept the trauma Rhonda had gone through, and eventually they were married.

When It Won't Go In: Vaginismus

Vaginismus is another big issue among women, particularly teenage women. This condition occurs when all the muscles in the vagina contract, preventing penetration by a sexual partner. Vaginismus usually occurs because of past sexual trauma, lack of trust, fear of intimacy, or the fear of losing control and being vulnerable.

Trust: How Not Having It Affects Sexual Function

Retarded ejaculation occurs among many men who grew up in alcoholic homes. These men have an erection and penetrate their partners, but being vulnerable and trusting is more than they can allow themselves. They believe that an orgasm would be the ultimate release of self. This release requires a level of recovery that is hard for some men to reach. Using the Good Sex Program, as Scott did, helps them discover their sexual selves.

A thirty-two-year-old contractor, Scott had one year of sobriety when he and his girlfriend Gilda came in to see me. They had been together for five years during his drinking and cocaine days. Both of them had used cocaine, and Scott had been a dealer. "Sex wasn't important then," Gilda said. "Neither of us was ever interested, and we blamed it on the drugs." But in recovery, Gilda felt something was missing. Scott showed little interest in her, and when they had sex, he was unable to ejaculate inside her.

Scott's father had been an alcoholic and a rageaholic who had put the fear of God and masculinity into his son. The physical and emotional abuse he endured and saw his mother endure suppressed Scott's ability to trust enough to let anyone near him emotionally. Scott could not risk penetrating and ejaculating into his partner because he might be rejected and hurt.

Gilda and Scott followed the Good Sex Program together and gradually discovered how to nurture themselves and each other. Gilda learned how to masturbate Scott, and Scott learned to have Gilda on top during intercourse. They became playful and spontaneous. Eventually their relationship was consummated.

Many individuals whose partners encounter retarded ejaculation feel responsible for that dysfunction. Gilda voiced this feeling when she came to see me. She needed to realize that she was not necessarily responsible for the situation. Ironically, this guilt and concern is another adult child trait, an overdeveloped sense of responsibility.

When They Can't Have an Orgasm

Learning to have an orgasm alone and with their partners is difficult for many women. Those whose orgasms occur unreliably usually suffer from control issues, lack of trust, feeling vulnerable, and "not knowing what a woman is supposed to be like sexually." Polly had some of these issues.

"If I let go and have an orgasm, how will my partner react?" asked Polly, a thirty-two-year-old adult child. When Tod questioned her about what feels good sexually, she told him "Everything you do feels good," yet she never had an orgasm. Polly believed that lying about what she felt or did not feel was easier than telling the truth (another adult child trait) because she was not sure what she liked or wanted. Tod had no idea that she was not having orgasms, because she was good at faking them. When I asked her whether they had talked about this part of their sex life, she laughed. "What is there to say?" she wanted to know. The question she needed to ask was, "What haven't we said that needs to be said?"

Polly and Tod worked the Good Sex Program together and discovered what they wanted and needed in their sexual relationship. Essential for their growth was the development of good communication skills, something they lacked in several areas of their lives. They also learned how to get in touch with their bodies and how to respond as sexual beings, not as they had seen in movies, read about in books, or seen their parents pretend.

It is a myth that men ejaculate every time they have intercourse. Men as well as women sometimes forgo orgasm. The fact that some men are nonorgasmic is a secret because men feel threatened or less manly if they admit they have not had an orgasm and ejaculated. Their partners ask, "Why doesn't he love me anymore?" Here communication between partners is essential if the sexual relationship is to grow and nurture both parties.

Impotence Happens to the Other Guy

Impotence happens to all men at one time or another during their life cycles. Because many men do not realize this behavior commonly occurs, they believe that any episode of impotence is a harbinger of things to come. A pattern of impotence is reinforced when they keep playing the message in their heads, "I think I can't...I think I can't...," and so they don't.

Some impotence is induced by chemicals like alcohol. Most impotent adult children, however, have psychological impotence—the "I think I can't" syndrome. They believe they can't because they didn't have a healthy role model to show them what a man should be or how to behave, or they may have been sexually traumatized.

Dale had struggled with these issues for years. This forty-year-old man was raised to believe that women were "something you bang" because his father and brothers, all alcoholics, had always treated women that way. Dale remembered vividly how his father bragged about "screwing the old lady" and his brothers boasted about their one-night stands. Dale knew he didn't want to repeat their behavior, but he didn't know how to do anything else. He medicated his feelings for about fifteen years before he got sober. In sobriety, however, he had to deal with his impotency. Working the Good Sex Program and the Twelve Steps of AA for sexual recovery, he discovered the tender, open, and trusting authentic sexual man he was.

Overcoming "Don't Talk, Don't Feel, Don't Trust"

As adult children work their recovery programs, they discover that the inability to trust inherent in adult children blocks effective communication, including sexual communication. (Various tools to develop these skills are presented in chapter 13 and part 3.)

Sexual Addiction and Adult Children

The trauma of growing up in an alcoholic environment with various kinds of abuse leads to the repetition of that trauma by some adult children. Without wanting to or understanding why, some men and women may "repeat the sins of their fathers," engaging in sexually addictive activities that spring from their past traumas, some of which go back five generations among sex and romance addicts. This tendency to repeat behaviors from generation to generation is common.

Becoming Sexualized

The process of becoming sexualized—the growing awareness of one's sexual self—occurs during puberty, when the hormonal systems of boys and girls activate. Unfortunately, many adult children were sexualized earlier under traumatic circumstances, including neglect and abuse. Events such as child molestation, enemas, rape, and bondage cause people to shut down sexually or to exaggerate sexual activity and to keep repeating the trauma in an attempt to relieve the resulting pain.

Sex with animals also occurs among adult children. As children, many sought affection from their pets, and some of that need for love was expressed in a sexual way. This experience causes much shame and guilt. Although some clients have said they will take their secret to their graves, Virginia was not among them.

"The only love and affection I remember getting as a child was from my pets and farm animals," said Virginia, a forty-three-year-old store manager. She had been married three times and was single when she came to see me. She had been raised in the South on a farm and had been neglected and emotionally and physically abused. The comfort she had received from her cats, dogs, and pet lambs had been her only escape.

When Virginia and I first met, she had twelve years of recovery from heroin. While she was using drugs, she had gone from being a $2000-per-day prostitute to being unable to perform oral sex for $20. After hitting bottom, she successfully worked a recovery program for her chemicals, recovered from her eating disorder, and addressed her adult child issues. Still unresolved, however, were her sexual trauma issues. Although she had opportunities for human sexual comfort, she turned to her cats for sexual gratification. She had trained them to lick her clitoris, and she masturbated against them. Her cats provided her with the safe, warm feelings she had experienced as a child with her pets.

Co-Sex Addiction

"I keep marrying or getting involved with the same sex addict again and again," said Gloria. "The only change is in his name." Many adult children repeatedly find themselves with the same type of partner. Because they lack role models and an idea of what constitutes a healthy relationship, they think sex is love and that, if they control their partners, they will have the security they lacked in their childhoods. The tendency to be co-sex addicts corresponds well with several other traits, especially being extremely loyal when such loyalty is clearly undeserved.

Growing Up with Incest

The most common incest is between father and daughter, followed by sibling incest, mother with son, mother with daughter, and father with son. Men find it very hard to admit to childhood incest with a parent. Incest issues bring with them the question of boundaries, which adult children have not identified.

Successful recovery from incest issues depends on a solid foundation of recovery from the consequences of childhood in an alcoholic home. The amount of time between beginning adult child work and incest recovery varies. Many incest survivors cannot remember much of their childhood. As techniques such as hypnosis assist the recall of past events, the memories may come as slowly as a trickle or they may be a flood of images.

Myra's memories arose as flashbacks and body memories, the persistent physical reaction to traumatic or painful situations. She was a thirty-seven-year-old nurse who had been raised in Mexico, mostly by maids. She was the third child, with one sister and two older brothers. Myra's father was away from home most of the time. Her mother was addicted to pills and sex and was considered "crazy" by people in their town.

Although her parents neglected and abused Myra, her most painful flashbacks and memories concerned sexual abuse from her brothers. She recalled that, when she was nine, she was hiding in the corn field when her brother and his friend found her and assaulted her. Her body memories of this attack involved burning and other pain in her vagina and pain in her shoulders from being pinned down. Myra is now in recovery from anorexia and co-sex addiction. She completed an inpatient program for her sexual abuse issues and has a good prognosis for recovery.

Am I a Man or Woman? Gender Identity Crisis

Adult children with gender identity crises usually lacked proper role models. If a young boy has a father who was a violent alcoholic and a mother who told him, "Your father is horrible—he's always beating us and never works," that child will not want to grow up to be like dad. However, his only other role model may be his mother, so he may imitate her. Many men discover that, once they are in recovery, they need to validate their personalities. "I don't know how to be a man" or "I know I'm not a woman" is a common cry, because these individuals despised some characteristics they had associated with their gender, and they don't want to be like their fathers.

Estelle suffered the pain of not knowing what it means to be a woman. Her mother had been a chronic dieter who had not given her daughter any physical or verbal affection. Estelle's father was an alcoholic who molested his daughter continually for years. Estelle clearly had received inappropriate signals from both parents about women, whose nature she thought was evil. Somehow Estelle believed that it was her fault that her father had treated her badly; if she had been born a boy, she thought, everything would have been okay. She remained loyal and protective of her father despite his abuse of her.

Getting Better: General Therapeutic Approaches

Adult children tend to be givers and caretakers, often forgetting to take care of themselves first. Thus their initial issue in recovery is learning to be comfortable with themselves. Once they learn to acknowledge themselves as vital and complete individuals by working the Twelve Steps of AA adapted for adult children, they can discover their sexual selves using the Good Sex Program.

A Leap of Faith: Trauma Survivors

9

"I was voted most likely to succeed by my parents ever since I can remember." These words emerged bitterly from Nick, who had received scholarships to three prestigious Ivy League colleges, had completed two master's degrees, and at age thirty-two was working for minimum wage in a deli. He had seven years of sobriety from his chemical dependency and two years in recovery from sexual addiction. The sexual part of his relationship with his partner had gradually dwindled during the previous year. She was concerned about the loss, which she feared might be permanent.

During our sessions, Nick slowly uncovered the depth of his emotions associated with being labeled as bright and capable. Nick was expected to be the family hero in his alcoholic family. Although he could perform bright, six-year-old activities when he was that age, his parents pushed him to do high school algebra. When he was in high school, they were planning his doctoral program.

Nick learned to internalize his family's unrealistic standards, although they were impossible for any human to achieve. Realizing that whatever he did "wouldn't be good enough for them," he left graduate school, worked part-time, and shut off all his feelings. After he started a program of sexual recovery based on the Twelve Steps of AA, he began to have feelings, including rage, about this intellectual abuse. He used the Good Sex Program to learn how to share and experience these feelings with himself and his partner.

Peeling the Artichoke: Reaching the Core Issues

Picture an artichoke, plump leaves enveloping the inner heart. As men and women peel away the leaves of addictions and dysfunctions—in Nick's case, chemical dependency and lack of sexual desire—they reach the heart of the matter. Here the core issues hide, the reasons why people act and feel the way they do.

Recovery is a process of peeling away as many leaves as it takes to reach the core issue or issues. At the heart are feelings that were medicated with addictive behavior, which in turn causes more hurtful thoughts and feelings. People with post-traumatic stress disorder (see Appendix 9-1) have survived a devastating trauma or traumas, such as rape, incest, or child molestation, in which uncontrollable stress made a long-lasting psychological (and, some researchers now believe, a physiological) impact. In recovery, trauma survivors can learn to know, understand, and release the events that hindered them from emerging as healthy sexual beings.

Trauma: The Pervasive Experience

It is impossible to have grown up in modern society without having experienced some trauma. In order to assess the impact, the questions to be asked are, What was the duration and severity of the trauma? Was there a single incident, a series, or several different events? What is the psychological makeup of individuals who are coping with trauma?

Two people exposed to the same traumatic event respond in different ways. One may develop post-traumatic stress symptoms; another may be only mildly affected. Some may have symptoms for decades; others' symptoms resolve spontaneously; still other people may need therapy to gain new perspectives about the experience and ways to deal with it.

A recent theory is that a physical basis underlies post-traumatic stress disorder. Scientists have shown that a single overwhelming traumatic event can alter the brain chemistry of some people. This imbalance creates a sensitivity to adrenalin surges that may persist for decades. A traumatic event also can activate the part of the brain that blunts pain and causes emotional numbing.

Medicating the Pain of Trauma

Children raised in dysfunctional families or adults who have suffered different kinds of trauma look for ways to medicate those experiences. As children, they did not learn healthy ways to cope with these events, and as adults they often are unaware of ways to heal the pain they feel. Some carry the feelings of guilt, shame, and pain for decades. Ethel, a fifty-two-year-old secretary, came to me after completing inpatient treatment for compulsive over-eating. She had been in an asexual marriage for twenty-four years. As she brought her eating disorder into remission, she connected with her anger and her feelings of rejection about what was happening, or not happening, in her marriage.

As she thought back to the early messages she received about sex, she recalled that at age four, a teenage neighbor boy had invited her into his home, pulled down her pants, and fondled her. She had told her mother, but her mother shamed and blamed her for "what she had done." She was a "bad, naughty girl" who never should have gone to his house and "should have known better." The sexual shame as part of her core being was implicated in her asexual marriage and her eating disorder.

Ethel also processed the abuse she had suffered daily at the hands of her alcoholic, rageaholic father and her codependent mother. She began to see that she did not have to be a victim of her past anymore. As she separated the past from her present life, she realized that it was her parents' shame, not hers. Ethel also recognized that she had a right to live a healthy sexual adulthood.

The issues associated with trauma span mild to severe codependency; yo-yo dieting to life-threatening anorexia; mild to severe post-traumatic stress disorder and multiple personalities. Every issue pulled away and dealt with brings men and women closer to their core concerns and to recovery.

Pressure Cookers of Emotions

Trauma survivors are full of conscious or unconscious turbulent thoughts and feelings, waiting to boil over into addictions, psychosomatic illnesses, or psychological defenses such as hypervigilance or denial. It is not a question of if. The eruption *will* happen. The question is when people will feel safe enough to reveal to themselves and others what has been hidden for so long. Survivors can maintain happy, false selves instead of their authentic selves for some time. But as their defenses fail and they proceed more years into recovery from their addictions; as they get older and their defenses wear thin; as they find themselves in safer surroundings and can allow themselves to let down their defenses, they see more deeply into themselves. What emerges are the dark secrets that they tucked away long ago.

Releasing the Pressure

Nick, the former doctoral candidate, had repressed his rage in addictions and denial, living with feelings of worthlessness and anger, and turning off his sexual feelings. When he began recovery from his addictions, the unconscious memories emerged. At the core of the sexual dysfunctions and addictive behaviors was his childhood intellectual abuse.

Annie is another example of how suppressed childhood hurts can come out under pressure years later. She first came to see me ten years ago, concerned about her relationship with her lover, Doris. As we discussed Annie's lack of sexual desire and inability to have an orgasm, I learned that both women were active alcoholics. Having entered recovery, Annie now has ten years' sobriety. Doris, however, refused treatment, and the relationship ended.

Annie's recovery program included working through her adult child issues because she had two alcoholic parents. After her codependency, anorexia, and alcoholism were in remission, she came back to see me several years ago and wanted to address her sex and romance addiction as well.

Annie had many artichoke leaves to peel away. About one year into her recovery for sex and romance addiction, she began to have flashbacks and body memories of physical and sexual abuse. The body memories were pains in her vagina and burning sensations in her uterus. These feelings she had experienced in childhood when she had been sexually abused. Annie then began the Twelve Step Program for her trauma issues. With additional individual and group therapy, she is making peace with her past. She is dealing with her shame core and beginning to reclaim the precious child that was wounded long ago. In this process, Annie is touching her true sexual self, free of her addictions.

Types of Trauma

Trauma includes more than rape, child molestation, or incest. Emotional, intellectual, physical, sexual, spiritual, and ritual abuse are all trauma issues that affect people's functioning.

Mind Manipulation: Emotional Abuse

"You're a hopeless case!" "You'll never get it right." "You'll never amount to anything." How many people have heard those words or similar ones? Such statements, especially made to young children, constitute emotional abuse. But it is not limited to children. "Every day of our five-year marriage, my husband told me I was a cold, stupid bitch," said Brittany, a thirty-year-old woman who was an account executive for a large advertising firm. "Not until years later, after we were divorced and I had received therapy, did I realize how corrosive that daily barrage had been." Emotional abuse can occur at any time in people's lives and comes from work environments, family, spouses, lovers, friends, and social situations.

Keeping Women and Men "in Their Place"

A common form of emotional abuse is the "gender" trauma women and men face. Systematic intellectual abuse of women and emotional abuse of men in society keep each sex in the "proper" place. Many women have been programmed to "be beautiful, not smart," and to believe that "if you want to catch a man you must be submissive." They've been told, "You can't have it all," and have been chastised for daring to try to succeed.

Men also are victims of gender abuse. Despite the women's rights movement and an effort to educate both men and women about equal opportunities for both genders, many pervasive and abusive ideas still persist. Men are admonished not to feel or show their emotions, for fear of being labeled soft or wimpy. They are expected to be hard and competitive, the stereotypical breadwinner. Male hairdressers or interior designers or men who switch roles with their wives and become househusbands are suspected of being "less than" real men.

Abuse and shaming messages are delivered to both genders: girls are stupid and boys are smart; it's a woman's "job" to care for the children and the home, and the man's "job" to bring home the money; women should be thin sex objects, and men should be macho studs. When men and women grow up hearing these messages from their families and society, they believe they are expected to perform these rigid roles.

Intellectual Abuse

Emotional and intellectual abuse inherently go hand-in-hand. Shaming messages are verbal attacks like these: "Shut up; you're stupid." "Can't you do better?" "Everyone does better than you do." "Why can't you be as smart as your sister?" Such pitiless criticism corrodes a child's self-respect. Over time, children who experience this abuse from their parents decide that no matter how bright or capable or lovable they may be, they are totally inferior persons.

Sophia was a bright, precocious, beautiful child who, to the outside world, appeared to have sensitive, caring parents. At home, however, they abused her. Because she was so bright, they had expected great achievements beyond her intellectual development. Although their physical abuse was minimal, the emotional abuse was devastating. They repeatedly told her, "If you don't do what I say, I'm going to kill you." These threats were combined with the fact that no matter how perfect she was, her parents were dissatisfied. When she took Spanish, they said she should have taken French. When she preferred to go to Vasser, they wanted her to choose Sarah Lawrence.

This continuous no-win bind emotionally disabled Sophia most of her adult life. At the time she entered therapy, she and her husband of twenty-seven years had gradually stopped having sex because Sophia couldn't stand the thought of intercourse. When she started exploring her feelings, we found that she had a severe post-traumatic stress disorder associated with her abuse.

Not all trauma is inflicted in childhood, of course. Traumatic events that occur in adulthood can be equally devastating, as they were for Tracy. Often these events paralyze people until they do not know how to care for themselves.

"I had no right to be alive." Those words were the beginning of recovery and freedom from guilt for Tracy, who was severely dysfunctional with post-traumatic stress. She had been a nurse in Vietnam, and during the Tet offensive she was part of the operation that evacuated the babies. After she put the last of the babies on the plane, the plane departed and crashed, killing everyone on board. Still in Vietnam herself, she began drinking heavily.

Seven years later, Tracy achieved sobriety. After three years of recovery her husband gave her an ultimatum. He had hoped that, with recovery, her sexual interest would return. When it did not, he told her, "See a therapist, or I need to find another woman."

Tracy felt responsible for what had happened to the infants. Her survival seemed unjust when so many others had died. She believed she should be condemned to a life of death on earth. Gradually she accepted her innocence and initiated the grieving process she had never allowed herself to experience. As she did, she started to respond sexually to her husband.

Containment Abuse

Morgan came to me with eight years of recovery and told me he could not understand why he wanted to die. He and his lover had a very good, loving relationship. During treatment I began to see untreated adult child issues. His father had been a raging schizophrenic alcoholic, and Morgan had been the object of his father's delusions and abuses. Morgan finally ran away when he was thirteen.

As Morgan began to experience feelings other than those related to suicide, he picked up emotionally where he had left off. He felt anew the hopelessness and despair he had felt as a child when he had been locked in his room and his father taunted him from outside the door for hours until Morgan cried and screamed to get out.

Containment abuse is one of the most severe trauma issues. After Morgan underwent therapy and attended meetings, he began making peace with his past. When he worked Steps Eight and Nine, he discovered his desire to become a clown. He now volunteers as a clown several hours a week and does children's shows for neglected, injured, and battered children. While he is helping other children, he also is healing the child within himself.

Sexual Dysfunctions among the Sexually Abused

The primary forms of sexual abuse are rape, child molestation, and incest. The sexual symptoms and dysfunctions associated with these forms of abuse are generally, but not exclusively, common to all three.

People who have been sexually abused are tender. They come to me saying that they

- feel disgust about sex
- can't get enough

- treat sex like a job
- don't enjoy touching and being touched
- feel emotionally distant and dissociated during sex
- have disturbing sexual thoughts
- engage in one or several compulsive sexual behaviors
- are difficult to arouse
- cannot be intimate or bond with other people
- experience impotence, vaginal pain, or retarded ejaculation.

Accompanying physical symptoms often include headaches, asthma, heart palpitations, gastrointestinal disorders, pelvic pain, general body aches, and faintness or dizziness. These men and women also suffer from depression, anxiety, low self-esteem, self-abusive behavior, and stress.

Rape

Rape is unwanted, forcible, or violent sexual touching, fondling, and intercourse with someone who does not consent. The definition of rape has expanded to include assaults by dates, spouses, and strangers. Date rape is not a new phenomenon, but it is gaining recognition as people begin to understand personal boundaries.

The same can be said about marital rape. "I was told I had to put up with it," some women say. Many have been married for ten to twenty years and think that rape is sex; they don't know that they are being raped by their husbands. They were raised to believe it their duty to submit to their husbands' sexual demands. Many women therefore have been victims of sexual abuse that passed as "dating" and "marriage." They carry emotional scars of this sexual trauma.

Rape by strangers or accompanied by additional violence are the types most easily identified as assault. Rape survivors experience fear, shock, helplessness, pain, and a sense of lost control. They are usually reluctant to report these incidents, because they often feel they are to blame. They are convinced no one will believe them, or that they are cheap and dirty. This repugnance leads some to keep the event a secret for days or years. Others report it after seeking help at rape trauma centers or talking with trusted family or friends. Every rape survivor responds to the assault uniquely. Thus they bring into the post-traumatic period of their lives various degrees of guilt, shame, denial, fear, anger, and depression.

Marla kept her secret for six months. She was an untreated adult child and thirty-nine years old when she called to make an appointment with me. Six months before seeing me, she had been brutally raped on her way home from her job as a part-time book-keeper at a thrift store. The rapist had threatened to kill her with a gun.

As she talked about the event, she said, "I was going to die, and I was aware that I had not lived yet." Once she revealed this terrible thought, we focused her recovery on her memory of her childhood and the reasons she felt she had "missed out." For the first time, Marla felt the violation she had experienced during the sexual assault. Although dealing with the rage was painful, it helped her realize that life is fragile. She decided she wanted to "live before I die," so she returned to college, earned a bachelor's degree in architecture, and continued working toward her master's degree in environmental architecture. Marla's success in processing a life-threatening event and dealing effectively with the aftermath can be realized by other trauma survivors once they get in touch with their memories and feelings about the incident.

Rape survivors need unconditional love and as much support as possible after the event. The combination of sexual violence and the feelings of shame and guilt which it elicits leads to many problems in daily life. Survivors often suffer from disturbed relationships with lovers, friends, and family. Many find sex disgusting or adopt addictive behavior to medicate the pain and shame.

Child Molestation

By definition, child molestation involves a child younger than eighteen who is sexually seduced by an older person in authority. Generally, child molesters are classified as sexual sociopaths, sex-addicted offenders, or pedophiles. Sexual sociopaths victimize children and feel no remorse or guilt about their actions. Some are involved in "kiddie-porn" trafficking, child prostitution, and the exploitation of children in pornographic movies and literature. Since this type of sex offender considers children to be expendable, these victims are in danger of being hurt or killed.

Pedophiles are men or women who engage in sexual activities with children as their preferred or exclusive method of achieving sexual excitement (see "Paraphilia," chapter 3). These activities involve exhibitionism, the fondling of children's sexual parts, masturbation, oral sex, or intercourse.

Pedophiles often rationalize that they loved their victims or introduced them to adult sexuality for the children's good. Survivors of child molestation are consequently confused about their perpetrators' behavior. Many clients have reported that their perpetrators were "loving" or "gentle" during their encounters. The stereotypical picture of the dirty old man in the gray raincoat or the man who lures children with offers of candy are not true pictures of pedophiles.

Incest

Incest is any covert or overt sexual behavior that occurs between an adult or an older child, and a child who feels or is closely related. Many adults have repressed such childhood experiences.

After three weeks in a treatment program for alcoholism, Abe, a thirty-six-year-old school principal, experienced body memories from his early boyhood. These memories came out in therapy sessions, where he curled up in a fetal position, screaming in pain. He was referred to me immediately because it was clear that if he did not deal with his past he could not maintain sobriety.

Abe was severely depressed and needed antidepressant medication before he could work with his issues. As we pieced together his childhood, Abe attached images to the body memories. He recalled that someone unknown had hidden in his bedroom closet and had sodomized him when he was asleep. Initially, knowing the identity of the rapist was important to him, but gradually that need dissipated as his body recalled the pain. In the course of releasing the hurt, he had flashbacks of the rapes, but he worked through the memories and got on with his life.

Recognizing Incest Survivors

One factor links many of the men and women who have addictive behaviors and sexual dysfunctions: as children they were involved in incestuous relationships with one or both parents. (See Appendix 9-2 for signs and symptoms indicative of incest survivors.)

120

These survivors may complain of retarded ejaculation; they may lack sexual desire, or be hypersexual, nonorgasmic, or totally turned off by sex. Many of them also are codependent or have a chemical addiction or an eating disorder. Sexual addiction often is an issue for incest survivors. Because they themselves have undergone severe trauma, they are more likely to engage in child abuse, knowingly or unknowingly, repeating the pattern from generation to generation.

Self-mutilation is another common behavior among abuse survivors, who use physical pain to medicate the pain they feel inside. Cutting or carving patterns into their skin, burning their skin with cigarettes or matches, and pulling out their hair are some of the ways they hurt themselves. In related activities, sadomasochists cut or otherwise injure their own or partners' sexual body parts.

Survivors of incest and other trauma have difficulty being close to others, and sometimes they hate being touched. Chronic depression, guilt, shame, low self-esteem, and feelings of worthlessness also affect them. Physical manifestations include insomnia, gastrointestinal disorders, gynecological difficulties, and hormonal disorders.

Whatever the manifestations in behavior or physical symptoms, the core issue is always the same: incest. Survivors of incest cannot remember all or part of their childhoods or they have frozen feelings. When they can feel, they feel fear or shame. As they pull the leaves off the artichoke, they find they were injured by sexual abuse within their families. Perhaps they witnessed incest between other family members; maybe as adults they are the partners of incest victims. These indirect incest survivors also are injured. Witnesses or partners of victims have their own pain to live with as they repress the memories or watch their partners either deal with the issues or suppress them and flee.

Healing the pain of incest often means making therapy a "family affair," according to Mike Lew, author of *Victims No Longer*. Individuals who decide to reveal the secret they've been carrying for years usually upset their families, but they also open the door to recovery for all family members who choose to walk that path as well.[18]

---

18. Mike Lew, *Victims No Longer* (New York: Nevraumont Publishing, 1988), 196.

Facing the Issues, Healing the Pain

In *The Courage to Heal*, Ellen Bass and Laura Davis aptly observe the chronology of stages incest survivors go through. The first stage is also the one that initially prompts most people to seek help. Men and women in this **emergency state** have partners who threaten to leave, or they want to have a baby, or they are getting sober and cannot cope with flashbacks and memories that are intruding. In the **remembering** stage, pieces of the past float up into consciousness, and the pieces eventually fit into the complete puzzle. These memories are usually locked somewhere in the body, and they can be called up to consciousness by visual or auditory triggers, touch, or a smell or taste. These body memories are physical reactions to past events, and they can appear in any number of ways. Some of my clients report feeling "like someone is grabbing my neck," or "someone is pinning my arms to my sides," or "a burning, sharp pain in my vagina."

To deal with the memories as they come, some clients look at their old photo albums, recalling their school days, and using other methods to help them deal with body memories and flashbacks. Clients who do "inner child" work use meditation or hypnosis to go back (or regress) and look at those traumatic events that caused them to become "stuck" or frozen at some point in childhood. When they go back and get in touch with the personality that was not allowed to grow, they are safe, with the trauma in the past. They can recover their authentic selves; they are able to drop the masks. Clients who experience inner child work usually learn the reasons behind their addictive behaviors.

Next comes **believing that the trauma happened**. Many survivors of sexual trauma say repeatedly, "It really happened." For example, survivors of satanic rituals were intentionally programmed to disbelieve their own memories. This disbelief is denial, the first obstacle to recovery. Surmounting it is usually the hardest step for satanic ritual survivors, because the magnitude of the horrors they have witnessed or participated in is often hard for most people to accept.

Breaking silence involves survivors' going to therapists, clergy, family members, friends, or the perpetrators. It also involves finding sponsors and beginning to tell the truth to themselves and another. Sharing the pain is a cleansing and healing experience.

Understanding that it wasn't their fault relieves a great deal of survivors' guilt. Men and women believe that if somehow they had been smarter, thinner, bigger, a boy, or a girl, none of their anguish would have happened. They assume the guilt because the perpetrators feel none. Incest survivors need to understand that they were children when the incidents occurred. My clients therefore go to schools to observe children of the age at which their own personal abuse started. This exercise allows them to begin to realize that the incest was not their fault. They do not need to carry the responsibility for the actions of perpetrators any longer.

Making contact with the past is accomplished when clients locate family photographs of themselves, objects, stuffed animals, and dolls that represent the children within themselves. People commonly house several inner children of different ages—the children they were at different times in their past when they tried to deal with trauma. With help, a client can integrate those children, making sure that the survivor is in charge of the "committee."

Trusting themselves is a big step for survivors of sexual abuse, who are the least likely of all groups to trust anything they think or feel, because of the way they learned to survive. Their personal boundaries were violated; they therefore cannot trust or even know what they feel. Clients work with me to explore their feelings as they define their boundaries.

Grieving is another step in recovery. Incest survivors not only process the painful events they experienced, but mourn their stolen childhood. Adults seem to make peace with actual events more successfully than they accept the loss of what they never had. My clients' process of grief may involve planning memorial or funeral services for their childhood or painfully divorcing their perpetrators.

Anger, the backbone of healing, is an emotion so powerful that it is potentially destructive. To vent their anger, my clients use batakas and tennis rackets or chop wood; others write letters, put their thoughts and feelings on tape, or do anything they can to express their frustration and rage safely.

Healthy expression of anger is crucial for all survivors of abuse. Men and women who choose **disclosure and confrontation** tell their perpetrators or others involved in the abuse what they know about it. Other trauma survivors have no need or desire to confront the individuals responsible for the abuse. People who decide upon disclosure need to make this choice with the guidance and support of a therapist, sponsor, cleric, confidant, or other trusted individual.

Forgiveness is part of Steps Eight and Nine, forgiving self and forgiving the others involved. People need to forgive for themselves, not for the sake of the perpetrators. At this point, clients are willing to do anything to recover, even making amends for their character defects directly to the perpetrator if his recovery has begun. Forgiveness does not mean pardoning or whitewashing; it means accepting, surrendering, letting go of the event, and getting on with life. For their own sake, people forgive those who have harmed them; they are not condoning the behavior or releasing the perpetrators from accountability for their actions.

When Pope John Paul II was shot in 1981, he went to the prison to forgive his assassin. The pope felt the need to forgive his perpetrator, and he did so. Forgiveness is something people do for themselves. The assassin was not released from prison, nor was he absolved of his obligation to pay for his crime; he was simply forgiven. This act differs from a pardon, which is what President Ford gave Richard Nixon.

As clients let go of the past, they feel inner peace and comfort with themselves and God. They experience **spirituality,** a feeling of completeness that puts them in touch with inner strength. Some people describe spirituality as coming into the light after a long time in the dark. They feel well at last, rather than sick.

Trauma survivors also begin to see their own perpetration issues. As survivors, perhaps they have unknowingly injured others by being distrustful, distant, cold, angry, controlling, and judgmental, in their effort to protect themselves.

Resolution and moving on is the next natural progression. Survivors have combined acceptance with inner strength so they can go on with their lives. My clients use a wide variety of techniques during this process, depending on their own personal needs: journaling or inner child work; relaxation methods such as breathing and massage; psychodrama, in which groups act out life events, changing the endings. Twelve-Step groups, inpatient or outpatient treatment centers, and assertiveness training have helped other survivors. These many methods bring trauma survivors to integrate healthy sexuality and complete the process of their healing.

Sexual Abuse in Men

Men cannot easily admit having been sexually abused. Tending to interpret such assaults as threats to their masculinity, they are afraid to be labeled homosexuals or wimps.

As Ellen Bass says in *The Courage to Heal*, you can't forget what you can't remember. Gerald, a teacher in his early thirties with seven years of recovery, knew the truth of that statement. Increasing pain in his rectum was waking him up at night. Although he associated the pain with his childhood, he had repressed the source.

Under hypnosis, Gerald went back to an earlier age. He had flashbacks to a three-month period when he was sodomized by older boys in a juvenile correction facility. When he had been unconscious of the injury, he was paralyzed in his nightmares. After he remembered the assaults, he worked through the stages of recovery to heal his wounds. Then he could truly leave the past behind him.

Many men who are in touch with their physical abuse have a harder time identifying sexual abuse in their lives. Statistics show that one in three girls and one in seven boys have been sexually traumatized by the time they reach age eighteen.[19] Such stigma surrounds sexual traumas to boys and young men that many men interpret injuries as "getting lucky."

Alan totally repressed such memories. He was a twenty-eight-year-old married man with two children. Because of his pornography collection, drinking in strip bars, and paying prostitutes, he was going bankrupt. As he brought his sex addiction into remission, unbearable images arose of his father coming home drunk every day for years and physically abusing him and his sisters. He was beaten with two-by-fours, stripped naked, and forcibly confined in a closet. His father taunted him in front of his sisters, and failed to feed or clothe the children appropriately. Alan finally remembered that his father had sodomized him during a drunken stupor.

---

19. Ellen Bass and Laura Davis, *The Courage to Heal* (New York: Harper and Row, 1988), 20.

In the course of recovery, Alan admitted that he was reenacting on his son what had been done to him as a child. At that point, the boy was removed from their home until Alan learned how to feel his feelings, express them appropriately, and put structure back into his chaotic life. Today Alan has peace and serenity and three years of recovery. The family went through family counseling. Now Alan's marriage, although shaky, is much sounder than before.

Intergenerational Addictions and Abuse

Trauma, alcoholism, eating disorders, and sexual addiction often recur from one generation to the next, as began to happen between Alan and his son. Unresolved sexual issues go on for generations. The dynamics of such a family create a high risk for trauma of all kinds, including overt and covert incest. Alan's story illustrates how alcoholism was intergenerational, and child abuse was a real issue until he sought family therapy.

Spiritual Abuse

The attempt to dominate, manipulate, and control others who are defenseless to resist, in the name of God, Jesus, a guru, Buddha, or any other religious authority is spiritual abuse.

Phyllis is a good example of a woman subjected to such control. She came to see me directly from the treatment center for cocaine recovery. Her husband Ted was a devout Christian who believed that "good" wives always obey their husbands. They had two children after fifteen years of marriage. Phyllis had lost all sexual desire during the previous few years. Ted was an out-of-control sex addict, demanding that she service him sexually two to three times a day. Phyllis was afraid he would leave her and the children if she did not give in to his demands. The only way she could cope with him, however, was to stay high on cocaine.

In sobriety, Phyllis returned to her normal state before cocaine use, which, after being made to obey her husband all those years, was sexual numbness. Working together, we discovered that she was torn between obeying her husband as a "good Christian woman" and following her own heart and soul to healthy sexuality. She wanted to work through her sexual trauma issues and own some power and control over herself and her body, without disrupting the relationship. Unwilling to give up his drug, Ted refused to let Phyllis continue therapy.

126

Another woman, Ursula, a forty-three-year-old college administrator, was three years into recovery for an eating disorder, exercise addiction, and sexual addiction. As those issues came into remission, memories emerged about her childhood in a very strict Catholic family. She had been sexually traumatized by priests and nuns in her school years between the ages of six and nine, when her perpetrators told her that her participation in these sexual acts was pleasing to God, Mary, and Jesus.

Yolanda, who had been brought up in a fundamentalist religion, came to me complaining of chronic pain and lack of sexual desire. As we worked, I realized that she much preferred the physical pain to the emotional pain of confronting her mother's "desertion" and her own subsequent sexual abuse by her grandfather, who was a peer in the church. Yolanda was an orphan who had lived with her grandparents from age three after her parents were killed in an automobile accident. Her grandfather convinced her that, in the eyes of God, their sexual relationship was healthy, and she must acquiesce in order to be God's servant.

Ritual Abuse

Like other forms of abuse, ritual abuse is something most people pretend does not exist. Such denial allows it to continue. Ritual abuse is any systematic practice or pattern whereby an individual or group harms or controls its victims. These victims are usually children or adults who are unable to resist or escape the abusive behavior. Some ritual practices appeal to a higher authority or power, such as satan, a guru, or other authority figure, as a way to justify or rationalize the actions taken by the perpetrators. This abuse may be mental, physical, emotional, spiritual, or sexual.

Perpetrators of ritual abuse deepen the silence of their already powerless, poor, young, innocent, or desperate victims. Victims are often forced to perform exhibitionistic or sadistic acts, or to participate in sacrifices involving torture, murder, cannibalism, and other cruel abuses. Some victims are programmed to kill themselves if they ever reveal information about specific rituals or the organizational structure and leadership of the cult. These threats are especially common in satanic rituals.

"It's like living in a continuous nightmare." "I felt like I was walking on eggs all the time." "Beatings became as much a part of my life as eating and sleeping." These words come from the people I see who have endured ritual abuses in childhood. My clients describe the diverse ritual ways people devise to hurt one another.

The routine Barry's father practiced was private, not a group behavior. He regularly came home drunk, found something to get angry about, beat his son, and then locked him in the closet without food or water for at least twenty-four hours.

Janet's abuse came from her older sister Brenda. Whenever the girls' parents left the girls alone, Brenda tied Janet's ankles together and, beating her with a belt, forced her to jump up and down the hall to make her behave. Janet underwent this abuse for several years and never told her parents.

Walt was physically abused by his father, who tied him naked to the bed and beat him every night with a belt or piece of wood. Even though he had welts and could not sit, he was expected to go to school.

Satanic Rituals

Perhaps the most terrifying and devastating abuse that can be inflicted upon human beings is the emotional and physical trauma associated with satanic rituals, some of which occur during special holidays on the satanic calendar. Others, incorporated into daily life also, severely traumatize participants. Many ritual abuse survivors are introduced into the cults at a very young age or at birth. As adults, most of these survivors have deeply repressed memories of the rituals.

Jessica, thirty-eight years old, had two children and a sex addict husband. She was anorexic because, whenever she began to eat, she remembered being forced by her older brother, a cult member, to eat disgusting substances. Also, her mother, a drug addict, had used enemas on Jessica as a daily torture; the duration of the enemas was based on her mother's judgment of how "bad" she had been that day.

Cynthia was a teacher of the year. At age thirty-two, she had received a lot of therapy before coming to see me for biologic depression. After we brought that into remission, she began to remember her father, brothers, and uncles sexually abusing her in a satanic cult. She entered an inpatient treatment program for sexual trauma for thirty days and then wanted to control her flashbacks. With my group of satanic-ritual survivors, she began to piece together her "marriage to satan" and the continual rituals of abuse and torture. It took her many months to deal with her violent memories. A woman had been murdered during Cynthia's "marriage" ceremony. Babies and animals were killed, and Cynthia was baptized in a vat of blood filled with dismembered babies and animals.

Hector was a ritual survivor who had resolved his drinking and sex addiction, but he was severely depressed. When I first saw him he was in the hospital, where he was remembering satanic ritual abuse. After extensive work using Laura Bass's incest stages and the Good Sex Program, he established a good relationship with another man and has a productive life today.

Nancy had been a priestess in a cult. She came to see me because she and her husband were having sexual problems. "He wants it all the time and I don't care at all," she said. As we dealt with her aversion to sex, memories of incest with her father came to her. Behind those were satanic ritual memories. She entered treatment, dealt with her multiple personality disorder, and continued to work as a nurse.

Robin was the most traumatized satanic survivor I've seen. She had never had an orgasm and felt "I deserve one before I die." Robin had eight years of sobriety and five years of recovery from her eating disorder when she first came to therapy. We started on her sex history and used exercises that focus on the senses as a way to become more aware of feelings, wants, and desires. Robin began to realize that she had never been aware of her body. She had always dissociated herself from her feelings and sensations, never acknowledging that she wanted or needed anything. As she started to know and understand her body through these exercises, she felt heart palpitations and pains in her arms, body memories of being held down and raped. Flashbacks of her parents and their satanic cult rituals also troubled her. Today Robin is dealing with the fact that her husband is a member of the cult and that he brought her children into it.

10

Double Winners: What Gay People Need to Know

Alfred Kinsey explained the range of sexual preference: 10 percent of people are gay, 10 percent are straight, and the rest fall somewhere in the continuum. At some point in their lives, those 80 percent are afraid that they are gay. Many people owe their fear to a lack of sex education and ignorance of the fact that same-sex thoughts, feelings, and behaviors are a normal part of life and development. By age forty-five, 50 percent of men and about 28 percent of women have had a same-sex relationship, experience, or thought.[20]

The notion that homosexuality is a mental disorder is a misconception; it definitely is not. It is a normal variation. Homophobia, however, an intense fear of being gay translated into fear of homosexuals, is a certified mental disorder. In all the research that has been done, no one has discovered any "cause" or "cure" for homosexuality. That's because homosexuality is a characteristic that people need to accept; it is not a character defect.

Becoming Aware of a Homosexual Identity

Gay men usually become aware of their sexual preference before age eighteen. They tend to focus their relationships on their sexual activities with partners, an emphasis that once led to the prac-

---

20. Alfred C. Kinsey, Wardell B. Pomeroy, and Clyde E. Martin, *Sexual Behavior in the Human Female* (Philadelphia: WB Saunders, 1953, rev. 1966), 487.

tice of having multiple partners. The prevalence of AIDS has made this behavior less common.

Lesbians usually become aware of their sexual preference at a little later age than gay men. They tend to be the least sexually active people and the most monogamous of all couples; they have a lower rate of sexually transmitted diseases than either gay men or heterosexuals. They also seem to suffer the greatest inhibition of sexual desire, an issue many have resolved by using the Good Sex Program.

Many homosexual people who get sober then find that they need to deal with their sexual preference—the coming-out process. It is difficult for them to maintain healthy sobriety without making peace with their sexuality. Sometimes they are as homophobic as everyone else in the culture. The shame, guilt, and anger they feel about their sexual preference trigger relapses into addictive behaviors unless these people work through their conflicts.

"Am I Gay?" Chemically Dependent Men and Women Want to Know

A sexual issue that alcohol and drugs medicate is people's fear that they might be gay. Homophobia, an important issue among chemically dependent men and women, is especially prevalent among male alcoholics. Ninety percent of men in the United States are not gay, but what panics them is their *fear* that they may be gay.

Gay individuals usually lack healthy sexual role models because their parents were not gay. They don't know that during healthy psychosexual development—the twelve to fourteen years of same-sex play, scouting, camps, and paper routes—same-sex thoughts, feelings, and behaviors are normal. Ignorance results in fear. Chemically dependent women and men, who don't recognize their own emotions or trust others enough to talk intimately, stuff these feelings and experiences. They react to their fear by doing insane things to prove they're straight, when in reality nothing needs proving.

Like many other male alcoholics, Bert feared that he was gay because of several one-time, same-sex encounters during his drinking days. His fear drove him to use prostitutes obsessively. Lydia, another alcoholic, became so obsessed with thinking she

132

might be gay that she cruised the bars and picked up men indiscriminately. It is not unusual for this proving process to get out of hand for many chemically dependent individuals.

On the other hand, many men and women who are integrated and happy being gay begin to fear that they may be straight. This "heterophobia" sometimes occurs when gay women and men have opposite-sex affairs during their addictive days. Some worry about opposite-sex relationships they had before they recognized they were gay.

Facing Fears

Facing the reality of homosexuality is difficult and painful for some recovering people, especially those who began abusing substances early in adolescence because most are frozen sexually at that point. Once they stop drinking, they face their emerging sexual thoughts and feelings. They need to deal with this awakening honestly as part of their recovery.

Gay Alcoholics: Double Issues

As gay men and women discover their sexual preference, they often hold the same initial fears and opinions about homosexuality as uninformed heterosexuals do. Dispelling these misconceptions is necessary to acceptance of their sexual identity. Those who are both gay and alcoholic have to cope with double issues.

Many gay people use alcohol to deal with their feelings about their sexuality, and much gay social interchange revolves around bars and night clubs. It is in this social setting that much of the "coming out" process occurs. Drinking and being gay become inextricably linked.

Coming out is such a sensitive and difficult process for many gays that they often use alcohol and other drugs to delay it for years. As homosexuals become conscious of their sexual thoughts, feelings, and behaviors, they begin to label themselves and others, often erroneously, because they do not know what normality is. If they have sex seven times in one weekend, they must be sex addicts. If they eat a whole pound of chips, they are overeaters.

Geoff, a sixty-five-year-old man with fifteen years of sobriety, told me he felt suicidal. When he had become sober fifteen years ago, he had left his wife and four children, and he had avoided a sexual relationship since then. He learned in sobriety that he was sexually attracted to men, but his religious beliefs would not allow him to act on his feelings. He was tormented constantly by intense fear and denial of his sexual preference. Geoff's self-hatred finally drove him to suicide.

Stages of Emergence

Researchers have found that the coming-out process develops in six stages of growth. Often, but not always, people begin to become aware of their affinity to one gender or the other during adolescence or even before.

For Suzanne, that awareness came after she had had sexual experiences with men. A nineteen-year-old college student, she was engaged to be married and had been sexually active with her fiancé for almost two years. During that time, however, she had not had the bell-ringing experiences her friends talked about. As she worked through the Good Sex Program, she discovered that she was attracted to women. Initially, this fact was unacceptable to her, but she finally acknowledged that she could not return to a sexual relationship with her fiancé. She and her fiancé ended their engagement amicably. He was sad but relieved, and Suzanne eventually became involved in a fulfilling relationship that has continued for more than five years.

The process that Suzanne and millions of other emerging gay women and men go through varies with individuals and their circumstances. The stages described below are not rules, but merely a guide to the process that gay people commonly undergo as they awaken to their feelings and learn to accept themselves as they are.

Self-labeling. Some straight men and women erroneously label themselves gay if they have not dealt with sexual abuse or molestation issues and are unable to identify their preference. Others may have post-traumatic stress disorder or be adult children who cannot identify with the role models of their alcoholic parents.

Gay men and women, however, usually label themselves as homosexual for other reasons. As they become aware that they do not feel "normal" and they are attracted to same-sex people, they question what is different about them. These individuals need to

134

look at factors that may be associated with such thoughts and beliefs in order to understand themselves. Perhaps they found a same-sex partner who helped them realize their sexual preference. Maybe they met other gays and felt more comfortable with their life style than that of heterosexuals.

Before coming out. As they look at their feelings and thoughts honestly, gay individuals begin to look around the gay community and check out whether their suspicions are true. Many in the gay community call these fledglings "baby dykes" or "chicken meat." They may be very vulnerable to exploitation.

Coming out. While gay men and women are identifying their feelings and exploring in the gay community, they come to accept that their sexual preference is same-sex. This watershed period is very difficult. Many people suffer diminished self-esteem, feelings of inadequacy, body aches and pains, severe depression, and destructive behavior. Many of them begin alcohol and drug use in an attempt to medicate their feelings.

Exploration. As men and women integrate the knowledge that they are gay, they accept themselves and see their homosexuality as a characteristic, not a character defect. They attend gay activities, identify with the gay community, and feel comfortable in it.

First relationship. Some gay women and men seek counseling as they begin their first relationship. Having been raised in a heterosexual society, they lack a picture of what committed gay relationships look like.

Bret was a typical novice. This thirty-four-year-old man was in recovery from cocaine and alcohol addictions. Although he had lived with a woman for five years, in his first year of recovery he admitted to himself that he was attracted to men. He ended the relationship with the woman, went to a support group for men in transition, and learned about the gay community.

His first same-sex relationship was difficult; he had no road map for sexual behavior, love, or any sort of intimacy with a man. What Bret needed was "technical advice," information on what to expect from the experience, as well as moral support. He received both from the support group and from his first partner, Tim, with whom he has shared a mutually satisfying relationship.

Identity begins to integrate. In this final stage, gay individuals emerge as whole and unified personalities, at ease in their relationships with other people. They have learned to live an integrated life, comfortable with themselves as they are.

Gay Women Alcoholics

Claudette called me because she was not able to have orgasms. After several sessions, it was apparent that her sexual issues with her partner, Mallory, centered in Claudette's alcoholism. Sex was the symptom, not the problem, and the alcoholism had to be brought into remission before the couple could address the sexual issues. Claudette willingly entered a treatment facility.

Before she completed treatment, her relationship with Mallory ended. Therapy focused on her feeling of isolation as a lesbian and alcoholic. Like many gay men and women alcoholics, she benefited most from the Twelve Step AA program for gay people, which addresses their unique needs and issues, including their feeling of special isolation.

Now Claudette has more than eight years of sobriety. She established a healthy relationship with another recovering woman, and the orgasmic difficulties that occurred during her active drinking days are gone. Today she has a healthy, sober, sexual relationship and freedom from the feeling of isolation associated with being a gay alcoholic woman.

Sexual Identity Issues

Men and women with sexual identity issues are confused as to whether they are gay or straight. Many of them are married and think they may be gay; others in gay relationships think they may be straight, or a little of both.

Norman has been in a gay relationship with Bill for ten of his thirty-four years. He came to see me about the attraction he felt to some of the women he worked with in his office.

"I'm very confused," he said, "because I love Bill and don't want to leave him." Norman was afraid he was straight; if he were, that fact would destroy his relationship with Bill.

As Norman discussed how the pair spent their time together, he said that Bill's job had recently required him to be out of town for two to three weeks each month. This absence made Norman feel abandoned and sexually frustrated. Because their relationship was deteriorating, and they had not talked about their feelings, Norman was being attracted to other people. His attraction to women had occurred because his office was staffed entirely by women. If he had worked with men, his attraction would have been to men. It was a situational need for intimacy and affection, regardless of gender.

Sexual identity issues begin in childhood or adolescence. Many children or teenagers who start drinking early do not establish a solid sexual identity. When they achieve sobriety later in life, they may be confused about who they are sexually. They need reassurance and guidance to help them discover who they are as sexual men and women.

Homosexual Shame

When gay men and women feel absolutely ashamed about their same-sex preference (egodystonic homosexuality), what they need is not to change their sex preference, but to work through their feelings about themselves. As Geoff's story demonstrated earlier in this chapter, this condition is very painful and difficult; many people commit suicide rather than acknowledge their sexual preference.

A twenty-four-year-old homosexual named Gary had been battling his alcoholism for four years when he called for an appointment. This handsome man had been raised at a military base, and his father was a marine sergeant. Gary said, "I'd rather be dead than gay. Either tell me you can change me, or I'll kill myself." I told Gary the only thing I knew how to change was his attitude about being gay. A short time later he got drunk and drove off a mountain cliff to his death.

Nadine was a thirty-eight-year-old alcoholic with three kids and a loving husband, Peter. She had recently realized that her sexual preference was women, but she expressed her concern about the effect that orientation might have on her children. After six months of therapy, Nadine still refused to stop drinking or accept the reality of her sexual preference. Peter assured her that he and the children loved her, no matter what. He asked her to stop drinking and said they could work out their problems together. Nadine quit therapy for several months but returned after she met BethAnn and finally accepted the reality of her attraction for women. The two women moved in together. Peter and Nadine worked through their divorce with much sorrow, but maintained their respect for each other. Peter remarried and has a positive connection with her as a coparent.

The Good Sex Program offers gay men and women the resources and the support to achieve healthy sexuality. Like Nadine, Bret, Suzanne, and Norman, gay individuals become double winners when they work their recovery program. They can celebrate both the acceptance of their homosexuality as a healthy characteristic and the discovery of their unique sexuality.

PART THREE

The Journey of Sexual Recovery

What Sexual Wellness Looks Like: Stage 2

When I told Geneviere and Gustave, as I do all my clients, that I would work with them to create their *own* definition of healthy sex and not impose mine, they were surprised and disappointed. Shouldn't I, the sex therapist, tell them what is best? I expect that response, because it emerges from the lessons people have learned from their culture. Our institutions and customs dictate what "normal" sex and sexuality are, what is and is not healthy, and what intimacy should and should not include.

In my workshops, people include in their descriptions of healthy sexuality the values of compassion, tenderness, respect, honesty, warmth, commitment, kindness, gentleness, imagination, a sense of humor, expressiveness, intimacy, vulnerability, and trust. (Notice they don't mention penis or breast size.) I have broadened the concept of healthy sexuality and sexual wellness to include the fact that people's intellectual, emotional, physical, spiritual, and interpersonal functioning are interwoven. In Stage 2, women and men define for themselves how they want to function as sexual individuals. As they put the components together and view them on the surface, this concept of healthy sexuality seems complete.

However, what they have been taught to feel about sex, sexuality, intimacy, and normality may obstruct them. They need to rid themselves of any distorted negative views of their bodies and their sexuality. They also need to abolish the fear of an inability to measure up to society's expectations. Many men and women are so concerned about others' opinions that they have never discovered who they are as sexual beings. Here, in Stage 2, they look inside and find their unique selves, rejecting the false idols of perfectionism that were held up to them.

To begin this process, clients recall what they have already learned and look at themselves by working the AA Steps adapted for sexual recovery (outlined in chapter 2). Below is an account of how this process worked for Gustave and Geneviere, the composite couple.

The Twelve Steps of AA Adapted for Sexual Recovery: Gustave and Geneviere

With their addictions checked, Gustave and Geneviere were ready to begin their work in the Good Sex Program. Gustave's first Step was to admit that he was powerless over his inhibited sexual desire, his premature ejaculation, and his asexual relationship. Geneviere surrendered to her sex addiction, inhibited sexual desire, and inorgasmia. As the couple began to accept their powerlessness, they realized that the hope of recovery was in the second and third Steps. Believing that "I can't, but He can," they placed their trust for the promise of recovery in their higher power.

During his moral inventory in Steps Four and Five of the AA program, Gustave saw the character defects that had landed him where he was: he was a people-pleaser and a "good guy"; he never rocked the boat; he was afraid of his anger, could not ask for what he wanted, needed, or desired, and feared abandonment. These insights he now needed to share with Geneviere. He began to work the Sixth and Seventh Steps, asking for his shortcomings to be removed, but he had great trepidations. Although he was willing to have his character defects taken away, Gustave gradually learned enough patience to have them removed in God's time, not his own.

In the Eighth and Ninth Steps, Gustave began to make amends, not only to Geneviere for placating and people-pleasing, but also to himself as the person most violated. He began to take care of himself and to identify what he wanted and needed.

Geneviere surrendered to her powerlessness over what was happening or not happening sexually in her life. When we discovered later that she was an incest survivor and had suffered all kinds of abuse from her parents, brother, and two cousins, we dealt with those issues as well. As her feelings came to light, Geneviere began the Fourth Step, looking at her need to control and her self-centeredness, fear, shame, isolation, anger, and dishonesty.

In Steps Six and Seven, she asked that these character defects be removed. Steps Eight and Nine were critical for her, as she made amends to her mother, father, husband, and herself about the character defects she had uniquely developed out of her background. Making amends is emphatically *not* making apologies. This process is very tricky; it drives many people crazy. When they make amends, they are doing so for themselves, not for the persons to whom they make the amends. Some individuals choose to make amends to their perpetrators, an act recommended *only* when the perpetrators themselves are in recovery.

Making amends is a cleansing process. Geneviere was launching a clean start. She made amends to her parents for years of refusing to talk to them as human beings. With that new beginning, she could thaw her frozen feelings, let go of her resentments, and start healing herself. How her parents took her communication was ultimately irrelevant. Eight and Nine are especially important for people who have been victims, for these Steps help them avoid perpetuating the victim role. In this case, Gustave was a victim of Geneviere, and Geneviere was a victim of her parents.

In the home stretch, Gustave and Geneviere worked Steps Ten and Eleven, continuing to look for character defects and praying for God's will and the power to continue their work in the program. Couples commonly blame one another for their trouble instead of looking within themselves. Both Geneviere and Gustave had a good fix on what each had contributed to their situation. Once couples acknowledge that "it takes two to tango" and that the accusing finger they are pointing at their partners also needs to be pointed at themselves, they can begin a good recovery. This wonderful process acts as a springboard to the Good Sex Program for sexual recovery.

Modern Americans and Sexuality

Although society tells people that they don't measure up, in reality, most of them do. Most people are normal, but they don't know it. Only part of the population suffers from sexual dysfunctions and sexual addiction. The principal dysfunction is the false belief people have that they are not good enough just the way they are. They are looking for perfection, *but normality is not perfect.*

"Normality" must be defined, since normal, healthy sex depends on people's definition. Is it what they want, what they enjoy? Is it in harmony with their values and needs? Here it is helpful to repeat my definition: **Healthy sexuality is the positive energy of every person's basic nature, from birth through death, as a male or female, gay or straight. It is interwoven in one's intellectual, emotional, physical, spiritual, and interpersonal functioning. It is a positive statement of self. Everyone has many choices about how to direct this energy throughout the life cycle.** If partners consent to behavior which does no harm of any kind, that behavior is normal and healthy.

The recovery people strive for encompasses many facets of being, thinking, and feeling. Part of healthy sexuality involves putting aside the myths that bigger organs are better, more sex is better sex, and only thin bodies are alluring. The images promoted by Madison Avenue and Hollywood are big business, designed to keep people so dissatisfied with themselves and their partners that they want more, better, or different. These myths rob individuals of their unique identities.

Another strong current in American society is the Puritan ethic built on sexual repression, which many religious groups continue to promote. This influence can play an important role in sexual dysfunction. The sexual drive can be intense. Our culture has generally feared and squelched it, sometimes seeing it as evil and something to be controlled. Some churches, cultures, and countries know that, if sexuality can be controlled, so can their members.

Many distorted ideas of normality come from these influences. People need to realize that they were born sexual and remain sexual until they die. Sexuality is a state of being and not sexual performance. Basic sex education promotes that understanding, but many people have been inadequately informed or not informed at all. Some of my clients, for example, have no idea that masturbation is normal for men and women, married and single, throughout their lives. Nor do people know that normal frequency for lovemaking ranges from daily to monthly.

Sexuality Comes from Within and Without

Sexuality is not only instinctive; people also learn about its physical, emotional, psychological, and spiritual aspects from their environments. *If people are misinformed, partially informed, or not informed at all, sexual dysfunction may result.* No one need feel ashamed, confused, or guilty about not knowing or understanding any aspect of sexuality. Ignorance is not bliss.

Sexuality and the Life Cycle

The fact that humans are sexual beings from birth bears repeating. It is normal for infants and young children to be sexually curious. Sometimes sexual expression is discouraged because it disturbs parents who are fearful and do not understand the reason behind their children's behavior. The realization that such curiosity and activities are healthy and natural can dispel these fears. Masturbation among infants is common. Female infants experience vaginal lubrication, and male babies are often born with erections. By age five, many children play house, taking the roles of husband and wife; or they play doctor, exploring their own and each others' bodies. These interests are natural and are important for children in forming their sexual identities. Such activities can be acknowledged appropriately or perhaps gently diverted into other activities.

Age Five to Puberty

Between the ages of five and eleven, children gain experience identifying who they are as boys and girls. As they enter puberty, females (ten to twelve) and males (eleven to thirteen) undergo hormonal changes. Same-sex and opposite-sex thoughts, feelings, and behaviors are common, part of normal development. Some children explore same-sex relationships, which is also normal at this age. As they mature, masturbation and sexual fantasies continue to be natural for both boys and girls. Many adolescents begin to experiment with alcohol and other drugs, and sex when puberty arrives.

Adolescence

During adolescence, people's sexual thoughts, feelings, and behaviors increase. Adolescents have many questions but don't know whom to ask or where to get answers. They begin to separate from parents and bond with their peers. Experimentation and expression of their thoughts and feelings become important, and they begin to establish their own identities—not those of their parents, church, peers, or school.

Early Adulthood

People between the ages of eighteen and twenty-four, of course, launch their higher education, careers, and families. More delay marriage now than in the past. Social taboos are lifting for single adults who choose to live with adult partners, be they gay or straight. During this stage, most gay men and women become aware of their same-sex preference and begin the "coming-out" process, although many begin before eighteen.

Between the ages of twenty-four and forty, the issues of children, career, and relationships tend to fill up people's lives. Some persons feel confused about who they are sexually with themselves and their partners.

Jason and Debbie were experiencing some of this sexual confusion in their marriage. They came in for therapy because they feared "the thrill was gone" four years after the wedding. Both were twenty-four years old. Jason was working part-time and attending graduate school. Debbie worked full-time and took classes, planning eventually to complete her four-year degree. Before their marriage, they had agreed to delay having a family until they had settled into their careers.

They had enjoyed a very satisfying sexual relationship during their first three years, but their enthusiasm had diminished rapidly over the last year. When I spoke with them separately, each professed love for the other: but Debbie complained that Jason had been very irritable lately, and Jason said Debbie was "cold in bed more and more frequently." Both were afraid that something was wrong; they were "too young for the excitement to be gone."

Both had grown and matured sexually. They wanted more variety, longer foreplay, and sex at different times of the day. However, neither one had adequate communication skills to ask for something different, and this silence was affecting their relationship.

Debbie and Jason were experiencing a normal part of the life cycle as they established their personal identities and their careers. As they learned to communicate and discovered more about themselves, their whole relationship strengthened.

Midlife

The phenomenon of midlife crisis that occurs between the ages of forty and fifty-five is well known. Men and women begin to ques-

146

tion their roles as lovers, parents, sons and daughters, and employees. Lives change as careers advance, children leave home, parents die, marriages fail, and remarriages occur. These great shifts force people to reassess their lives and their sexuality. When individuals resist the aging process and the associated physical and sexual changes, they are caught in a battle they cannot win. People who recognize these changes as a natural part of life are more likely to become the best they can be in their middle years and not act like aging twenty-year-old men and women. Their maturity has enhanced their sexual, emotional, and spiritual self-image, and they can accept changes.

The Mature Years

The level of sexual interest and activity maintained after people reach fifty-five depends on their success in weathering life's challenges and on sexual attitudes and interests from their younger years. One couple who attended my class, "Healthy Sexuality over Sixty," said their reason for attending was that they wanted to get rid of "those feelings." They were afraid of being called a "dirty old man and woman" because their son had told them that interest in sex after forty wasn't normal. Natural aging entails hormonal changes and an increased incidence of disease and other disorders. When these conditions are treated or adapted to, however, many older adults continue sexual activity well into their seventies and eighties.

Sexuality is a normal, natural part of life, well into the mature years. One woman in my class was in her late seventies when she wrote this poem, in which she recalls the special sexual relationship she and her husband had shared until his recent death:

I Remember
After years of love, I am once again alone,
And I remember.
I miss you, yes, I miss you!
I miss our talks and sharing,
Touching, and caring,
The blissful delight of being nude.
I remember, yes, I remember,
My special place within your arm,
How our bodies touched,
And I was ready for that special part of you

That swelled with pride for me,
And how I welcomed its loving intensity
Deep within, to a place of comfort and love,
Where that special part of you
Became a part of me,
And I became a nest of love!
In blended ecstasy we knew not
Who gave or who received.
I remember,
Yes, I remember.

The Many Faces of Normality

Sometimes it is hard to understand that sexual thoughts, feelings, and actions can be separated. People need to realize that curiosity about a same-sex or opposite-sex encounter or about watching other couples having sex is not "wrong." These thoughts and interests are normal. Recovering people can choose what to do with these thoughts and feelings. Abnormality involves thoughts, feelings, or actions that make people's lives unmanageable.

Normality is not necessarily being orgasmic all the time. Both men and women need to be orgasmic often enough for their own satisfaction, not necessarily that of their partners. Normal sexuality involves being able to say yes as well as no—to having sex, to wanting to be touched, to initiating or receiving a sexual encounter. Normal people can choose celibacy; if they have sexual feelings, they allow themselves to acknowledge, feel, and choose not to act on these feelings. They feel okay, having made their own choice. The uncomfortable adoption of cultural dictates, however, stifles growth.

Sexuality Is Energy and Growth

Sexuality can be viewed as an energy force, like the ocean. There is continuity in it, an ebb and a flow, with pace and rhythm. Sometimes people ride tidal waves, and other times they are dead in the water. Most of the time, however, there is a rise and fall—and that is normal, from birth until death. Although healthy human beings can function sexually throughout their lives, messages from society and sometimes from the individuals themselves unfortunately discourage that function.

A healthy sexual relationship grows at its own natural pace. At times people want sex in the living room or outdoors, or they want to sleep alone on the couch, even when they're married. That is all normal and part of a healthy relationship. Respect involves acceptance of others' boundaries and a need for closeness, creativity, and space.

Another part of letting a sexual relationship evolve normally is the recognition that people's wants and needs change. People differ at different times in their lives; they need to give themselves and others permission to change. I asked Geneviere and Gustave to write out this permission and keep it in a visible place. Doing so, they acknowledged to themselves that the growth in them was right and good, and that change is the way of the world. They learned to be honest with themselves.

Being Realistic: The Sexual Life Cycle

Before people can enjoy healthy sex with intimacy and spirituality, they must acknowledge who they are and what they want and need. Because many men and women have in the past lived in denial or delusion or at present are trying hard to change, they cannot accept who they are and what they want and need now, at this moment.

The Twelve Steps help people who suffer from sexual problems to work with these issues. When people strain, trying not to masturbate or not to ejaculate prematurely, when they make an effort to be orgasmic, all that trying just gets in the way of surrender to the way things are. All of Gustave's and Geneviere's exertions only obstructed a healthy relationship. Until both of them admitted their powerlessness over their sexual difficulties and their addictions, recovery was not possible. At this point in their recovery, all of my clients take a good look in the mirror and ask themselves whom they see looking back. Are they forty pounds overweight and incest victims? Are they gay or have they been celibate for twenty years? They need to accept whatever facts they see. Being realistic may be painful, but unless they are honest with themselves first, nothing else can happen. They may get symptomatic relief or have nice times, but throughout their lives, they always will feel that something is missing.

What is normal and satisfying is personal and individual. Although the techniques and exercises introduced in this Good Sex Program can be practiced by anyone, what individuals and their partners derive from these experiences is unique to each person and each relationship. For example, the techniques that Gustave and Geneviere used to cure his premature ejaculation have been used by many clients. Yet each couple bring their own unique personalities, needs, and desires to any exercise. That is the beauty of the Good Sex Program and the importance of Stage 2.

Taking a Realistic Look

People who equate normality with perfection have unrealistic expectations. They need to ask themselves whether they should expect at the age of forty-five to be as sexually active or interested as they were when they were eighteen. Perhaps they should be more interested; were they inhibited at eighteen and now, in their forties, do they feel free? Financial concerns, falling in love, child discipline problems, retirement, career moves, loss of a job, death, and divorce all drastically affect people's sex lives. It is not realistic to be celibate on a honeymoon or accept ongoing asexuality in a relationship without mutual agreement.

Members of divorce groups tend to be fragile, angry, in pain, and uncertain about taking risks. Many elect celibacy or masturbation. These options are normal for people in this group. They need to be realistic about what to expect from themselves sexually during their divorce and trust that the recovery process will help them to move on.

Deciding What Was Realistic for Gustave and Geneviere

Gustave and Geneviere evaluated what was sexually realistic for them. They believed that they were both still young and vital and that their first goal was to bring their addictions into remission. Gustave confronted his codependency, co-sex addiction, eating disorder, and compulsive spending. He wanted to enjoy the moment and not worry about performance. He would work to recognize the sharing and intimacy of sexuality rather than "doing it" as a task. He needed to look inside himself and assess his own sexual likes and dislikes and then share them with Geneviere. As he learned to share himself and his thoughts with his wife, he saw how to become an equal partner in their relationship and not to be her parent.

Geneviere's goal was to deal with her chemical dependency, sex addiction, and eating disorder, as well as her adult child and sexual trauma issues. She also wanted to deal with the flashbacks of sexual injury so she could work through her inability to have an orgasm and her lack of sexual desire.

As a couple, Geneviere and Gustave hoped to learn a variety of sensual and sexual expressions that they could share. They wanted to be comfortable with initiating sex and with saying yes and no to one another. They also wished for a more spiritual and complete feeling of intimacy as sexual people, both alone and together.

Sexuality Is Part of Life

Since sexuality is not separate from other elements of identity, but is interwoven with emotion, body, and spirit, what is natural and normal varies for each person. A lesbian's sexuality is obviously different from that of a fifty-year-old married man. A nineteen-year-old anorexic woman faces different realities than an alcoholic man who is trying to cope with premature ejaculation.

Ride Waves, Not Ratings

Men and women often rate sex and sexual behavior. Sex is a performance for them, which is evident when they ask, "Did you come?" "How was it on a scale from one to ten?" "Did you score?" And "What do you mean, not yet?" These questions set people up for pain and rejection, for feeling not good enough. In reaction to their being rated, they begin lying to make themselves look good or to hide the fact that they didn't have a perfect "10" orgasm.

A major part of healthy sex is about people taking care of themselves. Although most people react negatively to the word "selfish," some enlightened self-interest in all relationships is healthy. Men and women want to give pleasure as well as receive it, and they should expect the same from their partners. Intimacy entails giving and receiving pleasure, trusting and being trusted, and respecting oneself as well as one's partner.

Intimacy: The Elusive Ideal

Intimacy means sharing feelings with yourself and others and becoming vulnerable. It is connecting with another person in a completely honest way, through the intellect, spirit, body, or emotions. It can mean holding the hand of a frightened geriatric patient. It can be a little girl hugging her new puppy. One famous symbol of intimacy is Michelangelo's portrayal on the Sistine Chapel ceiling of two fingers touching, God and Adam making the intimate connection.

Attempting a purely sexual relationship without integrating a deep level of intimacy is a gamble; the odds are that the relationship will falter. Integrating intimacy and sexuality is a real challenge, but one many are seeking to face. Couples need to communicate authentically and to risk vulnerability and commitment as they grow in a trusting relationship. Clients often call on great courage when they trust the universe to bring them intimacy. Typically they say, "Oh, God, that's too close. I can't handle it," or "If that happens, I'll blow away. I'll go into a black hole and never come out." The "fight or flight" impulse takes over.

The avoidance of intimacy often comes from fear of abandonment. One woman told me, "If I let someone in that close, if I'm truly intimate, look at all I'm risking if that person leaves me! I couldn't live through the pain."

Men and women need to become intimate with themselves before they can be intimate with another. I ask clients to take time to be introspective and learn who they are, feel what they feel, finish processing their past, and face the experiences that shaped their personalities. They need to examine family-of- origin distortions that may unwittingly affect their perceptions today, such as "The only thing men want is sex," "Women will trap you," and "I don't deserve a healthy relationship." After they look at these factors, they can build new selves based on healthy beliefs. When they know themselves, they can proceed on the road to healthy intimacy with partners.

Sexuality and Spirituality

To understand the connection between sexuality and spirituality, people need to recognize what spirituality is. Many people equate spirituality with religion, but the two can be very different. While religion is a practice of beliefs and rituals and may come from *outside* of people, spirituality exists *within*. Spirituality is the inner light and harmony that makes every person unique. It is the achievement of balance in all aspects of life.

Because many people regard sex as dirty and ugly, they don't believe it can be spiritual. However, healthy sexuality is integrated with spirituality. When men and women surrender to their issues in recovery, they can acknowledge their true inner selves and achieve spiritual sexuality.

Part of spirituality is the connection people make with their inner energy. That connection involves unconditional love—of self and others. Sexual intimacy is not merely a physical conjunction but a deeper connection that functions with emotions and intellect; spirituality is a natural part of the inner harmony.

All these aspects of self contribute to the ultimate intimacy people have with themselves, with their higher power, and with each other. The concept of intimacy therefore includes touching or caressing and other physical affection; hearing someone's joys and sorrows; or sitting with someone special and sharing silence.

The Peace of Healthy Sexuality

Once people discard popular opinions concerning intimacy and feel at peace with their sexuality, they can share those good feelings with their partners. That is the most satisfying experience they can have, because they act according to their own lights, rather than obeying preconceived notions and expectations.

Inner peace doesn't come from trying to fit an idealized picture. Health and normality come naturally from within when men and women realize that their higher power does not desert them at the bedroom door.

When individuals are comfortable with their own sexuality, they can approach a healthy sexual encounter feeling enriched—not degraded. Acting on sexual choices is never an emergency for them or something done of necessity to survive. It is, instead, a great option. No one imposed it upon them, not society or a sex therapist or a partner. They can savor the discovery of their unique sexual selves and then share when they choose.

Sharing the Discovery

When men and women share their personal sexuality and spirituality with partners, they make intimate connections. They know they can trust and are trusted; they know they are safe with partners who are safe with them. They can be vulnerable and enjoy unconditional love.

Authentic intimacy translates into honesty—with no ulterior motives on either side. It is being and existing in the moment.

Neither partner tries to control the outcome of the relationship or encounter. Mutual commitment and agreement about the nature of the relationship enhances intimacy. Commitment provides a groundwork of safety. Some of its components are trust, respect, and love, or at least liking for one another. These are the necessary factors for a deeper connection.

Fantasy and Intimacy: Having Fun along the Way*

The path to healthy sexuality need not be all serious. When people feel safe in an honest relationship, they can experiment, be spontaneous, play, and risk being foolish or silly. "Giggle sex" is okay. It's okay to make mistakes, to not "get it right," because there is no right or wrong. Sex may be play, shyness, tenderness, lustfulness, making love, and touching the depths of one another's soul. The physical expression of love may be messy.

After clients have established a basic trust or "okayness" with who they are and whom they choose as partners, they can free their imaginations. When they understand that fantasies are neither good nor bad, they can act on them or just quietly enjoy imaginary experiences. They also may choose to talk about their fantasies. What would sex be like with three lovers, for example, a same-sex lover, an opposite-sex lover, a new position or location? Once they feel unconditionally safe, some men and women share these thoughts with their partners.

Regardless of whether people create fantasies or talk about them, they are a normal part of sexuality and an option for people to enjoy. Americans tend to disapprove of imagination, playfulness, and fantasy, but my clients learn that their sexual fantasies are normal and healthy. They explore books on fantasy if they can't get started. Fantasies on the printed page somehow give them permission to begin.

Addiction versus Healthy Sexuality

Healthy sexuality and intimacy are possible only when people

---

*Sex addicts, co-sex addicts, and romance addicts who are addicted to fantasy need to talk to their sponsors before acting on this section. The crucial role of fantasy in their behavior is explained in chapters 3 and 5.

have their addictions in check, and the most successful way to achieve remission is participation in Twelve Step programs. Women and men can thereby develop the kind of relationship with themselves and others that they seek. People who are active in their compulsive behavior are married to their drug, and intimacy is impossible. When their addictions are in remission, they are open to healthy sexuality.

As men and women work the first two stages of the Good Sex Program and incorporate the Twelve Steps into their lives, they discover what is normal and healthy for them in their particular sexual lives and learn about the human life cycle. Often they also realize that their knowledge of their own sexual functioning is inadequate. Before they can use the tools, they need to become familiar with them.

12

Ignorance Is Not Bliss: An Operating Manual for Increasing Sexual Knowledge

Many people are uncomfortable talking about sex. Although they pretend to "know all about it," they are often unaware of how their bodies function sexually. Because they think they should know it all, they are often too shy, too inhibited, or too afraid to appear uncertain by asking their partners questions about sexual matters.

This ignorance, added to the myths fostered by advertising, movies, and other institutions of our culture, interferes with healthy sexual function. (Some of these myths are presented later in this chapter, "Dispelling the Myths That Inhibit Healthy Sexuality.") No one can recognize a glitch in the system without knowledge of the system's normal operation.

Gustave confessed, "I never understood what a woman's clitoris was or looked like or how to stimulate it." When he and Geneviere began the Good Sex Program, they took a sexual inventory of their bodies and learned how they work. The gaps in what they *thought* they knew surprised them. They found healthy, exciting ways to please one another and realized how important it was for both partners to learn sexual anatomy and physiology. Like Gustave and Geneviere, all of my clients go through a sexual parts inventory, an explanation of the sexual response cycle, and general information about human sexuality. That process enables them to assess where they are and want to be.

A Woman's Sexual Anatomy

Many women look in a mirror held between their legs, to locate their external sexual parts. First they notice two folds of skin that lie on either side of the vaginal opening and clitoris. The outer lips are called the **labia majora** and are covered on their outer surface with pubic hair. They protect the inner lips, the **labia minora**, which enclose the vaginal opening and the urethral opening. (See Appendix 12-1.)

The clitoris is the most important organ for women's sexual satisfaction. It is analogous to the penis in the man, and it contains a large and variable number of nerve endings that make it highly sensitive and responsive. It is the organ through which most women are orgasmic.

Fewer than one-third of all women have an orgasm with penis-vagina intercourse only. Usually the clitoris needs to be stimulated in some way for women to experience orgasm, but not every woman wants, needs, or requires the same kind of stimulation. This fact was important for Gustave and Geneviere. When they were working on partner genital sexuality (Stage Nine), both Geneviere and Gustave knew how the clitoris functions.

Some women prefer to have the clitoral hood rubbed indirectly during a sexual experience. Circular manual stimulation excites some women, while others like a direct touch. Each woman has individual preferences as to what pleases her sexually. Her response also varies, often depending on the time of the month. Women who are ovulating may be more sensitive than they are just before a period.

A muscular tube called the **vagina** extends from the opening between the labia to the cervix, at the lower end of the uterus. (See Appendix 12-2.) The penis enters the vagina during sexual intercourse. When women are sexually excited, this organ opens and elongates; after sexual activity it closes. Between the clitoris and vagina is the opening for the **urethra**. This tube-shaped organ carries urine from the bladder to the outside of the body. Because the urethra is close to the vagina, some women are prone to urinary infections. Urinating relatively soon after sexual activity helps prevent infection.

The **cervix** is the opening to the uterus through which sperm flow up and menstrual fluid flows down. It is also the birth canal, which explains why pregnant women infected with sexually transmitted diseases like herpes, syphilis, or gonorrhea can pass infection to their infants during childbirth.

A pear-shaped muscular organ that stretches to accommodate the growing fetus is the **uterus**. The uterine, vaginal, and anal muscles (some of the pubococcygeal muscles) contract during orgasm. They sometimes contract during menstruation as well, which causes cramping.

The **ovaries** regularly produce eggs from a supply of about 75,000. From adolescence, when women start to menstruate, until after menopause, at about age fifty, any eggs that are released without interference of birth control have the potential to unite with sperm and attach to the uterine wall, resulting in pregnancy.

On the front wall of the vagina is an area in some women called the **G-spot**, named after Ernest Grafenberg, M.D., who first described it. When stimulated adequately with fingers, an object, or the penis, this two-inch area swells, which may result in orgasm in some women. The existence of the G-spot surprised Geneviere and Gustave, and they remembered it as they went through the stages of sexual discovery.

The anus is the opening into the **rectum**, where the feces, or solid waste, comes out. It is part of the pubococcygeal muscle system that contracts when women have orgasm. It also can receive (gently with lubrication) fingers, hands, objects, or a penis during anal intercourse. **Even with the careful use of a condom, the latter practice is not safe; AIDS is easily passed during unprotected anal intercourse. It is more dangerous than vaginal intercourse because the rectum is not elastic, and the AIDS virus is transmitted through tiny injuries.**

A Man's Sexual Anatomy

In the male (Appendix 12-3), the **testes**, also called testicles, which produce sperm and the hormone testosterone, are contained in the **scrotum**, the loose pouch that hangs behind the penis. The **prostate gland** secretes most of the seminal fluid that is ejaculated during orgasm. Sperm are a very small portion of this ejaculate.

Extending from the testes to the prostate are the **vas deferens**, two firm tubes that carry the sperm. The **Cowper's glands** secrete a fluid that lubricates the urethra to allow the sperm to pass easily out of the body. Some sperm may be present in this fluid, which is often seen on the tip of the penis during sexual excitement before ejaculation. Therefore, women can become pregnant even if their partner does not ejaculate into the vagina. If the couple want to avoid pregnancy, they need to consider using some form of birth control.

The **penis** is the primary male sexual organ, composed mainly of three layers of spongy erectile tissue. During sexual excitement, these tissues fill with blood and cause the penis to enlarge. The most sexually sensitive part of a man's body is the **glans**, the cone-shaped head of the penis.

The **urethra** is a tube that runs from the bladder through the penis. Both urine and sperm travel through it, but not at the same time, as some men and women fear. Because the prostate surrounds the urethra at the point where it leaves the bladder, disorders like prostatitis (which occurs in older men) can cause urinary difficulties.

Both Gustave and Geneviere needed to learn about the male sexual anatomy and be comfortable with their knowledge. This information helped them understand the techniques they used to cure Gustave's premature ejaculation. (Gustave's progress with these techniques is followed in chapters 16 through 20.)

Sexual Response Cycle

Sexual response in men and women occurs in a cycle that is both physiological and psychological. Sex researchers have charted this cycle and refer to it in order to clarify the point at which dysfunction occurs.[21] Sometimes people know something does not feel right; unless they have a picture of what they are looking for and understand their sexual response cycle, however, they can't judge its function.

Phases of Response

The phases of the sexual response cycle are the same for all men and women: excitement, plateau, orgasm, and resolution. What differs most between men and women is the timing of their phys-

---

21. W.H. Masters and V.E. Johnson, *Human Sexual Response* (Boston: Little, Brown, 1966), 5.

ical reactions during each part of this process. Men typically reach peak excitement and plateau sooner than women. Some women experience more than one orgasm without a pause for rest. After men have an orgasm, they go through the resting phase before they are able to begin the cycle again. These phases and the gender differences are shown in Appendix 3-1.

This explanation is merely a guideline. No two people react the same way, nor does one person always react the same way every time he or she has a sexual experience. People's bodies respond not only to their own physical and emotional states, but also to their partners'. Understanding this fact was important for Geneviere and Gustave as they worked to correct his premature ejaculation and her inability to have an orgasm. Many of the techniques used in the Good Sex Program helped them to feel better about themselves so they could better deal with these issues.

Another couple, Jay and Linda, having learned that their bodies do not always respond in the same ways, stopped worrying about "doing something wrong."

"When Linda and I have sex," Jay said, "most of the time her nipples don't get erect, and sometimes she doesn't get wet. I used to think it was my fault or there was something wrong. But she tells me everything is okay."

Linda explained that she finds Jay very stimulating and sexy. "My nipples have never been very sensitive. And depending on the time of the month, I sometimes don't lubricate very well." She also noted that when she feels stressed from work, she may not be in the same mood as Jay.

How Men Respond

The many triggers of sexual response include touch, smell, sight, a thought, or anything that has sexual meaning for people. The body reacts by increasing blood flow into various body parts, increasing their size and often their sensitivity.

Men's lips, ear lobes, breasts, and penis become engorged with blood. Not every man achieves full erection soon after becoming sexually stimulated. Younger men often respond spontaneously; older men may need more time and direct stimulation to become erect. The testes retract into the scrotum and muscular tension increases throughout the body. Breathing rate, blood pressure, and heart rate increase. Some men get erect nipples, reddening of the skin, and involuntary spasms in their pelvis, buttocks, or facial muscles.

All of these bodily changes are reversible. If men become distracted or lose stimulation, or if the encounter goes on too long and they become desensitized, they may lose their erection or other signs of arousal. This experience is normal. Once they take "time out" and resume the activities that stimulated them originally, the plateau and orgasmic phases usually can be reached again. Generally, younger men return to these stages in less time than older men. Like women, men respond individually during these stages: some men are noisy and thrust vigorously; others are quiet.

During resolution, the phase after orgasm, the organs and body functions return to their normal or relaxed state. The penis soon loses about 50 percent of its rigidity and then returns to its flaccid state. A rest or refractory period follows the resolution phase for most men. During this time, they are not able to experience another erection for a while. The length of this refractory stage differs and depends on age, partner, length of time since previous ejaculation, and whether orgasm was achieved. It might be two minutes in younger men to two days or more in older men.

How Women Respond

In women, several external and internal responses usually occur. Most are associated with increased blood flow and breast and nipple size; elevated pulse rate and blood pressure; and swelling of the labia and clitoris. The amount of lubrication in the vagina varies among women and depends on several factors. As Jay and Linda noticed, vaginal secretions can be affected by the time of the month as well as age, stress, pregnancy, vaginal infection, or the use of oral contraceptives, hormones, or antibiotics.

During the plateau phase, breathing rate increases and the vagina continues to increase in diameter. The clitoris enlarges about 50 percent, elevating until it is partially or completely covered by its hood. This change causes some men to complain that after finding the clitoris, they "lose it," or "don't know where it went."

Rhythmical contractions of the pubococcygeal muscles around the vagina and uterus occur during orgasm. Breathing rate, pulse rate, and blood pressure reach their peaks. Like men, women react individually. Some flail about; others behave in a quiet, gentle way. Some are vocal, telling their partners what they feel; some moan or use erotic language; others are subdued.

Orgasms Are Like Snowflakes

What is interesting and important is that every man and woman experience orgasm in his and her own unique ways. Once Geneviere became orgasmic, she and Gustave set aside any preconceived ideas about how she "should" act or what she had done in the past. They focused instead on the present, the way their teamwork had evolved during sexual recovery. They needed to disregard the "Hollywood" version of orgasm on videos or the movie screen.

Such unrealistic expectations affect many couples. "I thought I was doing something wrong because Liz was so quiet when she had an orgasm," said Tom. "I admit I didn't believe her when she said she had one." Tom and Gustave are not alone in believing that the Hollywood orgasm—complete with moaning and thrashing—is the "real" or "right" way. What's real and right is different for each person.

Some women want to experience more than one orgasm and thus delay entry into the resolution phase. Others do not enjoy being stimulated again after orgasm. Women do not need a refractory period before they can reach orgasm again. Once resolution occurs, if women don't want to be restimulated, all bodily functions and organs return to their normal state.

Dispelling the Myths That Inhibit Healthy Sexuality

Many myths that have been perpetuated for years get in the way of healthy sexuality. The sex research conducted by Masters and Johnson disproved many myths that nevertheless still persist today. The size of a man's penis is not related to his sexual performance, for example.[22] The research also showed that women do not have two kinds of orgasm, clitoral and vaginal; they simply have an orgasm.

Two common and related fallacies are the beliefs that men want sex all the time, and women rarely want sex. Both men and

---

22. Masters and Johnson, *Human Sexual Response*, 19.

women sometimes "have a headache" or are "not in the mood." Sometimes women want more, and men may want less. How, when, and why women and men feel sexual depends on many factors.

FACT: Both men and women masturbate through all phases of their lives, including the times when they are in healthy sexual relationships. Masturbation is not only manual stimulation to the point of orgasm, but also casual pleasurable touch. It usually begins in childhood and normally continues until the day people die. It is a natural expression of sexuality, and while individuals are in a healthy sexual relationship, masturbation is not indicative of dissatisfaction or other sexual difficulties between partners. Many people masturbate to please themselves, when their partners are not interested, or when they are separated.

FACT: Many heterosexuals occasionally have same-sex thoughts or feelings. Similarly, many homosexuals have opposite-sex thoughts or feelings. None of these thoughts necessarily changes sexual preference; they merely reflect healthy curiosity about sex. Fantasizing during sex is another normal phenomenon. It does not lead to infidelity, nor is it bad in other ways.

"Sometimes when my husband and I make love, I pretend he's Richard Gere," confessed Marsha, "but that doesn't mean I don't love my husband."

Another woman, Monika, said, "My husband told me that sometimes he fantasizes that there are two women in bed with him when we're making love. I play along sometimes. I find it exciting." These couples know that the biggest aphrodisiac is imagination.

FACT: Treatment for premature ejaculation is fairly simple, very quick, and highly successful. The technique described in Appendix 12-4 helped Gustave and Geneviere and many others. Some men who ejaculate prematurely become so discouraged that they compound the issue by getting locked into performance anxiety. Once they learn to relax and use the corrective technique, they usually eliminate the problem.

FACT: Both men and women do not always have an orgasm. In our performance-oriented society, people need reassurance that such variability is normal. Shared sexual expression can be a complete experience without orgasm.

Biological Issues, Signs, and Symptoms That Affect Sexual Function and Sexuality

"I get so depressed I don't even want to think about sex, much less do anything about it," confessed Bonnie. "Nothing motivates me. My lover keeps pressuring me to make love, but all she's doing is pushing me away."

Everyone feels depressed occasionally, and most people can bounce back and deal with the issues. When it becomes severe or chronic and unchanging, it requires medical treatment.

Recognizing Depression: Is It Reactive or Biologic?

Depression manifests itself in two forms. Reactive depression is a response to a life event: the death of a loved one, losing a job, being forced to move, breaking a leg, having a breast removed, and so on. Biologic depression, however, is a state which cannot be attributed to an external factor. The precipitating cause is not based on any life events.

Establishing the distinction between reactive and biologic depression is especially critical in addicted individuals, who suffer a higher prevalence of depression than the general population.

Biologic Depression. The symptoms include low sex drive, extreme sleeping or eating habits, chronic fatigue, impaired concentration or thinking ability, lethargy, suicidal thoughts, and so on. (See Appendix 12-5.) Until the depression stabilizes, psychotherapy cannot progress as rapidly as it might otherwise.

Leslie discovered a long-standing biologic depression that was associated with her ex-husband's alcoholism. About seven years earlier, Leslie's marriage had started to go bad. She connected this deterioration with the fact that her thirteen-year-old daughter, Brenda, became anorexic at that time. For the next five years, Brenda was in and out of hospitals, and Leslie believed the stress and depression she felt was caused by her daughter's disease. When Brenda moved to Paris for two years, however, Leslie's depression did not improve.

Peter, Leslie's former husband, was an alcoholic, an issue she had denied. Although she had left him eighteen months before coming in for therapy, her depression persisted. She insisted that I fix her depression, which she believed was based on psychological issues. Although there were certainly serious issues in her life, her depression was mainly biologic. It is possible she had been biologically depressed for most of her life, but the condition had worsened as she aged.

For people in recovery especially, identifying the kind of depression and then treating it effectively opens the door to the rest of the issues. Addressing biologic depression first is crucial for recovery from sexual issues. This fact was apparent with Leslie, who could not work through her divorce or the situation with her daughter until her overwhelming depression lifted. After only four months of medication, her life turned around. Now she is practicing her career and living a happy single life.

Seeking Help

Men and women who want help in dealing with a biologic affective disorder need to find a psychiatrist trained to treat these conditions. Such professionals are sometimes called biologic psychiatrists or psychopharmacologists. Locating a qualified physician is important; about 70 percent of psychotropic drugs are dispensed, often in inadequate amounts, by family practitioners who lack understanding of the disorder they are treating.

Hormone Levels Affect Function

Normal function and regulation of hormone production and cycles is vital to everyone, since hormones control every system in both men's and women's bodies. A foreign substance like alcohol or other drugs, or external forces like psychological stress or physical trauma, can affect the hormone balance adversely.

One of my clients, Brian, had a hormone imbalance because of his fifteen-year history of alcoholism. When this forty-three-year-old broker came to see me, he had been sober for one year; the impotence he had experienced for five of his drinking years persisted into his recovery. "My friends tell me to try another Fourth Step; they say that I can't blame the Program for not giving me back my sexual function," he said. Compounding his depression about his impotence was the fact that his wife had left him for another man and filed for divorce.

Brian was suicidal. He was not eating properly and was on

the verge of drinking again when he came in for his first session. The medical workup I suggested showed that his testosterone level was that of a man in his eighties. The alcohol had done that much damage to his hormonal system. Once Brian began a combination of testosterone injections, sex therapy, and nutritional counseling, his potency returned—and so did his wife.

Hormonal imbalances are particularly bothersome in women, especially chemically dependent, codependent, and adult-child women. If their hormone levels have been disturbed by alcohol or other chemical abuse, extreme chronic stress, drastic weight loss or gain, or nutritional deficiencies, various sexual dysfunctions may result. These commonly include little or no sexual desire, sexual aversion, painful intercourse (dyspareunia), and shrinkage of the vagina (vaginal atrophy).

The effects of severe weight loss on Ellen, a twenty-six-year-old graduate student, were apparent even six months after she finished treatment for anorexia. Although she had not reached her optimal weight, she was well on the road to recovery and said she felt good most of the time. She had no sex drive, however, and her menstrual periods had not returned. Before her anorexia, she had had limited sexual experience. Now she was terrified that she would "be like this forever."

Ellen's doctor found an extremely low level of estradiol, or estrogen, one of the female sex hormones, similar to that of a woman in menopause. During Ellen's disease, her starvation cycle had shut down her hormone production. After she began taking estrogen and progesterone (another female sex hormone) to replace the substances her body no longer produced, her sexual desire returned within six months. "I had thought that my anorexia had ruined any chance for a normal sex life and babies of my own. But since my desire returned, I am much more confident."

Hormone Replacement Therapy. Replacement of hormones, especially those Ellen received, is a very important adjunct. Estrogen deficiency can cause vaginal shrinkage, loss of vaginal lubrication, structural changes in the pelvis, mood swings, depression, low sex drive, and hot flashes. Restoration of estrogen, progesterone, and testosterone can improve these conditions. The need for this treatment occurs in men and women as young as their early twenties and at any time thereafter.

Drugs and Sexual Function

The effects of prescription or illegal drugs on sexual function can be mild to severe, depending on the drugs. Alcohol and illegal drugs such as cocaine, marijuana, heroin, and crack impair sexual functioning (see chapter 4). In general, drugs interfere with sexual desire, erection, ejaculation, and orgasm in men. Negative effects in women include lack of sexual desire, vaginal lubrication, and orgasm.

Prescription and Over-the-Counter Drugs

Many over-the-counter drugs and prescriptions for physiological or psychological conditions also can contribute to sexual difficulties. (See Appendix 4-3.) Among the worst hazards to sexual function are antihypertensive drugs, which Gustave was taking. More than thirty-seven million adults in the United States take these drugs to control high blood pressure. Their use, a factor in Gustave's low sex drive, causes impotence in some men and lack of sexual desire in both men and women.

Other important agents associated with sexual dysfunction include antipsychotic and some tricyclic antidepressants. Among people who use antipsychotics, the most common sexual dysfunction is impotence. Tricyclic antidepressants occasionally have been associated with painful or delayed ejaculation. Other side effects include impaired sexual desire, sedation, and possible interference with sex hormones in both women and men. In addition, antibiotics sometimes cause inflammation and painful intercourse in women.

Sexually Transmitted Diseases

Sexually transmitted diseases are contagious infections that interfere with not only sexual function, but also general health. A common infection in women is **pelvic inflammatory disease**, or PID. It is usually transmitted during sexual intercourse and causes inflammation of the Fallopian tubes and ovaries, which results in blockage, pain, fever, and a stiff and swollen abdomen.

About 80 percent of women who contract **gonorrhea** (also called the "drip" or the "clap") observe no symptoms. Those who do, notice a vaginal discharge, a frequent need to urinate (which can be painful), and a red, irritated vulva. If gonorrhea is not treated, it may lead to PID.

Men with gonorrhea usually have acute urethritis (painful inflammation of the urethra). Fortunately, treatment for both men and women is a single injection of penicillin or another antibiotic.

Genital herpes causes both physical pain and emotional distress. Itching and soreness usually occur before the characteristic painful and highly contagious sores appear. There is no vaccine to prevent herpes and no cure, so flareups recur throughout a lifetime. Acyclovir has been very successful in suppressing the recurrence rate. With the help of their physicians, men and women with herpes can learn to manage their disease and lead sexually active lives. Those who do not may suffer feelings of guilt about being "diseased."

Syphilis, if detected within the first two years after infection (when it is most contagious), is usually curable. The first stage is identifiable by a sore or chancre that appears in the anal-genital area, the mouth, or on the lips or tonsils, between ten and forty days after infection from sexual contact. In stage two, a non-itching rash appears on the patient's trunk; swollen glands, headache, and low fever may occur. During the third stage, which can last for many years, syphilis is not contagious. Stage four is manifested in any organ, especially the skin, as ulcers, and eventually causes death.

AIDS the acquired immune deficiency syndrome, is caused by a virus, called HIV (human immunodeficiency virus) that destroys the body's immune system. It can affect *anybody*: all races, old and young, men and women, gay and straight, drug users and drug-free people. Because no cure has yet been found for this deadly disease, learning how it is transmitted and how to protect against it is simple self-defense.

The most common way to contract AIDS is through intimate sexual contact that involves the exchange of bodily fluids (blood, semen, urine, vaginal discharges), such as occurs during anal, vaginal, and oral sex. AIDS is also transmitted through use of contaminated needles or syringes among drug users or from a transfusion of blood donated by someone who has the virus. The disease cannot be transmitted by hugging, kissing, food service, or using the same toilet seat as someone with AIDS.

Because a person who has acquired the AIDS virus may not show symptoms for more than ten years, people need to know about the past of sexual partners before engaging in sex. This precaution is particularly important in women who are pregnant or who may someday become pregnant, because AIDS can be passed along to infants during pregnancy or birth. Signs and symptoms of AIDS include flu-like complaints that linger for a long time, unexplained weight loss, diarrhea, white spots in the mouth, and purple bumps on the skin and inside the mouth, nose, or rectum. People who suspect they may have AIDS or want more information should contact the local AIDS chapter or health department, or call the nationwide hotline at 1-800-342-AIDS.

Steps to help stop the spread of AIDS include the following:

- Limit the number of sex partners.
- Talk to sex partners about their sex history and AIDS.
- Use condoms and spermicides as protection.
- Avoid risky sexual practices, such as anal intercourse.
- Avoid use of intravenous drugs and avoid sexual contact with those who use them.
- Have a blood test done if exposure to AIDS is suspected.

Birth Control

Some people are so afraid to discuss birth control with their partners that, rather than talk, they avoid being sexual. Any dysfunctions men and women have may simply reflect their fear and inability to communicate with partners about whether to have children and what kind of birth control to use.

This fear of communication turned out to be a major issue for one couple in their early thirties. Art, an alcoholic, and Priscilla were surprised to discover a clue in Art's monthly alcoholic binges.

"He drinks all the time, but he really binges several nights each month," Priscilla told me. "I get so angry and confused that I can't stand the thought of having sex with him." This reaction was exactly the one that Art was seeking. Priscilla wanted to start a family, but Art did not. Rather than discuss the issue, he went

170

on an alcoholic binge whenever she was ovulating. He was enlisting his own form of "birth control." Priscilla had not known his feelings about children, and Art had not realized "how important a family is to Priscilla." Once they discussed Art's childhood experiences and his fears about raising a family, they were able to make plans.

After both partners learn how birth control methods work and consider the pros and cons of each, they can make informed decisions. They need to discuss how they feel about birth control. Do they have religious or moral compunctions about contraception? Does one method or another cause either partner embarrassment? Does either partner want a child, and do they agree on the question? Secrecy obstructs all kinds of intimacy. Couples who talk openly and honestly about these topics can sort out conflicts that would otherwise divide them.

On the Road to Recovery

When biologic issues underlie sexual issues, all the Twelve Step programs and therapists in the world cannot help. Identification and treatment of conditions such as hormone imbalances and biologic depression open the way to sexual recovery.

After men and women have taken inventory of their sexual functioning, they can learn to be themselves and share their self-knowledge with their partners.

Communication: Living Room Skills for the Bedroom

13

Communication, the cornerstone of relationships, is more than talk. It certainly requires people's honesty with themselves and their partners, but it also involves listening, to their own feelings and to one another. This kind of openness is important in all areas of people's lives. When men and women want to talk about sex, many of them blush, stammer, and outright avoid the subject. This discomfort hinders their personal development and the growth of relationships.

Another hazard to communication is codependence, the attempt "to live inside somebody else's head." Some people want to know their partners' every thought and feeling; to protect their privacy, these partners clam up. Others think that long-term partners should know one another's thoughts without their being spoken. These people are silent about their concerns, believing incorrectly that problems will resolve themselves, or they exchange angry words without calmly talking or listening to one another. The result is hurt and resentment.

Good communication begins within. Many clients who are uncertain themselves want to tell their partners how they feel, what they like and don't like, or how to indicate an interest or lack of interest in something. Before women and men can begin to communicate such information to others, they need to get in touch with their own feelings, desires, and fears.

Learning to Be Honest

Before couples move into the bedroom, it helps them to "talk it up" in the living room. Living room skills, like the capacity to lis-

173

ten and talk, to resolve conflicts and power struggles, to deal with past hurts and resentments, enable people to move more confidently and comfortably into the bedroom. These skills begin in self-knowledge.

As people use the Twelve Steps of AA in their sexual recovery, they are learning how to communicate, especially with themselves. People need to be honest with themselves and then tell their partners what pleases them, in the bedroom and out. The First Step helps them to admit that they have avoided certain issues in their relationship with themselves and others.

The key to communication with self is in Step Four and the personal inventory. In intimate relationships, especially sexual ones, many people find it easy to take inventory of their partners, telling them what is wrong. Many an absent spouse has sent the partner to a counselor to "be fixed" sexually, assuming that the "repair" will result in a good relationship between them. This approach mistakenly takes as separate entities what is, in fact, a unified system. If a relationship isn't working well, *both* parties need an honest assessment of their respective contributions to the problem.

The Fifth Step involves sharing and communicating with another person and a higher power. How effectively people communicate depends on the skills they have developed and practiced with their partners. When both parties can talk openly and admit responsibility for the situation as it is, they are less likely to deny their feelings, discount them, or act defensively.

Sharing responsibility for sex was difficult for Carol and Richard, who had been married fourteen years. "Isn't it Richard's job to take the initiative in sex?" she asked. "If I say I'm horny or want to be touched or held, won't he think I'm being too forward or acting like a slut? If he loved me, he would know what I want."

Richard said in one of our sessions that he wished Carol would be more seductive. "I can never tell whether she is interested in sex. Sometimes I wish she would make a move, but I don't want to have to tell her to do it. Then she'll think I'm too demanding. She acts like it's my job."

Just whose "job" or responsibility is it to initiate sex? Our culture generally places sexual overtures on men's shoulders. Misconceptions, such as this assumption about the division of sexual "labor" or the idea that partners shouldn't say no to sex because they're married, hinder many relationships. These false beliefs

174

can be corrected if people learn to communicate with themselves and their partners.

True, this directness is easier said than done. Saying out loud what they want or how they feel is difficult for most people. Although the exposure of feelings is a risk, it becomes not only easier after the first time, but also more rewarding. A couple find new ways to share and please one another.

Learning to Communicate in a Relationship

"I remember my parents telling us kids in hushed voices that sex was something you're not supposed to talk about," said Pamela, a forty-four-year-old divorcee. "So, I never did—not with my ex-husband or my kids." She believed that her marriage broke up because "we didn't communicate well at all. We always 'assumed' things, and not just in bed, either."

Lack of communication leads to many misunderstandings in relationships. These misunderstandings are perpetuated by several factors, such as people's lack of knowledge about sex, their confusion about sexual feelings, and their silence about their desires. Some men and women jump into sex because they believe it is expected of them or they are afraid to say no, even though they would prefer not to engage in sex at that time. Telling a partner how one feels or what one wants may be harder or more painful than giving in to an undesired sexual situation. Instead of an act of sharing and communication, the sexual relationship becomes a performance or an avoidance tactic.

Reflective Listening

One very effective tool of healthy communication in a relationship is reflective listening. Each partner listens to what his or her partner has to say during brief intervals, usually about five minutes each. The listener needs to sit quietly without preparing a defense, reading between the lines, or finishing the other person's sentences. Then the listener summarizes the high points and says them back.

The person who did all the talking accepts or corrects the listener's summary. Then the two switch roles and the process begins again. This simple yet effective method to develop listening skills helps people recognize that they have a right to their own thoughts and feelings, whether they seem irrational or rational. Often people do not take the time really to hear what their partners are saying. Not listening leads to misinterpretation, misunderstanding, and loss of an opportunity to grow and develop with a partner.

The revelation of misunderstood actions is one benefit of reflective listening. When people spend too much time in others' heads, they are not clear what is in their own. Reflective listening also is useful when people want to let off steam. Many clients feel cleansed and relieved if they can put feelings, especially anger, into words. Anger frightens many people, and some individuals have done destructive things with it. To control their anger and to talk about it, people go to their sponsors, friends, families, or therapists. (See Appendix 13-1, "Anger Dos and Don'ts.") Reflective listening can provide a catharsis in these situations. When clients can't release their anger verbally, they relieve the tension by beating a bed with a tennis racket or bataka, chopping wood, or working out with a punching bag. Controlled physical release is then an extension of verbal expression.

Conflict Resolution

Whenever couples tell me they never fight, I am more concerned for them than for those who do have open conflicts. Anger, pain, jealousy, envy, pity, fear—these darkside feelings exist in everyone. Unfortunately, our culture has taught people that these feelings are "bad." While it is socially acceptable to acknowledge good feelings, people often hang on to bad ones. What should they do with them—hold them in, repress them, deny them, project them onto someone else, or vent them in some way?

Fighting Fair

The most important tool for dealing with "bad" feelings is clean and sober discussion. When a problem arises, couples need to choose carefully the place and time for discussing the topic. Some clients contract with their partners to get together at the soonest convenient time to sit down, uninterrupted, and hear what they have to say. Most find that a neutral location is best. For example, bedroom issues can be discussed over a cup of coffee at the kitchen table or during a long walk. Some people need to send their kids to a neighbor's house, turn off their phones, take a long drive—whatever allows them to communicate in a relaxed atmosphere without outside demands.

Setting a time limit for discussion also is recommended. Each partner needs equal time to be heard, which is one reason why reflective listening works so well. A time limit helps prevent either partner's bludgeoning the other by monopolizing the discussion or simply talking louder or longer or with a condescending attitude. It allows for quiet, rational conversation, which is what Peter and Joan needed.

"In our eagerness to bring everything out into the open," said Peter, "we found ourselves progressively talking louder and interrupting each other more and more until we accomplished nothing after an entire hour." Each of them felt that if the other *really* understood, he or she would do it "my way." Such controlling behavior is counterproductive. Peter and his wife of six years left too much unsaid during their sessions.

"We were basically talking just to hear ourselves talk," said Joan. "We each analyzed everything the other said, paying attention to facial and body expressions without coming right out and asking what we really meant or wanted." They were going around in circles.

Another trap Joan and Peter had fallen into before they came to therapy was straying from the original subject. Both admitted that they often dredged up the past or brought other people, like in-laws, into the conflict. This habit hurt them even more by renewing past hurts. The major goal is to focus on the current issue.

Those Are Fightin' Words

Certain words and phrases can help guide a discussion. When people use "I" statements, such as "I need a massage," "I feel sexy now," "I would like to listen to that music tonight," they tell their partners how they feel and what they want. The same is true of "When you...I feel" statements. The statement, "When you drink too much, I don't feel intimate," reveals true feelings; there is no second guessing.

If people approach the same situation with statements such as, "Why do you have to drink so much?" or "Are you going to drink all night?" they have not opened the channels of communication or spoken for themselves. The direct approach is best. When men and women say to their partners, "Do you think the music is too loud?", what they are really saying is, "I think the music is too loud. Do you mind if I turn it down?" The first question does not convey a feeling, and it invites a counter-opinion and a cycle of resentment. The second question is direct, tactful, and honest, and allows the couple to exchange ideas and feelings in a calm atmosphere rather than an accusatory, resentful one.

Lashing Out at Loved Ones

Sometimes people use verbal or physical abuse in conflict as a way to vent their anger, fear, and other feelings. Men and women often direct these feelings against those they love. One example of such lashing out occurred with Mark and Karin.

During their three-year marriage, her interest in sex had diminished until she admitted, "If I never had sex again I wouldn't care." Before they married, Mark and Karin had decided they would start a family after a year, when they would both be twenty-eight. But their sexual encounters had turned into crying and shouting matches, and they had not had sex in six months.

When I saw Karin alone, she said she loved children and definitely wanted a family. "But I'm so afraid they're going to be stupid, just like me," she said. Mark had completed a college degree. Karin, although bright, had barely finished high school. Mark had been calling her stupid and ignorant, accusing her of "not having enough ambition or brains to go to college." Karin, who worked as a data entry operator, had begun to believe him.

When I spoke with Mark alone, however, he revealed that he loved his wife very much and said that "she has more common sense than some of the people I work with." He confessed that his attacks were "lashing out because I was frustrated about my job and because we had not started a family yet. But we didn't talk about it." Mark's intellectual abuse of Karin had led to her sexual aversion. Because Mark and Karin had never communicated honestly about how they felt, they were operating with misunderstandings and misinterpretations.

Intellectual abuse, like that between Mark and Karin, occurs when people tell others that their thoughts are stupid or their opinions are wrong. Attempts to shame others with words or actions are emotional abuse. Spiritual abuse is an attack on one's

178

heart and soul, making love and regard conditional. "I'll love you if...." "God will love you if...." "If you just tried harder, I'd love you." These statements are examples of spiritual abuse.

Settlement of differences between partners happens in two steps: the confrontation and the compromise. Days after partners have vented their feelings about a certain topic, when the heat of the battle has cooled, they may talk through the issues again and reach a solution.

Hurts, Resentments, and Shame

Many people carry around hurts and resentments of people or past events. These emotions may affect the way men and women feel about sex or themselves as adult sexual beings. Until hurts and resentments are acknowledged and expressed, they tend to contaminate people's lives.

Charlene carried resentments about her family for fourteen years. This bright, articulate administrative assistant had shut off her sexual feelings and had been celibate for most of her adult life. After several therapy sessions, she admitted that, when she was sixteen, she had had an abortion at the insistence of her family. "I hated them for making me have that abortion," she said. "I always wonder what my child would have been like. Now, the thought of a physical relationship scares me."

Charlene realized that she needed to let go of her resentments because they were only hurting her. She gradually released the anger she felt toward her parents and the frozen grief and shame she had locked inside. Having acquired skills in communicating with herself, she was better prepared to communicate with a partner.

Repressed resentment like Charlene's about events, or about careless remarks made by adults to pubescent teenagers about the size or appearance of their breasts or penis, may haunt teens into adulthood. A drunken father may say to his teenaged daughter, "Those tits of yours are going to make some guy very happy some day." The remark he thought innocuous may make her ashamed of her breasts, or she might infer that they are her only asset. These feelings may result in her inability to be caressed or touched in a healthy way when she is older.

As a teenager, Robert had been ridiculed by his father and brothers about the size of his penis. Until he could communicate the shame and hurt he felt and realize that there was nothing abnormal about his size, the thought of a sexual relationship with a woman terrified him.

"I even avoided public restrooms and health club locker rooms," he said. At the age of thirty-four, he had carried around his shame for more than half his life. Once he began dealing with the hurt and shame, he also realized he was very resentful of his family for giving him that false image of himself.

Many chemically dependent people, codependents, and adult children discover in recovery that they have stored past hurts and resentments which they never dealt with. These old injuries come up when one member of a family is in recovery for chemical dependency and the entire family is part of the recovery process. Together they develop a plan for sharing the hurt and anger in therapy. Use of "When you...then I" statements are important tools in these situations. The structure and neutral ground of a treatment center, clinic, or therapist's office help families to reveal themselves. Some couples work out their hurts and resentments privately; others include family members to put the feelings associated with the disease behind them.

Doing It Their Way: Power Struggles

"Our whole problem was a failure to communicate," said Barbara. "That's why we broke up." Often when this sentiment comes up, the real reason for the conflict was a power issue; one person in the relationship didn't do something the way the other person wanted it done. Such power struggles are normal in any relationship—between spouses, business partners, lovers, parents and kids, and so on. The struggle for control and doing something "my way" cannot be denied. After it is acknowledged, people can negotiate a compromise.

Communication is effective when people simply state their preferences and are heard. When thinking is locked in a narrow interpretation of good/bad or right/wrong, understanding is impossible. People often mistakenly think that the mere statement of feelings will result in a partner's changed behavior. All men and women can ask for in a relationship is that their partners listen to them. The purpose of effective communication is the conveyance of feelings and thoughts. What those who receive the information do with it is up to them. Trying to manipulate or control the out-

180

come creates resentment and subversive behavior and ultimately destroys good feeling.

Relationships are like corporations, with shared values, goals, tastes, and interests. Each individual in that corporation differs. Yet many people approach their relationships like criminal lawyers, defending their cases. Relationships need two people working side by side, not on different sides of the courtroom. Partners can learn to shift from defensiveness to cooperation once they recognize they are in a power struggle and learn to communicate.

Cecelia didn't realize that a longstanding power struggle between herself and her husband, Martin, was the reason behind her inability to have an orgasm. She came in to see me in a last effort to become orgasmic and thereby save her marriage. She revealed that Martin had been an officer in the military for twenty years. He had run the family, which included three children, like a military camp. He had emotionally and physically abused the kids and had always dominated family life.

"Our sex life is normal, I guess," she said. "I get aroused, but I never have an orgasm. We don't understand what's wrong." As an aside, Cecelia mused, "It's strange that on nights when we make love, I wake up at two o'clock, having an orgasm in my sleep. What could that mean?"

What it meant was that because of the power struggle going on in her family, the only thing she could control was her orgasm, and the only way she could release it was unconsciously.

Good Talk Opens Doors

The power of good communication is far-reaching and fulfilling. Between partners, it can open doors and help to build foundations. Before women and men can communicate in the bedroom, they need to learn how to connect in the living room, or the dining room, or the park. Communication skills prepare people for sexual discovery and recovery.

An anonymous poet summed up the issue of communication well:

When I ask you to listen to me
and you start giving advice,
you have not done what I asked.
When I ask you to listen to me
and you begin to tell me why I shouldn't feel that way,
you are trampling on my feelings.
When I ask you to listen to me
and you feel you have to do something to solve my problem,
you have failed me, strange as that may seem.
Perhaps that's why prayer works,
sometimes, for some people,
because God is mute.
He doesn't give advice or
try to fix things.
"They" just listen and let you
work it out for yourself.
So, please listen and just hear me.
If you want to talk, wait a minute for your turn,
and I'll listen to you.

To Be versus To Do: Discovering Sexuality by Nurturing the Self: Stage 3

When clients reach this part of their sexual recovery, they have gotten past the hardest part. Like Gustave and Geneviere, they have brought their addictive diseases into remission and have worked the Twelve Steps for sexual recovery. Now men and women start doing wonderful things for themselves and their partners, if they choose.

Sex therapy can be a short-term process, and it is very successful. What people learn becomes a part of their daily life and behavior patterns. It becomes a part of them, not something they put on and take off like a winter coat.

The most common sexual issues men and women want to resolve are lack of sexual desire, inorgasmia, painful intercourse, impotency, premature ejaculation, and sexual aversion. People who suffer from any of these conditions need a program that helps them to actualize themselves as human beings. In Stage 3 of the Good Sex Program, they take responsibility for their own nurturance. Stages 4 and 5 are explorations of their own sensuality and sexuality. These three stages are also the best way to address codependent sexual behavior, a common issue in addictive individuals.

In Stage 3, people celebrate the core of their sexual being. They let go of the doing and getting in life and relax enough to enjoy merely *being*. Affirmations and various other techniques show them how to nurture themselves.

Affirmations

In recovery, people focus on growing toward their authentic identity. Affirmations help them develop a healthy perspective on sexuality. (See examples of affirmations in Appendix 14-1. Countless others can be found in literature listed in the Bibliography or in various Twelve Step programs.) Individuals choose affirmations that express the needs and goals of their own program and use them daily.

Because both Gustave and Geneviere had eating disorders, for example, they daily reminded themselves, "I accept my body as it is today, with or without imperfections." Geneviere affirmed that she could forgive herself any past sexual misbehavior, such as her affairs. Gustave affirmed his forgiveness of his codependency and could let go of Geneviere's past behavior.

Beginning to Self-Nurture

To understand self-nurturing, people review the Twelve Steps. They look back at Step Four and remember how they came out of their addiction. They recall the character assets and defects they listed in their moral inventory. Perhaps they are unstructured or excessively structured, or they are out of control, perfectionistic, jealous, judgmental, and so on. They recognize that their faults, whatever they are, distort reality and prevent a balanced and intimate life. They also look at Steps Eight and Nine and review the amends they made to themselves. They allow themselves peace of mind, so they can work for harmony.

Balance Makes Better Lives

At this stage of sexual recovery, clients assess their emotional, intellectual, spiritual, and physical relationships. A well-balanced life is conscious, undistorted, functional, and nurturing. That is the foundation on which people work and from which healthy sexuality springs. (See Appendix 14-2, "Recovery Check List," for an idea of what a balanced life looks like.)

For example, if a man is working on his doctorate night and day, nothing is happening from the neck down. Since his entire world is the library, any intimacy with another human being is impossible. Some intelligent women have been unable to fulfill their intellectual potential; without a framework for expressing their feelings, they are unable to meet their own needs. Women and men can achieve the goal of fulfillment and healthy function by creating greater awareness at every level of their lives. Especially in sexual issues, the people they have hurt the most are themselves. Now they can make amends by self-nurture. They need to forgive themselves, let go of the judge in them, and release their perfectionism, shame, and guilt to the universe.

Self-Nurture: Everyone Deserves It

When men and women do not take time to relax, play, or do things they truly enjoy, they are cheating themselves and their partners, families, and friends as well. People need to believe that they deserve inner peace and healthy sexuality, but many people do not know where to start.

The kindly care of oneself helps to prevent relapse. Unlike those who are so busy that they take no time for personal enrichment, others are faced with free time that they did not have while their disease was active. Many men and women relapse because they don't know what to do with their leisure time.

People nurture themselves in widely diverse ways, depending on their personalities and taste. Each person responds uniquely to experience. Clients therefore develop their own programs, exploring the options to discover what suits them best.

Sensate Focus: Becoming Aware of Self

Sensate focus techniques are an excellent place to begin because they allow individuals to do as little or as much as they want. Clients say that these exercises are revealing and healing. They help people to focus attention and heighten awareness of their bodies, feelings, and physical sensations.

Clients can learn sensate focusing techniques from the many books on the subject. One popular and successful technique that Gustave, Geneviere, and many of my other clients have used is easy to do. First, I suggest that people go to a quiet room where they can be alone and undisturbed for about fifteen to twenty minutes. Wearing comfortable, loose clothing and no shoes, they lie down in a restful position with their arms at their sides. With their eyes closed, they concentrate on their breathing, focusing on sensations as the chest expands and contracts. After several minutes, they visualize their feet and toes and concentrate on how they feel. In their minds, they slowly move up to their ankles, calves, knees, thighs, and hips. When they reach their genitals, women focus on their vagina and clitoris and men on their penis and scrotum. They concentrate on each body part for about one minute and think about whether each part feels warm, cool, heavy, achy, tense, relaxed, or light.

Proceeding upward, clients concentrate on the chest, arms, and hands. They let their hands go limp and imagine that any tension in their arms is draining out of them. After they release the tension, they center attention on the face and notice any smells in the room. Some people try to detect more than one smell and then separate them. Others prefer to focus on one in particular, perhaps a perfume or cologne they are wearing. As they move up past their eyes, they release any remaining tension through the top of the head. Slowly, they refocus on their breathing and continue to relax for another few minutes before becoming conscious of their surroundings again.

Other Activities

Gustave, who had been a workaholic, scheduled enjoyable and relaxing events, such as a baseball game or a concert, to nurture himself. He was so accustomed to filling every moment of the day with work that he had to make a conscious effort to plan relaxation time. He started slowly. First he blocked out fifteen minutes every day at his office when he locked his door, turned off the phone, and used a variation of the focusing exercise while seated at his desk. After several weeks, he added a short walk after work each day so he could unwind before he went home. He listed events and places where he felt relaxed, and he scheduled one or two of these activities each week.

My clients are enormously creative in the ways they find to nurture themselves. They schedule time to enjoy books they always wanted to read; visit the zoo; enroll in a photography class; meditate; treat themselves to a massage; or visit a friend for lunch. Geneviere enjoyed wandering around the art galleries in town, an activity which relaxed her, but which Gustave had never wanted to share.

Bodies as Temples

Many men and women have lived in shame and guilt and do not believe they deserve anything except the crumbs of life. When they learn how to nurture themselves, they find a way of being in the world that fosters their healthy sexuality. "I deserve" and "I am worthwhile" are affirmations they need to make. For some people, it is a revelation that they deserve shoes and underwear that fit. The concept that their clothes do not always have to be hand-me-downs or clearance goods can open a new sense of self.

Human bodies are temples to be cared for and revered. Rather than degrading their bodies with junk food, smoking, and hours of sitting in front of the television, my clients develop a nutritional plan or exercise program. They begin to experience their bodies as good, sacred places in which to live. Others turn to meditation, yoga, inspirational readings, or prayer to nurture their spiritual and emotional selves. Many of these people have abused their bodies with drugs, too much food or a lack of it, excessive exercise or none. They have neglected simple hygiene. Once they see that their bodies are indispensable, they can care for them properly. They go to the dentist, get a haircut or schedule a prostate examination, eye test, or mammogram.

Geneviere's years of chemical abuse and irrational eating had left her with some nutritional needs. She took care of herself by joining a women's health spa, consulting a nutritionist, and adopting an exercise program that made her feel good about herself and her body.

Getting a Little Help from Friends

Some men and women get so caught up in "I deserve" that they become compulsive spenders as they keep thinking me-me-me. Others get into a cycle of you-you-you thinking, which is codependent self-sacrifice. They need balance, not the wild fluctuations seen in addictive behavior. Sometimes people need the help of a therapist, counselor, sponsor, or significant other to develop self-nurturing activities. If people have never done kindnesses for themselves or are out of practice, a little help from others can give them new perspectives.

What's Good for the Goose Is Not Always Good for the Gander

Self-nurture is different for men than for women. Women tend to recognize the pleasures they want to give themselves. They know a greater variety of ways and go about them differently than men. They may take time out for a bubble bath or a manicure. They may meditate or buy sexy nightwear.

Men generally get caught up in a more punitive style of self-nurturing. When I ask them to name some self-nurturing activities, they say training for a triathlon or becoming a bodybuilder, being successful in business, making a lot of money, or driving a fast sports car. Gustave was uncertain how to reply. Initially he said that he supposed he should improve his position in his department or chair another committee.

American society's sexual stereotypes limit men's pleasures, which tend to be viewed as self-indulgence. But men can have satin sheets, feed their babies, get a massage or a manicure, or wear sexy underwear. Where is it written that men cannot spend time cooking special foods they enjoy? Some men are unaccustomed to such a simple joy as sitting before a fire sipping hot cocoa, or allowing themselves a twenty-minute nap.

Before men can begin to nurture themselves, they must break away from the need to compete. They need to enlarge their conception of kindness to themselves, beyond the success mode. Although wishing to compete or to be successful is not especially unhealthy, it can be limiting. When men approach self-nurture as a way to "prove" their masculinity, it becomes just one more task or job to be done, which defeats the purpose. This stage of sexual recovery is not a job; it is an adventure.

When men and women feel good about themselves, they have a foundation for the next stage of growth.

Awakening the Senses and Discovering Self-Sensuality: Stage 4

15

When people learn to connect with their five senses and explore the potential there, they become more sensual and sexual men and women. Stage 4 is about making that connection comfortably. Healthy sexuality depends upon persons' knowing, loving, and caring for themselves. Then experiences can be shared with a partner in both sexual and nonsexual ways.

Few people appreciate the power and range of their five senses. Realization of that potential is an awakening process, as Gustave and Geneviere discovered. At Stage 4, they experimented with separate agendas. Initially some clients are apprehensive about trying new things. As they gently discover themselves through their senses, however, they enjoy their own sensuality. We hand down countless myths from one generation to the next: real men don't cry at sad movies or become secretaries or eat quiche; women should not be company presidents or refuse sex to their husbands. These and other damaging assumptions can be dispelled when women and men gain an inner knowledge of themselves and their needs and desires. Then they understand that they need not adhere to the whims of society.

Much sexual dysfunction results from misguided rules about gender. These fallacies hinder people's exploration of their own sensuality and sexuality. Such distortions restrict freedom. At the same time people are *doing* physical acts of sex or being sexual with a partner, they also need to explore their human *beingness*, as sexual men or women. They need the integration between heart, body, and mind.

189

Experiencing "Beingness"

People learn to be sensual by exploring the range of all five senses—sight, smell, touch, hearing, and taste—and trying to focus totally on one experience at a time. That is one of the main purposes of the exercises that Gustave and Geneviere used in Stage 3—to show people how to concentrate and focus on sensations.

The range of activities in Stage 4 is nearly endless. As they make discoveries about themselves, people develop their sensuality and sexuality.

Sensuality versus Sexuality: What's the Difference?

Sensuality is the feeling of pleasure people experience as they use their senses to connect with themselves and their environment. Sexuality is the feeling of erotic pleasure that people derive through stimulation of the senses. This feeling arises from their core, which encompasses their emotional, physical, intellectual, spiritual, and interpersonal energy. People can be sensual without being sexual, and sexual without being sensual. Ideally, they can be both at the same time.

For example, a man might be sitting quietly in the woods with his eyes closed. He focuses on the sensations around him: the coolness of the wind, the cheerful songs of birds, the sweet smell of wildflowers. He might become aware of how the breeze makes the hairs rise on his arms. The birds' song may remind him of being awakened in the early morning; the flowers' aroma may bring memories of how his partner's body smells when they have sex.

At first, some people are shy or feel silly about trying some of the techniques. As they become more comfortable, people shed any cultural expectations of how they "should" respond. They relax and act as unique individuals, creating their own variations on the exercises. Before applying the following ideas, many clients like to use the focusing exercise or some similar method to awaken their senses.

Getting in Touch with the Earth

My clients learn not only to get in touch with their senses, but also to connect with the natural elements of water, fire, wind, and earth. When people integrate their senses with the environment,

190

they become alive and aware and establish a vitalizing relationship with nature.

I asked Gustave to go to the park, for example, take off his shoes and socks, and walk barefoot in the grass. Then he walked through sand, gravel, and water. He enjoyed the sensations of the different textures on the sensitive skin of his feet.

Using this sensate tool, clients pay attention to how their feet feel. Are they hot, cool, uncomfortable? Are the textures rough, sharp, soft, smooth, or hard? The sense of hearing can be integrated—the sound the feet make, walking through each medium. Then people add the sense of smell as they breathe in the aroma of the grass, the water, and the earth. Gustave reported that the sound of walking through the water was "meditative."

Touch

The skin is the biggest sex organ. I teach people how to touch their bodies—lightly, roughly, gently, softly—using their fingertips to feel the texture and coolness or heat, and to locate areas that are ticklish or sensitive. Clients experiment in the bath or shower with water jets or shower massages to enhance their sense of touch.

Geneviere enjoyed using a water massage and adjusting the jets until she felt "little sharp yet stimulating dots" that made her feel "alive in my skin." She also liked using bath oils, something she "never seemed to get to" in the past. Body brushes, bubbles, and sponges also are fun to experiment with in the bath.

A massage—either a self-massage or one by a professional masseuse—awakens the skin. (Because this stage is about self-sensuality, partner massage is delayed until later.) These massages include whatever body part or parts individuals want to try: hand, foot, face, legs, arms, lower back, or whole body. Geneviere enjoyed foot and facial massages the most. To heighten the sensual experience, she used scented body oils on her feet and legs.

Taste

Although most Americans don't think of eating as a sensual act, many foreign cultures appreciate the significance of food, beyond nutrition. My clients go to grocery stores, delis, and gourmet shops and decide which foods are sensual, distasteful, nurturing, or meat-and-potato items.

Geneviere went to her favorite fruit and vegetable market

and looked for exotic items to sample. She decided that apples and pears were "boring," but that kiwi, bananas, and grapes were sensual. Eating grapes reminded her of the scene in *Cleopatra* where the queen is being fed these juicy morsels. Gustave had a different shopping list. He found that spaghetti was sensual when he sucked it off the fork. The stickiness of the juice of grapefruit as it dried reminded him of how two bodies feel after sex.

Other clients talk about the sensual pleasure of peeling and eating a banana, about licking the juice of an orange as it runs down their chins, or the sweet gooiness of fudge and the coolness of ice cream as it melts down their throats.

Everyone has taste buds that can distinguish four different tastes—sour, sweet, bitter, and salty. I ask clients to separate these tastes or combine them. They may try sucking on a lemon slice, then licking the salt from the rim of a glass. They dip a salty pretzel into melted chocolate, or taste plain yogurt alone and then add crushed strawberries. As people take the time to experience each kind of taste and texture in their mouths, many discover that they never really tasted their food before. As they experience their sense of taste, they increase their own self-awareness and their connection with their environment.

Sound

Neutral noise is constant in cities. We are constantly immersed in sounds that we tune out—music in shopping malls, restaurants, and elevators; the drone of traffic; the hum of conversation in public places. My clients have a lot of fun awakening their hearing. They experiment with different kinds of music, especially kinds they usually do not listen to. They make their own music by combining both natural sounds, like humming and singing, and created sounds, made by clicking spoons or tapping something hollow. Those who are musically inclined play musical instruments.

Other kinds of sounds, however, have been repressed. Groaning, grunting, or moaning makes many men and women feel self-conscious. To help overcome their embarrassment, I ask my clients to pretend they are cats, bears, wolves, or opera singers to get their vocal cords going. This activity helps them shed some of their inhibitions about making sounds that are not words or conversations.

Clients also listen to the sounds of nature—running water,

waves hitting the beach, crackling fires. When people become aware of natural sounds, as Gustave did when he walked barefoot in the grass and water, they cultivate an appreciation of their connection with the universe.

Sight

People become so used to the way something looks, they do not realize that it isn't quite right. I suggest, for example, that clients evaluate the appearance of their bedrooms. If pill bottles are everywhere, if pictures of in-laws are disturbing, if smelly socks and laundry are piled in the corners, a rearrangement may make this important room more comfortable. The bedroom needs to be an oasis, a place where people can feel safe, warm, and sexy. It may turn them off if it reminds them of their last doctor's visit, an argument with in-laws, or chores like the laundry. One client felt better when she removed the exercise bike from her bedroom. "I'm getting back in shape, but I don't want to be reminded of that all the time," she said. People whose children or parents live with them may need to put a lock on the bedroom door.

When Gustave and Geneviere looked at their bedroom, they admitted that, although it wasn't too bad, it did feel "sterile." They changed that by putting Gustave's scattered textbooks out of sight, painting the white walls a pastel blue, and putting mirrors on one wall.

My clients also cultivate their awareness of the human body's beauty. They look at art books and erotic photography to see how male and female forms have been depicted throughout the ages. Women need to appreciate the bodies of men, and vice versa, as a way to heighten awareness of their unique and spiritual qualities.

Another exercise I ask my clients to do is to pretend they are seeing themselves for the first time. Standing fully dressed in front of a full-length mirror, they noncritically tell themselves what they see: hair, eyes, chin, mouth, neck, breasts, arms, legs, hips, thighs, calves, and feet. This is strictly a "what you see is what there is" exercise, not an occasion to judge or criticize. People usually practice this technique several times before their image of themselves begins to change. Some people are comfortable with asking a friend's help with this exercise.

After men and women feel secure about "telling it like it is," they begin to add the sense of touch. They explore each part of their bodies and think about whether it feels bony or soft or muscular. This exercise builds an appreciation of their bodies as they are at that moment.

Smell

Smell is probably the most undervalued sense. Like other creatures in the animal kingdom, human beings need the sense of smell to bond with other people. A baby knows its mother's smell; a musky odor is associated with sex. Yet men and women spend time and money to eradicate their natural aromas and then spend more on perfumes, deodorants, and douches to substitute more "acceptable" scents.

A technique that clients use to become comfortable with themselves is to touch their genitals and smell their natural odors on their fingertips. I ask women to smell the aroma of their vaginas, and men to taste their semen; both men and women rub their sweat and smell it.

Learning to Stay Physically Present

If they are to be present and aware of their bodies, individuals need to establish boundaries. The metaphor of a sleeping bag helps to explain the concept of an immaterial border where the world stops and the self begins. The bag is like the skin; the person is inside that skin and functions "skin-in," while the world is "skin-out." A zipper on the inside of the bag enables the person to decide what to let in and out. Boundaries let people know that they can take care of themselves, safe from others' abuse or violation.

People who lack boundaries have an impaired sense of themselves. These individuals may be severe codependents or trauma survivors or adult children of alcoholics. Those who have undergone much trauma are either beside themselves, outside of themselves, or not at home at all. As people recover, using the Twelve Steps, they establish their boundaries and learn to stay inside their bodies or their "bags." For some individuals, especially trauma survivors, staying skin-in can be a lifetime task.

Fortunately, several good tools can help clients maintain their boundaries. One is deep breathing while listening to evocative music. This exercise allows people to get in touch with their inner selves so that healing can occur. Leaders trained in this technique can take clients through altered states of consciousness.

Another exercise, rebirthing, also involves deep breathing as well as visualization; music is optional. People breathe deeply, in a relaxed state, while their partners prompt them to visualize themselves first outside of their bodies and then in their bodies as complete, functional men and women. This second visualization works best when people envision themselves in a safe, secure, and loved place. After practicing several times, clients can use this visualization to center themselves when they notice their boundaries breaking down.

These techniques allow people to experience changes in mood and to be present in their bodies. Breath work is very useful in recovery therapy. Other excellent tools are yoga, meditation, and tai chi.

Healthy Parts Are Sensual Parts

People who are in touch with themselves take an active part in maintaining their health. I suggest that men regularly examine their genitals and that women examine their breasts and labia. Many excellent books describe these easy procedures (see section 3 of the Bibliography), or a physician can teach them. At this stage of sexual recovery, these self-explorations increase people's familiarity with their bodies and functions.

Kegel Exercises: Not for Women Only

Both men and women benefit from doing Kegel exercises to strengthen the pubococcygeal muscles, which, when squeezed or contracted, stops the flow of urine. These muscles also contract during orgasm; strengthening them increases control over them and the degree of sexual pleasure.

To identify the pubococcygeal muscles, I ask clients to imagine that, while they are driving, they need to urinate, but the next rest station is forty miles away. Women pretend they are squeezing a pencil in their vaginas. Concentrating on that image, they inhale and contract the muscles for a count of three, then relax and exhale. I recommend one hundred repeats, three times daily. A slightly more difficult variation on the exercise involves squeezing and releasing rapidly without counting to three. People can do Kegel exercises anywhere—while they watch TV, talk on the phone, stand in line at the bank, or wait at a stop light. No one will know.

Although they were originally recommended only to women, Kegel exercises also help men to control their erections and maintain them longer during lovemaking. For this reason, the exercises were one element of Gustave's treatment for premature ejaculation. Because they allow women more control and more intense sensation, Geneviere also practiced them to intensify her orgasm.

Sexual function involves the pelvic muscles. They weaken and wither from nonuse. The stronger these muscles, the better the orgasms. Use them or lose them!

Seeing the Body As It Is: Body Image Exercises

Many men and women never see their bodies from the neck down. Body imaging enables them to become aware of what their heads are resting on. These exercises help many people realize that they have a distorted view of their bodies, or even none at all.

I ask men and women to tell me what they see, what they are telling themselves about it, what they can truly accept, and what they can change. Many trauma survivors cannot even see their faces, so visualizing their genitals is impossible at this point. Dissociation from their bodies helped them to survive.

Body image exercises can be done at home, for thirty minutes in each session, three times a week. After clients have practiced several times fully clothed, they work up to doing the exercise nude. The procedure is similar: they look noncritically at themselves and begin to accept their bodies as they are. They think about the idealized American image of men's and women's bodies, perfectly proportioned and flawless in every respect, and they consider the falsity of that ideal. This stage is about acceptance of their normal physiques. Because many people are not realistic about what they see and say and what actually is there, they may need some help with this technique. Discussing their feelings with a therapist, sponsor, or partner can help bring into alignment their images and their bodies' actual appearance.

Self-imaging allows men and women to know how they feel about everything from their hair down to their toes. This increasing familiarity helps them to deepen their sense of themselves as physical creatures. Some clients even draw their whole bodies on butcher paper to get a more accurate sense of who they are.

Imaging the Genitals

When they have grown comfortable with their vision of their whole bodies, clients learn to focus on the genitals. Standing or sitting in front of a mirror, they spread their legs and take inventory of what they see. Men touch their genitals and write affirmations about them. This exercise helps them to experience the connection between the rest of their bodies and their genitals. This exercise was important to Gustave as he worked out his feelings about his premature ejaculation and tried to be more comfortable with his genitals.

Women also need to get over the uneasiness they feel about their genitals and those of partners. Both men and women need to believe these body parts are perfect the way they are. "My body is a temple." "I am a child of God." "My body is beautiful." These are some of the affirmations clients have written. No matter how people feel about their genitals, they need to voice any shame, embarrassment, and guilt. Once they express their fears, they can begin to change those thoughts in their heads by saying affirmations and practicing other positive techniques.

Clients also turn to art and poetry for positive images of human genitalia. Art history books contain photographs of muscular Greek figures, older than two thousand years, and the voluptuous women Rubens painted four hundred years ago. These masterpieces not only illustrate the great range and variance of normal physiques, but also show the changes that occur over the centuries in the ideal of beauty.

Many people keep a journal to record their feelings before they begin these exercises, notes of their perceptions while they look in the mirror, and their later conclusions. Thus they see their progress spelled out on paper, black-and-white evidence of their learning. Journals are a valuable tool throughout the recovery process.

Fantasy*

Fantasy can enhance sensual and sexual experiences, either in solitude or the company of a partner. Although many people think that fantasies are right or wrong in the same way that actions are, fantasy is not reality, and imaginary actions need not be carried out. People can have thoughts without action or even feeling, and they can stop the process anywhere.

People entertain all kinds of fantasies, especially people who have been traumatized sexually or physically. They were taught to associate sex with abuse, spankings, enemas, rapes, and other traumas. When they fantasize about such things, they feel shame, incorrectly assuming that something is wrong with them as men and women. They need to realize that these fantasies are a predictable outcome of their traumatic pasts, not reality requiring action, and can be changed.

The distinction between erotic and pornographic fantasy is unclear to some individuals. Pornography is visual or auditory material that degrades and dehumanizes both sexes, shows hostility or violence, and is destructive. Erotica, which makes a connection between love and sex, exhibits artistic and literary values. It provides materials to feed the senses, increase awareness, and heighten the experience of sensuality. It includes good poetry, books, music, videos, movies, and magazines. What stimulates erotic feelings in some people does not in others, so individuals experiment with different materials to find their preferences.[23]

---

* **A Word of Caution to Sex and Love Addicts**: Fantasy triggers addiction and relapse in some people. They need to skip this section. Before they can create healthy fantasy, they need a period of abstinence or celibacy from unhealthy fantasy.

---

23. Masters and Johnson, "The Sexual Response Cycle of the Human Female. III. The clitoris: Anatomic and Clinical Considerations," *Western Journal of Surgery, Obstetrics, and Gynecology* 70: 248-257, 1962.

16

Discovering Sexual Identity through Masturbation: Stage 5

Men and women express themselves sexually in infinite varia-tions. The sexual liberalism of the 1960s and 1970s gave way to circumspection in the 1980s with the emergence of AIDS. Now we are seeing new attitudes about monogamy. One attitude has remained constant with my clients, despite the radical social shifts during these decades: their intense fear, shame, and embar-rassment about the "M" word—masturbation.

In fact, masturbation is critical to sexual development and growth. It also is a fact of life that many people "fudge," deny, or lie about; the sexual dysfunctions of men and women who seek counsel show their ambivalence about it. People who want to masturbate, but are ashamed because they feel it is "dirty" or wrong, deprive themselves of an innocuous pleasure. Perhaps they don't know how to masturbate and are too embarrassed to ask, preferring to remain uninformed or misinformed.

I am not advocating masturbation as the only true way for sexual expression. Healthy masturbation is a sexual alternative, however, and a way for people to experience their bodies, which is the focus in the fifth stage of sexual recovery. On the other hand, those who engage in compulsive masturbation are sex addicts. People in recovery for sex or romance addiction or those with re-ligious scruples about masturbation may want to check with their sponsors or religious leaders. Is it an expression compatible with their abstinence contract, a pleasure they could enjoy as a normal fact of their lives? Masturbation is a personal matter people need to evaluate according to their beliefs and values, with the help of a therapist, sponsor, or other person.

For people who are not sex addicts, masturbation is a sexual option. If vagina-penis intercourse were the only way to express or experience sexual energy, men and women would be truly limited. Masturbation allows people to be comfortable with their bodies and to nurture tenderness that they might share with partners if they choose.

Sexual energy is a state of being: how men and women use it is an individual matter. Some masturbate when they want or need the option of solitary sexual enjoyment. Masturbation comforts people during illness. It is a healthy sexual alternative for people who do not have a partner or who have chosen celibacy, for whatever reason.

People Getting Comfortable with Their Bodies

It is critical during sexual recovery that people learn to please themselves and work through embarrassment, guilt, or shame. As a sex therapist, I cringe whenever I hear the myths about masturbation that still exist. The techniques my clients use during Stage 5 are intended to help them overcome embarrassment, misinformation, and awkwardness about masturbation.

Because each person holds unique beliefs, not every exercise is appropriate for everyone. What I offer here is one path; more information, including specific methods for masturbation, appears in books listed in part 3 of the Bibliography. Readers may want to refer to the body inventory in chapter 12, the discussion of sexual parts, their location, function, and response as they learn how to masturbate and be sexual with themselves.

"Won't I Grow Hair on My Palms If I Masturbate?"

Masturbation is a natural behavior, engaged in by children, adolescents, men, and women throughout their lives. It is a celebration of self that is not available in any other way. Nevertheless, myths have grown up around this normal behavior. Despite all our imagined sophistication, many of these myths persist.

Countless men have told me about their parents' repeated warnings that "it would fall off"; the boys would go insane or blind if they "touched themselves like that." Many boys also suffered threats that their parents would cut off their penises if they con-

200

tinued to masturbate. How many children dreaded the warts or hair they anticipated would grow on their hands? The practice also has been blamed for nosebleeds, "masturbator's heart" (irregular heartbeat), nymphomania, offensive body odor, headaches, and tender breasts. Some religious institutions forbid masturbation as an "unnatural act" because it has no procreative purpose and only gratifies oneself.

The masturbation taboo even survived the '70s, the era of liberal sexual behavior. Men and women were wrapping themselves in plastic, swinging from chandeliers, and having group sex, but when I asked them about masturbation, the shyness and embarrassment of the centuries came out. "We can't do that," they said. "That's infantile." Then they blushed and looked away. Masturbation was still getting a bad rap after the sexual freedom of the '60s and '70s. Even today, people who believe more is better still shy away from masturbation as a way to learn more about their sexual nature.

In Stages 1 through 4, men and women build their foundation and a self-nurturing and self-sexual environment. In Stage 5, they move past their shame about masturbation and learn to please themselves.

What Experts Say about the "M" Word

According to SIECUS (Sex Information and Education Council of the United States),

> Sexual self-pleasuring, or masturbation, is a natural part
> of sexual behavior for individuals of all ages. It can help
> to develop a sense of the body as belonging to the self,
> and an affirmative attitude toward the body as a legiti-
> mate source of enjoyment. It can also help in the release
> of tension in a way harmless to the self and to others, and
> provide an intense experience of the self as preparation
> for experiencing another. Masturbation, and the fantasies
> that frequently accompany it, can be important aids in
> maintaining or restoring the image of one's self as a fully
> functioning human being.[24]

---

24. Sex Information and Educational Council of the United States, Inc. (SIECUS), SIECUS Report 18, no. 2 (December 1989/January 1990).

With official permission granted, men and women can look at their concerns about masturbation.

Men Look at "M" Myths and Techniques

Somehow men believe that they are less masculine if they masturbate; they fear that it shows that they can't attract a partner. According to Alfred Kinsey, more than 96 percent of all men have masturbated. [25] Even if they approve of masturbation before marriage, however, many men believe that afterward it demonstrates defective masculinity.

Sex is more than the five-to-seven inches between men's legs. When they learn to feel sensual all over, men begin to realize that sensuality and sexuality involve the whole body. The sensate focusing techniques explained in Stage 3 help people do that, as does masturbation.

How People Feel about Masturbation

Two important reasons to masturbate are that it feels good and it relieves sexual tension. Mutual masturbation both to orgasm and before orgasm also is pleasurable part of partner sexuality. (See chapters 19 and 20, Stages 8 and 9.)

Male clients practice masturbating so they can learn to appreciate their bodies and its sensations. Doing so, they learn to time their orgasm so they can share it with their partners. This control was one of Gustave's goals, and the method he practiced in this stage helped him to overcome his premature ejaculation (see "Masturbation As Part of the Cure" later in this chapter).

Before men and women practice masturbation, they need to rid themselves of any negative or distorted beliefs about it. They analyze the myths and thoughts playing in their heads and decide *for themselves* how they want to behave, giving up the fancied obligation to satisfy others' expectations. Some Catholics, for example, have asked clergy for dispensation to masturbate after their therapists deemed it medically necessary as a step toward healthy sexual expression.

As people masturbate and go through the sexual response cycle, they focus on their physical sensations and emotions. Do

---

25. Kinsey, et al., *Sexual Behavior in the Human Male*, 499-500.

they feel positive, joyous, degraded, fulfilled, or humiliated? People need to identify their feelings and turn the negatives into positives in order to stay firmly on their path of sexual recovery.

Gentlemen, Attention Please

Both women and men find it helpful to begin each masturbation session by setting the stage and the mood. Men need the right atmosphere for their masturbation exercises just as women do, not just thirty seconds in the shower. I ask them to remove their sports and car posters from the walls and replace them with peaceful pictures, mirrors, or perhaps a wall rug. Since comfort and sensual pleasure is what they need, I also ask them to make their beds with aesthetically pleasing blankets, pillows, and sheets. Music sets a good mood, and men choose everything from classical to hard rock. Candles and incense also help them relax.

These masturbation sessions requires some time alone, fifteen to twenty minutes three times a week. Men need at least this long, because one of the most common causes of premature ejaculation is the way men learned to have an orgasm in the first place—quick and quiet. As adolescents, they masturbated behind barns, in alleys, or secretly in their rooms, terrified that someone would catch them at it. In the military, when they masturbated in their bunks or in the field, they had little time to waste and couldn't make any noise about it. The quickest kept their secret.

Ways to Masturbate

Men experiment with different methods and then choose one or more that are the most comfortable and provide the most pleasure. A variety of positions are workable: lying down on the bed or floor, sitting, standing, reclining against the back of the bed or a chair. Each man has his own preferred situation. Comfort and relaxation are the important elements.

Clients start with the basics and then experiment as they become more comfortable and make progress. I suggest that, after they have chosen a position, they use a focusing technique (see chapter 14). They masturbate with a dry hand during the first few sessions and then add a lubricant later. Saliva is a natural lubricant, but many men prefer commercial ones—KY jelly, petroleum jelly, body oils, or lotions.

I ask men to focus on their penises as they are stroking, being aware when they approach their point of no return, and then backing off. Because the purposes of these masturbatory exercises include an increased sexual awareness and control, men refrain from ejaculating during the fifteen-minute session. After the session, they may choose to ejaculate or not.

Fantasy can be a part of masturbation. Erotic literature, magazines, and videos are common aids. Men fantasize about past sexual experiences, group sex, romantic settings, or whatever else stimulates them. Some visualize the most erotic scene they can imagine and vocalize their feelings while they masturbate. They moan, make animal sounds, groan, yell, use sexually explicit language, or otherwise express their feelings in order to weaken their inhibitions about being vocal during sex. These sessions are their opportunity to experiment and to become comfortable with their bodies.

Masturbation As Part of the Cure

When I talk to men about using masturbation to cure retarded ejaculation, impotence, inhibited sexual desire, and premature ejaculation, they insist that they want a pill or a miracle, anything except THAT! "Real men use women," they say. Men need to allow themselves to feel feelings and let go as they progress through the masturbation exercises. They need to get past their distorted thinking and into the pleasures without shame and embarrassment.

As Gustave and many other male clients have discovered, masturbation also is part of a very effective treatment of premature ejaculation, explained in detail by Michael Castleman in *Sexual Solutions: An Informative Guide* (see Appendix 12-4). At this stage, Gustave practiced the first part of Castleman's method. He chose a comfortable setting and relaxed using a focusing technique. Then he masturbated with a dry hand for fifteen minutes, concentrating on how his penis was reacting, how his entire body felt during the experience, and not allowing himself to reach orgasm. He focused on his sexual response—noting how long it took him to reach excitement and plateau, and stopped masturbating when he felt himself approaching orgasm. When the feeling subsided, he resumed masturbating. This technique he practiced three times a week until he felt he had control. He repeated the technique with a lubricated hand three times a week until he had control, and then he alternated these two methods for several weeks.

As part of the treatment of premature ejaculation and other ejaculatory problems, solitary masturbation teaches men to control ejaculation. These men believe erroneously that ejaculation is involuntary. They learn that, although ejaculation itself is an involuntary reflex, they can delay it voluntarily.

Ejaculation and orgasm are two different things. Men can ejaculate without an orgasm; they also can have an orgasm without ejaculating. The treatment described here helps them know how far they can go without going over the edge.

Wrong Way Down a One-Way Street: Retrograde Ejaculation

In China, some men practice a form of birth control in which they control their ejaculation, forcing the sperm up into the bladder instead of out through the penis. They eliminate the semen later during urination. This "retrograde ejaculation" may occur unintentionally in recovering alcoholics. When some men are coming off alcohol, their systems do not operate optimally. Some very upset men have called me in the middle of the night to tell me they just had sex for the first time since they had been sober and that "it went backwards instead of forward." For them it is a sex crisis, but it is common among recovering alcoholics and men who have undergone urinary surgery until their systems normalize.

Women Look at "M" Myths and Techniques

Women have been told that their genitals are "dirty" and "icky." "Don't touch down there," adults tell little girls; "save it for the man you love." What are they saving for that man? Do they understand or know their own sexual needs and desires or their bodies' capabilities? Women say, "If he loved me, he would know how to bring me to orgasm," or "I'm too embarrassed to tell him what I like or what turns me on," or "I don't know myself what I like." Fifty percent of women are not having orgasms, and I believe that is because they are relying on another person to find out what they need rather than figuring it out for themselves and then sharing their knowledge of their bodies with their partners. Like men, women have been trapped in stereotypes which have made them sexually dysfunctional.

Let's Try It, Ladies

Women need more time for masturbation exercises than men—thirty minutes to one hour three times a week. They begin with a focusing technique. When they reach their genitals, they focus on their vagina and clitoris. Then they practice the Kegel exercises, contracting the vaginal muscles as if they were trying to hold onto a pencil with their vagina. Then they can take the focusing technique to its conclusion.

After several sessions, women add masturbation to their routine. Masturbation allows them to find those pleasure spots on their bodies that bring them to orgasm—ears, neck, nipples, vagina, inner thighs, clitoris, the G-spot—and experiment in a safe setting; so they can share what they learn with a partner later if they choose to.

This was Geneviere's goal—discovering what stimulated her so she could share that knowledge with Gustave. Because she had experienced sexual trauma, getting in touch with her body and feeling good *about* feeling good were important. Focusing helped her relax before she tried masturbation. After several weeks, she began to explore her genitals and eventually learned to identify the sensitive spots that aroused her. Once she was comfortable with her feelings, she tried several different positions and techniques.

According to *The Hite Report: A Nationwide Study of Female Sexuality*, more than 70 percent of women do not achieve orgasm through intercourse alone and need additional stimulation.[26] It has also been shown that the most intense orgasm is experienced through masturbation for both men and women, yet most people prefer to share their sexual orgasm with their partners. What men and women learn about self-masturbation at this stage can be shared later with their partners if they choose.

Positions women use during masturbation depend on the individual. Some women lie down on their backs, sides, or stom-

---

26. Shere Hite, *The Hite Report: A Nationwide Study of Female Sexuality* (New York: Bantam, 1981), 229-232.

achs; others sit up and lean against the wall or bedboard with their legs spread in front of them. When lying down, women may use a pillow, a rolled up towel, or a stuffed animal between their legs for pressure and stimulation.

For added stimulation, some women experiment using dildoes, vibrators, erotic literature or videos, or feathers. If they have nightwear or underwear or garters that make them feel sexy, I suggest they wear them while masturbating. Some women clients try rubbing their body with different textures and materials, such as silk scarves, satin, or feathers. Saliva and vaginal secretions are natural lubricants, but KY jelly, massage oils, petroleum jelly, or body lotions also can be used.

Fantasy: Mind Sex for Fun

Fantasy helps women to bring the mental and physical aspects of sex together for total sexual release. The content of fantasies used to enhance masturbation can be any memory or imagined experience that is stimulating and fun—a remembered sexual encounter; a sexy stranger on a beach; sex with a man who ties his lover to the bed with silk scarves. These private thoughts about sex need never be acted out. They allow people to get into a sexual mood and augment their stimulation. In addition, fantasies help women to take responsibility for their own arousal, rather than expecting their partners to turn them on physically and mentally. Some women clients use romance novels or erotic literature, magazines, or videos to help them with fantasy. Several excellent books are available about women and their fantasies (see part 3 of the Bibliography).

Why Is Masturbation So Important?

Masturbation is a powerful sensate focusing technique that allows men and women to observe various physical responses and thoughts during the sexual response cycle. This awareness reveals whether any unwanted thoughts and feelings get in the way of orgasm.

Women can masturbate in a safe environment, controlled and created by themselves. This security was particularly important for Geneviere, as it is for many women—especially those with little or no sexual desire, those suffering painful intercourse, and those with a sexual aversion. It allows them to relax enough to discover their own characteristics, which they listed in Step Four of the Twelve Steps adapted for sexual recovery. Such knowledge helps them identify obstructions to their full sexual expression. In that safe place, they can experience themselves, listen to the tape playing in their heads, and bring themselves to orgasm.

Learning to masturbate and become sexual with self is very helpful to trauma survivors because it allows them to feel they have control over their environment and their bodies. As trauma survivors increase sensual awareness, body memories often come out of the trauma. For that reason, they need to work with a sponsor, therapist, or partner to resolve their past trauma during this process and put it into the background.

Faking Orgasm—on Purpose

One technique many women enjoy is pretending they are actresses and role-playing an orgasm. The Hollywood, male-oriented version of what women look and act like is a distorted view that many women have believed. Women experience orgasm one way on the silver screen and another way in reality. When they play-act orgasm, barriers may reveal themselves; women can then learn how to break them down so they can experience full sexual release.

Many women report that, when they are masturbating, they feel more and more quiet as they approach orgasm—a quiet like the calm before the storm. Men have been taught to expect flailing excitement, like they see in the movies. These stereotypes need to be put aside. Masturbation sessions allow women to become comfortable with their bodies and their own unique orgasms, and to recognize the changes in their bodies and thoughts as they experience sexual release.

The intensity of orgasm changes, depending on fatigue, anger or other emotions, and the degree of intimacy and comfort with self and partner. There are no "right" or "wrong" ways. The orgasm may be centered in the vagina or the clitoris or somewhere else; it may be superficial or felt throughout the entire body. Some women moan or cry out, some are silent; some are active, while others lie still, or their bodies become rigid with sexual tension.

On Vibrators

Some women have become addicted to the use of vibrators. When a vibrator is the only route to an orgasm, both the women and their partners are frustrated. I recommend that such women abstain from using the vibrator for a three-month period and then resume only occasional use for variety thereafter. It is best to view vibrators as an enhancement only, not as the sole route to orgasm.

Sharing What Has Been Learned

At this point in sexual recovery, people have become aware of and comfortable with their bodies, feelings, and actions. Now it is time to share those experiences and feelings with a partner. Gustave and Geneviere and all gay and straight couples who use this model find a lot of excitement and discovery in the next part of the process.

17

Fore-Foreplay: Discovering Sexual Potential by Nurturing Partners: Stage 6

After men and women have learned how to nurture themselves and to be sensual and sexual with themselves, they can begin to share their good feelings with a partner if they wish. At this stage of the Good Sex Program, they work on developing a safe, healthy atmosphere for themselves, their partners, and their relationships so they can continue their exploration of healthy sexuality. They do this by establishing mutual trust, respect, vulnerability, and openness, and by basically liking each other and enjoying these positive feelings.

People who come out of alcoholic homes and addictive environments adopt the code, "Don't trust, don't feel, don't talk." With that motto hanging over their beds, sexual relationships start off tainted. Using the sexual recovery model, couples now use the communications skills discussed in chapter 13 to share what they've done so far. These skills enable them to resolve conflicts and power struggles and work through past hurts and resentments. With those issues settled, couples can create the kind of environment necessary for healthy sexuality.

First, Time Out

Men and women seek my help as a sex therapist expecting to learn "new, improved" sexual tricks, like acquiring new aerobic skills When I ask them to take time out from their usual sexual behaviors, to abstain, they think I'm crazy. Before they can become

211

what they want to be sexually, they need some down-time to assess what they have been and what they are now. This period of reflection is the fore-foreplay part of the sexual discovery, walking before they run.

In addiction treatment and sex therapy, people often talk about "the insanity of the disease." This "insanity" means repetition of the same behavior over and over again, with an expectation of different results each time. That change is just not going to happen until the addictive cycle and sexual dysfunction cycle are broken.

What Do You Mean, No Sex?

To escape from this insanity, some couples adopt an abstinence contract, particularly those caught in a sexual dysfunction cycle, or recovering co-sex addicts, sex addicts, romance addicts, or sexual trauma survivors. Temporary celibacy enables them to see what life is like outside of their dysfunctional cycle.

The typical experience of an alcoholic man who is fighting impotence is a perfect example of this cycle. He believes that, if he tries to get an erection just one more time and has one more drink to do it, he'll be successful. But when he can't get it up again, he thinks, "Just one more drink and next time I will," which leads to failure again. Many men and women who are not alcoholic play out a variation of this scenario, believing that if they try one more time harder or better, the next time will be different. It won't. Performance anxiety is part of this failure cycle. Healthy sexuality depends upon people *being* who they are as men and women, and not in *doing*. They need comfort in being themselves, not an Olympic performance. They need acceptance of their own nature, not "if only I were thinner/stronger/taller/prettier" myths.

The abstinence contract allows people to get away from the cycle of failure. Every time the cycle repeats, it traumatizes both partners, and the relationship as a whole. This contract prevents that reinjury.

A respite for healing is particularly important for sex and romance addicts because their sexual energy comes out of their disease and not health. Abstinence gives them a rest from the emotional high of sexual addiction and brings it into remission before they begin afresh. Sexual trauma survivors who are having flashbacks and remembering their past trauma also need a time out. The expectation that they can maintain sexual intimacy during this time is unrealistic because they associate their current sexual experience with past trauma.

Time out means having spontaneous, childlike fun without engaging in sexual activities. Individuals return to where they were before their sexual experiences if there is a point they remember: to dating and being affectionate, kind, warm and considerate, to the fun and joy of life before sex. (Remember?) Laxity about courting is easy, especially after years in a relationship. People forget how to do the little things for one another—holding open the car door, giving flowers or cards, hugging spontaneously, holding hands, saying "I love you." Partners who are nurturing one another are relearning how to play, to be spontaneous and affectionate, without the fun's necessarily leading to sexual intercourse.

Affection Does Not Equal Sex

Some people believe that any signs of nurturing or affection from their partners means they must have sex. "I just know that every time Jerry comes up behind me and kisses my neck he wants to have sex," complained Penny.

"When Ramona starts to give me a back massage, I always think she expects sex in return," Jon told me. "Sometimes I just feel like cuddling. I don't think she knows that."

Couples can break down this damaging myth, learning that they can touch and show affection without running into the bedroom. A nurturing relationship is possible in which hugging and caressing and holding hands, nonverbal expressions of love, are not necessarily preludes to sexual intercourse.

Gustave and Geneviere enjoyed rediscovering variety in expressions of love. Geneviere is especially touched by words; she needs to hear "I love you," "What has your day been like?", and "You look wonderful today." Gustave, on the other hand, likes hugs. Unless Geneviere gives him loving pats, holds hands, and makes other physical displays of affection, he feels she does not love him. Although Geneviere loves Gustave and tells him so, he does not hear the love; he wants to feel it.

Sex-History Time

Good communication is crucial in this stage of sexual recovery, which is why my clients do a sex history now. Their stories allow both partners to know one another's past. The last part of Step Nine, "...except when to do so will injure others," needs to be remembered here. In the sex history, people share with their partners whatever parts of their sexual past can tactfully be shared. Too much damage has been done in the name of honesty. The saying that men and women are as sick as their secrets does not imply that they must tell their partners about every relationship or flirtation they've had. Thus Geneviere did not share with Gustave all the sordid details of her promiscuous college days before she met him, nor the particulars of her affairs. It was enough for Gustave to know that, although this type of behavior had occurred, it had ceased, and Geneviere was in recovery. (See Appendix 17-1 for an example of a sex history.)

Finding Where Boundaries Are

Three elements generally compose a relationship: each individual and the relationship itself. A relationship is only as strong as the individuals in it. Partners in a relationship therefore need to know where their own boundaries are so they can determine where the relationship begins.

The relationship between Gustave and Geneviere serves as a good example. As man and woman, they are two separate circles. The third factor, their relationship, begins where they meet and compromise—the overlapping of their individual tastes, thoughts, feelings, values, and interests. The compromise is where individuals contribute or take away from the sharing process with their partners.

Picking Up the Pieces

At this stage of sexual recovery, men and women bring together the little things that they do for themselves, acts that affirm that they are good, vital, sexual people and share these pleasures with their partners. Nurture includes self-grooming and grooming each other. Sometimes people have been with partners for so long that they take the small personal touches for granted. Many couples voice this complaint.

"Leo expects me to be turned on, yet all he wears around the house is ragged sweat pants," said Bonita. Jeremiah noticed that his wife Dara had stopped wearing perfume except when they were going some place special. "It was always such a nice little turn on," he said. The little extra time courting couples spent cleaning their nails, trying a new hair style, changing into something more attractive, or wearing special perfume or aftershave is often forgotten as their relationships get older.

Can't Live with Them, Can't Live without Them

"Stan expects me to shut off the fact that we've just had a big argument and suddenly get sexy five minutes later, when he wants to hit the bedroom," complained Juanita. "I can't do that." On the other hand, some men say, "All she wants is to be touched and held. She wants all the love and affection but the last thing she wants is sex." How can men and women be so different and expect to live together in peace?

Gay or straight, couples need to achieve a balance within themselves and in their relationship to live together in harmony. The genders approach sexuality differently. Men focus more on the physical aspects of sex. Women tend to have a broader focus and are more affected by their emotions. To help bring these two sides together so healthy sexuality can thrive, couples need to talk.

Fore-foreplay involves the practice of good communication skills. Couples use conflict resolution exercises such as reflective listening or role reversal to help them achieve a balance in their relationships. Fore-foreplay means they resolve their power struggles and conflicts in the living room before they share with their partners sexually in the bedroom. (See chapter 13.)

Establishing Sex Roles in Nurturing

A strong sexual relationship is a partnership. Both partners need to share their feelings and expectations about one another and their relationship. This exchange requires that they put aside any stereotypical ideas about what men and women are "supposed" to do or say. Instead, they focus on their own particular needs and desires. Their relationship is unique, and whatever parts they mutually agree upon are okay for them.

The Parts People Play

Some people tend to perceive a relationship as adversarial. Although many people can share their most intimate secrets with their friends, when they try to share these same thoughts and feelings with their partners, they begin thinking in terms of more than and, less than; win or lose; good or bad; superior and inferior; mine and yours. Instead of entering a conversation with their partners with the intention to share, they go in wearing boxing gloves, ready to spar for power and control. This attitude prevents their meeting in the middle for compromise and balance.

People need to depart from the extremes of socially prescribed sex roles, and instead to find a middle way. When people wear the stereotypical masks imposed by culture, they project false selves. At this stage of sexual recovery, couples work to recognize that their relationship is a partnership, a family, a corporation. Two co-chairpersons head that corporation, and sexuality is a cooperative venture between the two partners. A partnership can thrive only if the partners are willing to communicate effectively and nurture each other.

How Men and Women Nurture Each Other

To establish a starting point at this stage, I ask people what they thought their parents' sex lives were like and what they told my clients about sex. Men and women discover that, when they piece together these thoughts and memories, they understand better where they are sexually at that moment. It doesn't always matter whether their parents told them the whole truth about sex. Some people say, "No one really talked to me about it, but I could tell by the mutual trust, respect, and love they showed that things in the bedroom were probably good."

Little Things Are Fun

What are some of those signs that things "were probably good"? The list of little kindnesses is endless. Some people call one another in the middle of the day to say "I love you." One might cook a favorite meal as a surprise, give little gifts for no special occasion, hold hands, wink or pat a beloved, write love notes, or pull out chairs and hold coats. Clients love these partner nurturing "homework" assignments, and many people come up with their own lists. Partner nurturing provides an opportunity for a couple to have fun and to be good to one another.

When couples share these caring signs, they truly seem to enjoy each other and emanate celebration and joy. They stop taking partners for granted. Considerate people call when they're going to be late, put the top back on the toothpaste, or stop to pick up something at the store.

Doing "It" and Not Doing "It"

Couples in this stage realize that they can be affectionate and nurturing throughout their life cycle, and that sexual intercourse does not need to be the "goal" or end result of these signs of affection. When men are between eighteen and twenty-two, their sexuality is driven by their hormones. As they age, the hormones diminish, and men need more physical stimulation to become sexually aroused. As this need increases, they can enjoy greater sexual fulfillment if they learn how to be more sensual with themselves and their partners. As women age, they reach their peak sexually. They begin to appreciate their bodies and their sexual needs more, and they become more open and sexual with their partners.

Some couples are in their fifties and sixties when they seek therapy. Their children have left home, and now either one or both of them is ill or has had surgery. At retirement age, they may see that they have gradually drifted apart until they don't touch at all. They are almost afraid to touch, because they have learned that touching means they will do "It." Some wives tell me, "Why bother touching and leading up to it when it's something he probably can't fulfill." When couples learn to nurture themselves and their partners, they realize that sexuality is not limited to genital sex. Other kinds of expression are not only fulfilling in themselves, but also enhance the pleasure in sexual intercourse.

Sex and Romance Addicts Learn to Nurture Partners

When sex and romance addicts reach this stage, sexual activity stops so they can determine whether they have anything else in common with their partners. These men and women need to do a personal inventory to see whether anything besides sexuality or the lack of it is the focus of their relationship. This time-out allows them to participate in activities they did not try during their addiction. Together they involve themselves in volunteer projects or spiritual gatherings, develop hobbies, read new books, attend cultural events, and enjoy any number of other good times that replace their addictive sexual activities.

Creating a Growing Space

Stage 6 is also the time when men and women create an atmosphere in which their healthy sexuality can grow. People who believe that sexuality is only performance set themselves up for failure. I ask that couples set aside at least one hour three times a week just to be together. This meeting is a time for companionship and conversation, not sex. Without that kind of intimacy, nothing more can happen.

During this special time, couples practice communication skills. "When you...I feel"; "When we're sexual again, let's try..."; "I like it when you..."; or "I have a fantasy I'd like to share with you." Here again, people need to practice tact. Fantasy is not reality and not something that must be acted out. Although people may wish to share fantasies, some partners may not be the persons with whom to share them.

How to Say No

When couples share nurturing time, they are in a secure environment, without pressure to be sexual. These special occasions are the perfect times to clear up misread or misunderstood communications. "How do I know if he's ready?" a woman may wonder. "He's had a bad day, I'd better lie low." "She has her period," a man may think, "and we never...." Now they can tell partners everything they always wondered, but were afraid to ask. Reading each other's sexual signals, deciding whether either person is ready for sex, takes communication. Men and women cannot be truly sexual until they have the ability, willingness, and courage to say no. "No" is how people set boundaries. People need to learn how to decline before they can assert with confidence, knowing that is what they truly want.

The myth is not true that men are ready for sex all the time.

Many men unconsciously want control and the role of initiator because they think that a woman can be sexual whether she is ready or not, and that, if a man doesn't have an erection, it's a "no go." Some men complain that women are not assertive and don't initiate sex. Men want the option to say no, too, and they need to learn how to say it. They also need to learn to ask women to initiate sex and not feel threatened doing so.

Feeling Safe to Move On

This stage allows men and women to experience a neutral, sharing environment in which they can communicate without pressure, where the risk of being hurt or rejected is reduced. Sharing with their partners what they have learned about self-nurturing paves the way for them to share their sensuality.

The Scenic Route: Discovering Sexual Potential by Sharing Sensuality with a Partner: Stage 7

18

Truly to appreciate and share healthy sexuality, people need to slow down, put aside their expectations, and take the scenic route. The road to healthy spiritual sexuality is open only to people who are relaxed and present in their bodies. They neither take their partners for granted, nor view them too seriously. They enjoy the present moment without striving to perfect performance as if life were only a string of tasks.

After they have practiced and learned how to be sensual with themselves, most men and women want to share those experiences with a partner. In Stage 7 of sexual discovery, people incorporate what they have learned about their own sensuality into their relationships, without crossing the line into sexuality. They also focus on getting rid of their hurts and resentments and talk about their fears, likes, and dislikes with their partners. This verbal exchange is a part of sharing sensuality in a relationship.

Where's the Fire?

Very often couples are in such a hurry to go for the gold—the big O—that they forget to savor the pleasures of the journey. They get caught up in the mechanics of sex, and they miss the experience of enjoying their partners' companionship.

Many women complain that their partners think foreplay is

221

a kiss on the lips, two gropes at their breasts, and then a lunge for the crotch. Some men talk about women who want two hours of cuddling and then fall asleep before sex. These are legitimate complaints. When people narrow sex down to genital friction, it becomes a masturbatory experience, not a sexually intimate one. A mere holding session is not sexually intimate.

Communicating and Compromising toward a Healthy Balance

One of the most common complaints is that one partner wants sex more than the other or, "He's hot when I'm not." Compromise is a skill, discussed in chapter 13. The compromise here is for the sake of the sexual relationship, the center of the partnership.

When people discuss a child's proper bedtime or the restaurant where they want to dine, they are negotiating. It is usually easier to learn negotiation on neutral issues than those that involve sexuality because sexual compromise is more embarrassing or uncomfortable for many people.

Rarely do two people like the same thing all the time. Negotiating techniques enable couples to resolve conflict about sexual variations or any other issues in a healthy way. If they think of their conflicts as arenas for deciding winners and losers, their relationships are lost. Working together to share healthy sensual experiences with their partners, men and women create a win-win situation.

When Saying No Really Means No

During Stage 7, clients continue to practice what I call "yes-yes" and "no-no" skills, learning how to say no and how to ask for what they want. This kind of give-and-take is difficult for many individuals, so they either don't talk about what they want or they respond in a way that hurts their partners or themselves.

Some people give in to sex, for example, because they don't want to hurt their partners' feelings. Rather than practice skills, looking inside themselves to see what they really want and then sharing that with their partners, they submit or don't talk about their desires. This omission causes resentments and hurts to build. I ask couples to use reflective listening and then to compare what they hear from partners with their own inner longings.

Gustave and Geneviere

I recommended that Gustave and Geneviere, like all my couples, practice these skills in the living room, on walks, sitting by the pool, and in other comfortable, safe settings. Often the bedroom is too threatening an atmosphere for people to open up their authentic feelings. They need to hear "no" as a positive statement of what the other person truly feels and not as a personal attack.

When Gustave told Geneviere that he did not like to have his ear lobes stroked, it was not a personal attack on Geneviere or her identity as a sexual woman. It was his personal preference, and he followed up his statement by telling Geneviere something she did that he did like. Thus they did not criticize one another, but affirmed the sensual bonding they were sharing.

Couples need to establish whether their words and actions come from anger with one another or something else. (See Appendix 13-1, "Anger Dos and Don'ts.") Mind-reading and guessing games lead to misunderstandings and resentments.

Removing the Shame That Blocks Progress

In Steps Six and Seven of the Twelve Steps, people work to remove shame and embarrassment by surrendering it to their higher power and then making amends to themselves and their partners. Then in Steps Ten and Eleven they continue to take moral inventory. Men and women in sexual recovery return to Step Ten at every session to keep tabs on themselves and anticipate any reappearance of their character defects. In Step Eleven, they reaffirm that their higher power is with them on their journey, capable of intervention in their behalf.

Bringing in the Senses

Sensuality exists on a continuum, from very public to very private situations. As couples go through some of the exercises together that awaken their senses, they begin to share with their partners what they've learned about themselves and their preferences. What were more or less two separate circles now overlap in the middle, and the partners compromise and determine their preferences as a couple.

Pleasure and Hangups Begin in the Mind

Sexual pleasure begins and ends in the mind, not between the legs. That's why couples affirm themselves, to allay any shame they may have brought to their sexual encounters. The suggestions below have helped many couples become more aware of how they can please partners through their senses.

Sound

Couples choose music they both find soothing, sexy, or stimulating. They discuss how different music makes them feel and which songs bring their partners to mind. Some couples like to pick songs that are "theirs." Mutual experimentation with new music, nature sounds, or music of other cultures can add a new dimension to their sexual exchange.

The inflection, tone, emphasis, and intensity of the human voice are dimensions that most people don't think about exploring. How many times have people commented, "It's not what he said but how he said it"? Couples practice saying phrases to one another in different ways. They discuss how they felt about what they said. "I love you" or "Why did you do that?" can mean different things, depending on how they are said. This exercise makes people aware of their manner of speaking and the power of their voices. Geneviere was very aware of voice, tone, and inflection because she needed vocal affirmations of Gustave's love and affection. They made creative use of this exercise.

Smell

The musky smell of fresh sweat is a common sexual turn on. Some men and women sleep in their partner's shirt or pajamas when the other person is away or out of town, because their partners' smell lingers on the clothing. For others, comfort with partners' natural smells is a new pleasure to be cultivated.

Trying different fragrances can also be fun. Every individual has a different body chemistry, so the same fragrance smells different on different bodies. Some clients choose potpourri, scented candles, or incense that they both like. Natural smells, such as flowers, the forest after a rainstorm, the muskiness of a cave, or the scents arising from the pounding surf evoke special memories for couples. Smells of cooking food also recall shared memories or experiences, such as a special Italian restaurant or a barbecue.

Taste

Gustave and Geneviere went shopping together to pick foods they wanted to cook together and share. They enjoyed choosing foods they found sexy or sensual, and then they prepared the food in a Chinese wok and fed one another and themselves using chop sticks. They also bought kiwi, bananas, and whipped cream and fed each other the fruit and cream.

Tasting does not have to be confined to food. Couples learn to taste each other, and sometimes they enhance the experience by adding food. After showering, but without adding any perfumes, powders, or lotions, couples can explore each other by licking their partners' earlobes, throat, the inner surfaces of the arms and thighs, or fingers and toes. Some couples spread whipped cream, fudge, honey, or any other suitable food on their partners' skin and lick it off. French kissing after eating something sweet, sour, bitter, and salty can be a new shared experience. Tasting a partner's vaginal fluids or semen helps people to become acclimated to one another and can be a prelude to oral sex.

Sight

Sharing the sights of nature together—sunsets, walks on the beach, drives in the country, moonlight hikes—is another mutually sensual experience. I suggest that couples go to a quiet natural setting they have never visited before and share it as a new experience and make it their own. Such shared activities establish couple preferences, like meeting at a special little cafe or a favorite area of the park.

Some couples find that dressing for each other can be a sensual experience. They discuss some of the clothing they would like to see their partners wear, what appeals to them as attractive, sexy, and flattering. Shopping together for clothing is a good way to share this experience.

Couples need to share the sight of each other while nude and grow comfortable with that experience. In Stages 3, 4, and 5, men and women established boundaries and built up a comfort zone of thoughts, feelings, and behaviors for themselves. Now the individual circles, each with its own comfort zone, are touching and interconnecting. As these circles overlap, the partners may stretch their zones gradually as they become more comfortable. Here couples negotiate and talk about how comfortable they are with nudity.

People can explore this question by sitting across from one another while nude. They may sit cross-legged on the floor or, if they are uncomfortable initially, at a table. Each partner takes a turn reaching out to touch the other and expressing feelings about the part of the body being touched. For example, Leona places her hand on Rudy's chest and tells him, "I love to run my fingers through the hair on your chest." Leonard touches Michael's thighs and tells him, "I see such strength in your thighs." Staying with affirmative statements in this exercise helps to reinforce a sensual bond.

Our culture has done men and women a great disservice by keeping the human body secret and hidden, exploiting it in the media, and giving it a charge of negativity or obsession. Many men have been so deprived of seeing women's bodies in a healthy way that all they see are nipples or crotch. Women are repelled by male genitals because they can't see them as part of the whole persons they love. The awareness techniques throughout the Good Sex model and others suggested in books listed in the Bibliography help people to appreciate and revere their bodies and to treat them appropriately.

Touch

The skin is the biggest sex organ (sorry, men), and touch is the primary sexual sense. Bringing the skin alive increases people's consciousness and the intensity of experience. At this stage of sexual discovery, men and women develop an appreciation of touching their partners, not in a sexual way but in a loving, sensual, caring way. Here people build on what they learned previously about nurturing their partners: touching, petting, and caressing each other are ways to nurture each other, which need not lead to intercourse.

"Scratch My Back and I'll Scratch Yours"

Three times a week for an hour, Gustave and Geneviere gave one another hand, foot, or facial massages while they were clothed. During these massages, they talked and otherwise showed one another what they liked and did not like. As they became more comfortable, they did back massages with clothes on and then gradually with clothes off. As their comfort increased, they did massages with just the chest bare and then eventually totally nude, but not touching the genitals at this stage. These exercises build people's awareness of what pleases them in a sensual way.

Trauma survivors and others troubled by painful body memories or flashbacks, deal with these issues as they occur, in order to find out what stands in the way of their enjoying healthy sex. They experiment with exercises in the bedroom, out of the bedroom, at night or during the day, and work around whatever triggers the memories so they can begin to enjoy positive sexual experiences.

Shampooing each others' hair, bathing or showering together, mutual stroking while watching television, giving each other loving pats—all of these touching activities increase people's awareness of self and partner and affirm their pleasure. Cuddling and holding are among the sensual pleasures. Many people, especially older individuals, like spooning—holding one another and sleeping side-by-side like two spoons touching. The mutual pleasure strengthens a couple's bond.

A Healing Part of Sharing Sensuality

At this stage of sexual recovery, Gustave and Geneviere returned to the method for treating premature ejaculation. Gustave taught Geneviere how to stimulate his penis, first using a dry hand and then a lubricated hand, but not to the point of orgasm. To do this, Gustave focused on responding sensually rather than sexually. He also massaged Geneviere's genitals in a sensual way.

The purpose of these techniques is the heightening of sensual awareness in a nonsexual framework, without orgasm as the result and goal. Separating the sensual from the sexual—affection from sexual advances—creates comfort with the knowledge that not all touching leads to genital sex.

The Fun Never Ends

Couples can share many ways to be sensual with each other. For fun, they build mutual fantasies about activities and places they would both enjoy. Sometimes I ask couples to experiment with each other's boundaries. Partners sit across from each other and reach out to each other to discover where each of them begins and ends, feeling each other's energy. Some people become uncomfortable when they are approached in a certain way or when certain areas of their bodies are touched. This exercise allows people to notice how they and their partners react to being approached.

Staying in the Body

Trauma survivors particularly need to know whether they are focused "in their bodies." When men and women are physically present, they are fully aware of their feelings. I teach couples to notice whether their partners have "left" their bodies. They may appear distracted, tend to stare, be slow to respond verbally, or hold their bodies stiffly. Often trauma survivors are not aware they have dissociated themselves. I train their partners to pick up the signs and supply the means to bring an absentee back to the present.

One tool is concentration on breathing. When people focus all of their energy and thoughts on their own breathing or that of their partners, they increase their body awareness. Gustave and Geneviere used this technique because, as a trauma survivor, Geneviere tended to dissociate during her sexual encounters with Gustave. Many couples enjoy this exercise while they are giving massages or spooning.

Show and Tell

Adult "show and tell" can also be sensual fun. People share what they've learned about their bodies and how they function, as well as what they've learned about a partner's body. This exchange gives couples a chance to talk about what they found that was interesting, new, or perhaps unpleasant.

And the Goal Is....

The goal is to be goal-less. Men and women give up their goal-oriented activities and learn to be joyous as sensual individuals. Having freed themselves from constraints and learned to share that freedom, they are ready to be sexual with their partners.

Closed for Repairs: Discovering Sexual Potential by Sharing Sexuality without Intercourse: Stage 8

19

When I was a sex educator for a family planning organization, I gave sex education lectures in high schools. At the time, I wished that many of the young men could be impotent for at least two years so they would learn ways to be sexual other than intercourse. Not only men, but also women have suffered as a result of the narrow perspective on sexuality. Many teenage girls are having their first sexual encounters with sexually misinformed boys and thinking "that's all there is."

American culture suggests that if the penis or vagina does not work, no sexuality is possible, but people can continue to be sexual and manifest their sexual energy in various other ways. Healthy sexuality is about negotiation, making peace with the differences and accentuating the similarities, not about what culture dictates is wrong or right. Sexual behavior which two consenting adults agree affirms them is acceptable behavior. Partners need a balance among the physical, emotional, spiritual, and intellectual factors of their sexual activities.

Sexuality Is More Than Penis-Vagina Intercourse

Many people unnecessarily deprive themselves of sexual expression because they believe the myth that penis-vagina intercourse

229

is the only way. I began to appreciate fully the multitude of variations on human sexuality when I worked with people who had spinal cord injuries and diabetes. Many of the men with spinal cord injuries, had been hurt during wartime, when they were sexually in their prime. They taught me the many places where orgasm occurs other than the genitals, such as nipples and neck.

People can discover new ways to be orgasmic through their senses, especially the skin. The paralyzed men could be orgasmic at a point just above the injury, whether it had occurred above the waist or the chest. Nursing mothers, who often report orgasm when they are nursing or sleeping, bear out this fact, and some women experience orgasm during sleep.

Re-Enter the Senses

Clients often view this stage of sexual recovery as a return to their courting or petting days, when they were afraid to do "it," and therefore tried other means of sexual expression. As adults, they know they can choose from many more options, a few of which are described below. (Materials listed in section 3 of the Bibliography present a wealth of others.)

As clients share sensory experiences with their partners in Stages 6 and 7, they focus on nurture and sensuality, the fore-foreplay. Next they explore ways to stimulate and arouse their partners sexually without penis-vagina contact. Some clients are skeptical about this stage, but they find that the path of sexual discovery is more exciting when there are unexpected curves in the road.

Men and women need to call into play all the sensual expressions and techniques they learned in previous stages. The dimensions of sound, taste, smell, touch, and sight, added to the sessions suggested below, enhance sexual encounters. Some of these sensual and sexual exercises, sexually explicit videos, erotic poetry, dirty dancing, even conversation about sexual activities can result in orgasm. As the patients with spinal cord injuries explained, arousal has much to do with the way people think and focus their sexual energy.

Sexuality without Intercourse

People can be sexual together using the hands, the mouth, and the anus, rather than the genitals. Each approach involves techniques that can bring men and women to orgasm without penis-vagina intercourse.

Manual Stimulation

All that women and men have learned about self-stimulation in the previous stages can now be shared with their partners. Many clients now discover the benefits of the Kegel exercises. For Gustave and Geneviere, manual stimulation was a natural step because they had practiced sensual massage in the previous stage and were ready for sexual massage.

Gustave and Geneviere began by getting comfortable in a place where they would not be disturbed for at least one hour. After centering themselves, they began stimulating one another manually. Partners can caress one another simultaneously (mutual masturbation), or they can alternate. Either technique is a good starting point for people who have never felt safe in the past.

They begin by slowly caressing their partners, applying different pressure, and perhaps using body lotions or oils to enhance the experience. Some clients rub feathers, silk scarves, velvet, or satin against the skin. Men and women share the experience by focusing on their partners' reactions and their own feelings during the massage. There is no need to talk much. It is the experience itself that is being shared. The first few times they do this technique, people avoid the genitals and breasts, which are so sensitive that merely touching adjacent areas arouses sensations. The goal is an awareness of exquisite sensitivity.

After Geneviere and Gustave had caressed one another for twenty or thirty minutes, they discussed the experience. What did they like and not like? What made them uncomfortable? What would they like to change next time? In these conversations, couples are looking for the positive feelings that came from the session and creating new affirmations.

In another exercise, couples watch their partners masturbate and explain to one another what they like. Many men and women fantasize about such an experience, which can be very arousing. This sort of activity is a workable compromise when one partner wants sexual intercourse more often than the other. The one who wants sexual activity can masturbate while the partner observes, or the partner who declines can masturbate the other.

This method also can be used when one partner is ill or incapacitated. Both individuals can get pleasure from sharing the feelings and the experience.

As clients feel more comfortable and adventurous, they often add little sexual enhancements to their sessions. Vibrators, both clitoral, vaginal, and anal, and dildoes can be enjoyable for both men and women. A whirlpool, shower, or hot tub is a good place to use water jets or shower massages for mutual or self-stimulation. (DO NOT INTRODUCE WATER UNDER PRESSURE INTO THE VAGINA; DOING SO CAN BE FATAL.)

Gustave and Geneviere especially enjoyed learning massage techniques from a book. The hospital backrub is only one limited kind of massage. Others include massage of the breasts and front of the body, the entire back side, the face, hands, feet, genitals, and anus. Any of these massages can bring about an orgasm, without penis-vagina intercourse.

Manual Stimulation of the Anus

Another kind of sexual massage involves stimulating both the genital and anal areas. Many men and women find this type of massage arousing, but it is a matter of personal preference. This technique is more common among gay men.

A centering technique is an excellent preface to this exercise because many people find it hard to relax for anal stimulation. The anal muscles are tighter than the vaginal muscles, so stimulation or penetration needs to be slow, with the use of a lubricant. It is best to start by gently massaging the anal area, then slowly and gently inserting a lubricated finger or penis into the anus only as far as is comfortable for the partner who is receiving the massage. In order to be receptive to partners, some men and women insert a finger into their own anuses to see how they feel about it. After one finger feels comfortable, some people can accept two.

Enhancements of this exercise include the use of anal vibrators or dildoes inside and around the anus. Gently pulsating water jets also are stimulating. Some men like to have their prostate massaged. To prevent infection, any object that has been in the anus must be washed with soap and water before it is inserted into the vagina. THE AIDS VIRUS CAN BE SPREAD THROUGH PENIS-ANUS INTERCOURSE. The use of condoms is essential;

232

this sexual practice is so risky, in fact, that it should be avoided entirely.

Oral Stimulation

Most people think of oral sex as involving oral stimulation of the genitals and the surrounding area, but it also includes oral stimulation of any other part of the body, such as the breasts, ear lobes, fingers, tongue, neck, palms, and toes. Clients to whom oral sex seems alien or uncomfortable can begin with centering exercises and a discussion with their partners of their fears. Contact between the mouth and the genitals (called *cunnilingus* when it involves the mouth and vagina and *fellatio* when it involves the mouth and penis) offends and unnerves some people because of genital odors. A woman may worry that her partner might come in her mouth or that she might gag on her partner's penis. The couple needs to talk over these concerns before they try oral sex exercises.

In the atmosphere of love and trust that Gustave and Geneviere established, they discussed these issues before doing exercises. Although Geneviere had been quite "wild" in her drugging days, now she had qualms about oral sex. She and Gustave showered together before their sessions and then did about fifteen minutes of sensory focusing exercises, including mutual masturbation and a centering technique.

Gustave knew that Geneviere feared he might ejaculate into her mouth. They decided that Gustave would tap on his wife's shoulder or tell her vocally when he was going to come so she could withdraw her mouth in time. Because of the trust and communication they had been building, this arrangement was agreeable to both of them.

Couples choose among many approaches for oral sex. Some approach one another face-to-face, starting at the neck and ears and slowly making their way down to the genital area while stopping to lick and stimulate other erotic areas along the way. The receiving partner can be sitting or lying down for this approach. If partners decide on mutual oral stimulation, the "69" position is popular, with both partners lying down feet-to-face so they can stimulate each other simultaneously.

There are many variations on these approaches. Those who are receivers can manually stimulate their partners or simply lie back and enjoy the experience. Partners can alternate, each spending fifteen or twenty minutes stimulating the other separately and then simultaneously. Some couples concentrate on just one or two areas at each session, such as the clitoris and the penis one time and the labia and the scrotum another time.

Techniques to stimulate the penis, scrotum, clitoris, vagina, breasts, anus, and labia can be found in any number of books (see the Bibliography). Couples often come up with their own ideas after they feel comfortable with oral stimulation. Foods such as whipped cream, chocolate syrup, or pudding can be spread on various parts of the body and licked off. Some couples wear eatable underwear and "snack" in bed. For many couples, oral sex has opened new doors of sexual understanding and pleasure. It is an opportunity to share sexual experiences with a partner without engaging in penis-vagina intercourse.

Phone Sex

Couples who are separated can use the phone to maintain their sexual relationship. They talk about their sexual relationship, fantasize, read erotic stories or poetry to each other, or use other imaginative ways to sexually arouse one another. Usually each partner masturbates during these conversations, at the same time or separately.

Phone sex is an effective way to release the sexual tension of couples who must be separated for any length of time. It allows couples to stay close emotionally and sexually while they are physically apart.

Sexuality without Intercourse for Trauma Survivors

The road to sexual recovery may be longer for trauma survivors, than for others. When the road is closed for repairs, these survivors need to be reintroduced slowly to sexual activities. As they near the end of the Good Sex Program, they need especially creative sexual positions and alternatives to intercourse, because man-on-top or woman-on-top or any other overt sexual behavior may trigger flashbacks. Both trauma survivors and their partners need to be aware of this possibility. For example, rape survivors may need to spend much more time learning to be comfortable with self-stimulation, before they are ready for the rest of the process. Once they reach Stage 8, their partners may need to explore more indirect or less threatening exercises for a longer time before moving on to genital contact. Rather than do whole-body massage, rape survivors may need to spend more time on kisses and hugs, hand or back massage, or techniques to heighten the other senses before they can feel comfortable with genital touching.

Gay Sex: What's It All About?

About 25 percent of my clients are gay. Some of my heterosexual clients have asked, "How are gay people sexual?" This question shows how limited their range of knowledge is about sexuality, a limitation which exists in both heterosexual and homosexual circles.

Some issues are special to gay men and women, but basically they experience sexuality in the same way heterosexuals do: through vaginal, oral, anal, and manual contact. They may substitute objects such as vibrators or dildoes for penises. They may also make other compromises about which partner leads and which follows, in both the relationship and sexual sharing, and these arrangements may change.

Sharing It All

All the sensuous and sexual experiences men and women encounter in Stages 1 through 8 of the Good Sex Program bring them to the time when they are ready for a complete sexual experience. In Stage 9, both partners share all their learning with their partner in sexual intercourse.

Going All the Way: Discovering Sexual Potential through Genital Sex with a Partner: Stage 9

20

Sexual intercourse is just another way of touching, of making skin-to-skin contact. When men and women add sexual intercourse to their relationships, they seem to experience what Stephanie Covington, author of *Leaving the Enchanted Forest*, calls a "mysterious impulse to fuse and merge" with their partners.[27] Looking at a relationship that way, people can begin to correct culturally based misunderstandings. When I work with individuals and couples on the Good Sex Program, I am careful not to ask them to do anything that could violate their beliefs for the sake of their relationship. If they do not want to try something, that's okay. If they try something once, they never need do it again. There are many ways to express and experience sexuality, as the previous stages demonstrated.

People need to take each stage of sexual recovery slowly and stretch their comfort zones to incorporate new ideas, experiences, and behaviors. Their larger repertoire frees them from habitual behavior and the doomed hope that the same old actions could yield new results. That is why I ask couples to look at their character defects to see whether they obstruct healthy sexuality. This

---

27. Stephanie Covington and Liana Beckett, *Leaving the Enchanted Forest* (San Francisco: Harper and Row, 1988), 119.

assessment involves their looking inside to their core and honoring that identity.

Same Old, Same Old?

At this stage, couples explore genital sexuality, incorporating it into the broadened range of experience they have been practicing. Although the missionary position (man on top) is the most common, men and women need not limit themselves to such a narrow menu. The variations are only as limited as people's imagination: Woman on top, side-to-side (either facing each other or spooning), both seated face-to-face, both seated facing same direction, rear entry, standing face-to-face, standing facing same direction, one seated and one standing, both kneeling. What matters is mutual agreement and comfort with the positions chosen. Sexuality is a joyous celebration of self, and sexual expressions reflect that joy. Many have reflected this feeling in music, painting, dance, sculpture, theater, movies, and the printed word. *The Joy of Sex* and *More Joy*, by Alex Comfort, are just two books that fall into the latter category.

Stimulating Each Other

When clients reach Stage 9, they look back at the knowledge they have garnered together. Some have experimented with stimulating their partners to orgasm without involving the genitals, as Gustave and Geneviere did. Those skills they can apply now, adding genital stimulation.

Learning how to stimulate the clitoris (or even finding it) can be a new experience for men. I ask women to show their partners where the clitoris is and how they like to be stimulated (which they learned in Stage 5 on masturbation). Gustave and Geneviere shared these experiences in the previous two stages. They were ready to apply what they had learned about stimulating each other during sexual intercourse.

At this stage, Gustave and Geneviere also completed the cure of Gustave's premature ejaculation. After she had masturbated him both with a dry hand and a lubricated hand, she took his penis into her vagina and simply held it there while Gustave moved just enough to maintain an erection for about fifteen minutes. After he was able to remain erect without an orgasm for fifteen minutes during several sessions, Gustave held still, while Geneviere moved just enough to help Gustave keep his erection for about fifteen minutes. During each of these exercises, Gustave and Geneviere focused on the amount of stimulation Gustave needed and their feelings during the experience. After they were able to do this successfully several times, Gustave started to thrust and pull out before coming, when he wanted to.

The Variations Go On

This stage brings in all the techniques and knowledge learned in the previous stages and incorporates them into love-making. Couples begin with focusing exercises or they shower together, give massages, or feed one another foods they both find sensuous. Some couples try different positions or locations or even a different time of the day—spontaneously in the middle of a Saturday afternoon, say, or during a shower. Practicing Kegel exercises during intercourse can enhance the excitement and help individuals control the timing of their orgasm. They can read erotic poetry, watch videos, or use feathers. Whatever they want to do, they need to learn how to be comfortable and how to have fun.

The relationship of one couple I know exemplifies the playful joy people can take in healthy intimacy. They express their feelings by setting up special evenings together. Marvin, a florist, buys every kind of food fantasy—chocolate-covered graham crackers to steaks, brie to kiwi—whatever he and Shirley may want to enjoy together. He has a hot tub with a gazebo, and he floats rose petals in the water. Shirley and Marvin use massage oils, satin sheets, fans, and X-rated films. They never let their evenings become boring or routine, but flow with whatever feels right at the time.

"From the minute we get together until the next morning, we feel as if we were having an adult slumber party," Shirley said. Their playfulness continually refreshes their relationship.

Snow on the Roof, Fire in the Oven

Men and women who accept the physical changes as they age and work with them can stay sexually active. If they simply feel the pleasure of their sexual experiences and don't focus on orgasm all the time, they can have fulfilling sexual relationships with their partners at any age. As men grow older, some need more direct stimulation to get an erection and keep it. Many women notice that they have less vaginal lubrication, a problem which they remedy easily with saliva or commercial jelly.

It's Not All Push and Thrust: Vaginal Containment

There is a misconception that the penis needs to be erect before sexual intercourse can start. A variation of the "gotta-be-hard" approach to intercourse is called vaginal containment. This way is sometimes called the "stuffing technique," or quiet intercourse, because the man puts his semi-flaccid penis into his partner and then neither partner actively moves. Contraction of the pubococcygeal muscles (Kegel exercises), mutual caressing, sharing sexual fantasies, and simply savoring the time together are the stimuli that gradually cause the penis to become erect without thrusting or movement from either partner. If time passes before the penis hardens, all the better; the pause enables partners to share quiet while they focus on their breathing and the sensations of their touching bodies.

Coming Together, Coming a Lot...Maybe

The idea that partners "should" have an orgasm at the same time sets people up for disappointment. If they do, great; usually, though, one has an orgasm and then he or she takes care of the other partner. Usually men see that women come first, but in today's liberated society, many partners take turns. They are realizing that, when they focus on the total sexual experience, they share with their partners and do not get caught up in the performance mentality. In *Becoming Orgasmic*, Julia Heiman and Joseph LoPiccolo suggest that when partners experience their orgasms separately, each person has the opportunity fully to appreciate the moment.[28]

Both men and women are capable of multiple orgasms. Because women do not go through a refractory phase after orgasm as men do, they can return to the plateau phase after an orgasm and soon have another one. (Remember the sexual response cycle?) After the refractory phase, men are capable of another orgasm.

---

28. Julie R. Heiman and Joseph LoPiccolo, *Becoming Orgasmic* (New York: Prentice Hall, 1988), 196.

Faking It...and Other Things That Did and Did Not Happen

"How do I say that I'm not finished?" "Have I failed because my partner had only one orgasm?" These are some of the questions men and women ask me. They need to experiment to find out what they are capable of, which is what the stages have helped many people do. Some couples have divorced because of their inability to bring one another to orgasm. Women have come to me hysterical, saying, "I know he's faking orgasm, there was nothing wet. Doesn't he love me?"

The truth is, both men and women fake it. Fakery does not necessarily mean they don't enjoy the experience. Sometimes intercourse simply goes on too long without orgasm for one partner. Although this circumstance may not be fair, it is normal. Couples need to talk about what they feel and don't feel, without blaming one another.

Sex during Menstruation

People's feelings about sex during menstruation vary. It turns on some couples, some say it's okay, and others are repelled. Some women use a diaphragm to hold back the blood flow, if that is what concerns them or their partners. Sex during a period, which relieves cramping in some women, is a personal choice, not something dictated by physiology or custom.

Ready for the Final Leap

After men and women have shared all their private experiences with their partners in sexual intercourse, they've achieved healthy sexuality, right? Almost. The final element, the one that brings their entire experience together, is spirituality.

The Ultimate Orgasm: Discovering Sexual Potential When Spirituality and Sexuality Merge: Stage 10

21

People's sexual wounds reach to their very core, and the only healing that can truly touch their core—their souls—is spiritual healing. A spiritually satisfying life is the vehicle through which to transcend the anguish and find true sexual healing. This healing is possible because *spirituality and sexuality both arise from the same source.* They are internal power and energy, affirming feelings of harmony that come from a person's core.

Spirituality and Sexuality: Making the Connection

Love exists in many different forms: love of children, love among siblings, erotic passion, love of God, love of friends, and so on. Although these kinds love are all available to people, passion and love of God are the most difficult forms that cause people to stumble. When they try to integrate sexuality and spirituality, they often fail to see the connection between these concepts: Sexuality is a God-given energy force, arising from the same inner source as the love of God. Sexual energy is spiritual energy. Accepting these articles of faith, people begin to trust that spirituality is integral to healthy sexuality.

243

When people faithfully work the Twelve Steps of AA adapted for sexual recovery and the Good Sex Program, they achieve spiritual sexuality. They fulfill the promises that the Program offers them. AA is a fundamentally spiritual program. For men and women who are caught up in addictions, or making money, or doing, rather than being, the Steps hold the road to new freedoms and new happiness. When people stop their insane behavior long enough to look at the Steps, the program assures them that their feelings of uselessness and self-pity will disappear. They will develop a new outlook and fresh attitude on life. Fear and insecurity will leave them. Perhaps most important, they see that their higher power can help them in ways they cannot help themselves.

People find that they can release past hurts and concerns about outcome when they work Step 3. They turn their sexuality over to the care of their higher power. Letting go allows the emergence of the authentic sexual self, either alone or with a partner.

As people take personal inventories and proceed on their own paths of recovery, they can connect with the love that is in them, be that their higher power, God, nature, or other people through whom this energy is revealed.

Sexuality and spirituality are identical. People can use their spiritual energy to affirm, celebrate, and transform themselves, or they can use it to perpetrate injury, degrade others, or shame themselves. Although sexuality and spirituality began as one, in our society, people have learned to divide the union. It seems that many people made an unbearable choice very early in their lives. They would be religious, good, successful, God-fearing and contributing citizens of this earth. Or they would be sexual beings, which they erroneously took to mean worthless, depraved, sex maniacs on a path of destruction. The illusion that spirituality and sexuality are separate and mutually exclusive categories deadens them both.

Spiritual Healing Is True Healing

Addiction is called an intimacy disorder, a dissociative disorder of the soul. The only true healing of addictions found so far is spiritual healing. When individuals seek solutions to their sexual problems, they need to start at the beginning, with the "Big Book" of AA. A passage from that work touches the heart of the matter:

...Acceptance is the answer to *all* my problems today. When I am disturbed, it is because I find some person, place, thing, or situation—some fact of my life— unacceptable to me, and I can find no serenity until I accept that person, place, thing, or situation as being exactly the way it is supposed to be at this moment. Nothing, absolutely nothing happens in God's world by mistake. Until I could accept my alcoholism, I could not stay sober; unless I accept life completely on life's terms, I cannot be happy. I need to concentrate not so much on what needs to be changed in the world as on what needs to be changed in me and in my attitudes.[29]

When men and women use the Twelve Steps for any issue, including sexual ones, when they stop blaming things that are "out there" for "what's been done to them," they begin to accept that whatever has happened is perfect as it is. Then they can focus on what needs to be changed in themselves and their attitudes. These are the only changes they are empowered to make in the status quo. They frequently reflect on Step Eleven, seeking through prayer and meditation to experience their sexuality without expectations and asking for God's will and the courage to carry it out. When people place their sexuality in God's hands, they accept their sexual experiences; questions like How long? How hard? How many? do not concern them.

Men and women use the Twelve Steps to accept impotence, incest, ritual abuse, sex addiction, inhibited sexual desire, and homosexuality. When they take the spiritual path of the Steps, they not only can change themselves and their attitudes, they also can cease to be victims of their circumstances. The fact that life dealt them a certain set of cards does not relieve them of the choice to change their perspective on those circumstances. They have the option to accept the cards and take a spiritual path to wholeness, beyond hurt and resentment.

"Spiritual sexuality" is a phrase that cannot be found in a dictionary, but the phenomenon is present in the lives of the men and women who have practiced the Good Sex Program. One thing that my clients agree upon when they reach this final stage is that each person has a unique way to express what spiritual sexuality

---

29. *Alcoholics Anonymous*, 3d ed. (New York: Alcoholics Anonymous World Services, Inc., 1976), 83-84.

means. They are anxious to share what they feel, and many of them say that it is hard to describe the energy and emotion that come from their deepest selves.

Luke is one of many clients who wanted to express what spiritual sexuality has meant in his life. His cocaine addiction and compulsive masturbation had resulted in feelings of hopelessness and his hospitalization for a rectal injury. During his recovery, he came to believe that it was one of God's miracles that his life was spared. He says that his sex addiction should have killed him; "there must be a patron saint for addicts" that saved him.

Every time Sarah had a sexual feeling, memories of her father's pornography collection came back to her. During her sexual recovery, she saw that she had lived her life in fear of her father and his drinking and rage. As she worked Steps Six and Seven and the fear and obsession with her father's pornography photographs were removed, the vacuum within her filled with love and serenity. She felt she was blessed with "a fearless, Godly loving energy."

For Jolette and Harvey, spiritual sexuality was a shared experience. Jolette learned to let go of the control she thought she had over Harvey's drinking and to experience her sexual feelings. As she surrendered her control, she not only shared her authentic sexuality with Harvey, she also came to believe in a power outside herself. The work Jolette and Harvey did together led them to be comfortable with their sexual feelings for each other, and they now plan to have another child.

Many of my gay men and women clients have said that their real feeling of spiritual sexuality occurs when they accept their homosexuality as God-given. For Claudette, that sense of spirituality came when she affirmed that she is gay, alcoholic, and a trauma survivor. She felt as if she had risen "from the depth of all my wounds" and reached an entirely new level of life, energy, and goodness.

For my clients who are survivors of ritual abuse, true healing is not concerned with religion but with spirituality. Robin's recovery process had included eight years of sobriety and five years of remission from her eating disorder before she addressed her trauma. She came to realize that the men and women who had sexually abused her as a child were truly evil and that a healthy energy coexists on the planet with that evil. Robin believes that her faith in a "divine spiritual light" was the only thing that helped her through recovery. For Hector, another satanic abuse survivor, the resolution of his alcohol and sex addictions also preceded the work on ritual abuse issues. He found his spiritual peace when he accepted his homosexuality as a gift from God and began a satisfying relationship with another man.

Some people say, "Surrender to God's will? That's fine for my job or my kids, but my sexuality is too personal, too important. I'm too embarrassed." When they surrendered their addictions, recovery opened up; when they release their sexuality to God's will, they will receive the promises they have sought. As men and women work the Twelve Steps for sexual recovery, and follow the other principles of the Good Sex Program, they are creating the space in which God's will may be done. What is so ironic about sexual wellness is that people have searched everywhere to get fixed. All the while, the solution to many of their sexual problems was, and is, spiritual.

What a paradox! I've come to believe that God truly does have a sense of humor.

EPILOGUE

More than twelve years ago, it became clear to me that there was a direct correlation between people's addictions and their sexual dysfunctions. Equally apparent was the fact that between eighteen months and two-and-one-half years after men and women thought they had "fixed" their addictions by working Twelve Step programs, they were relapsing. What had they done wrong?

It wasn't a question of wrong; it was a matter of not going far enough. The Twelve Step work had dealt with their addictions as separate entities, without accounting for the integral part sexual dysfunctions played in the recovery process. To complete their recovery, these men and women needed to address the sexual issues that accompanied their addictive behaviors. To make this necessary connection, I integrated the healing process of the Twelve Steps into a sexual recovery and discovery model. The Good Sex Program that evolved from that conjunction allowed my clients to find their own unique healthy sexuality while being free of their addictive behaviors.

Thus this book was born from the joys, fears, triumphs, and courage of the dozens of men and women, gay and straight, who have practiced the Good Sex Program. It is my gift to all who still suffer with the confusion and shame of sexual issues, in the hope that they will find the safe and loving road to sobriety and healthy sexuality.

Those who choose to walk the path will not be alone; many have traveled it before them, and many are on it now. Although the path is not an easy one, the Good Sex Program promises all who complete the journey a life of joy and serenity as healthy, sexual, spiritually intimate men and women in the light of a power greater than themselves.

About the Author

Sherry Sedgwick, M.Ed., is a certified sex therapist and addictions counselor, as well as an educator and lecturer. Her dual certification in addictionology and sex therapy, as well as her own personal history of recovery, generated her pioneering work in the interrelationship between these two disciplines. The success of this combination therapeutic approach has been proved again and again both in her private practice in Tucson, Arizona, and in her work in treatment centers.

Sherry Sedgwick is retained nationally by therapeutic facilities as a consultant whose mission is to integrate the important component of sexual recovery into addictions programs. She is also well known for her video and lecture series on human sexuality. Information about her programs can be obtained by writing to Serenity Recovery Services, 3661 North Campbell Avenue, Box 586, Tucson, Arizona 85719.

In *The Good Sex Book*, she demonstrates that interrelated sexual issues and addictive behaviors have common origins, and recovery from one is not realistic or enduring without recovery from the other.

Appendix 3-1

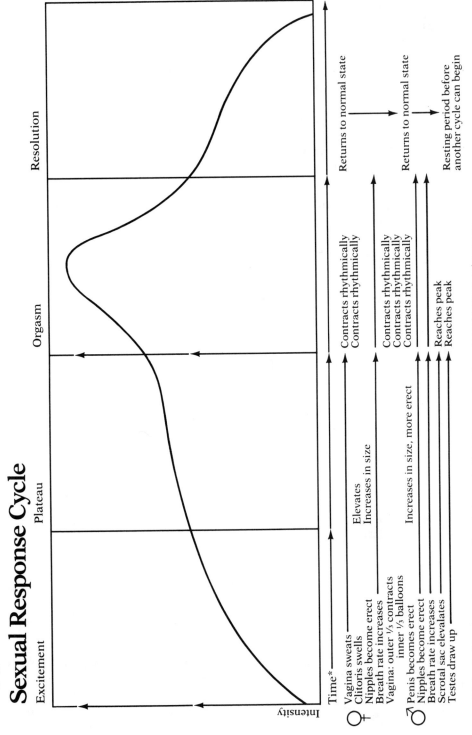

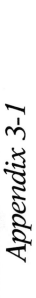

Appendix 4-1

Diagnostic Criteria for Chemical Dependency

Must Meet At Least Three (3) of the Following:

1. Alcohol and/or drugs often taken in larger amounts or over a longer period than the person intended.

2. Persistent desire to cut down or control the use of alcohol and/or drugs.

3. A great deal of time spent in activities necessary to get, take, or recover from the use of alcohol or drugs.

4. Frequent intoxication or withdrawal symptoms when expected to fulfill major role obligations at work, school, or home.

5. Reduction in social, occupational, or recreational activities.

6. Continued alcohol and/or drug use despite knowledge of consequences.

7. Increased tolerance.

8. Characteristic withdrawal symptoms.

9. Alcohol and/or drugs are taken to relieve or avoid withdrawal symptoms.

10. Defenses include: aggression, righteousness, grandiosity, perfectionism, anger, rigidity, charm.

11. Feelings include: guilt, shame, pain, hurt, fear, low self-esteem

Reprinted with permission. American Psychiatric Association, *Diagnostic and Statistical Manual of Mental Disorder*. Third Edition, Revised. Washington, DC, American Psychiatric Association, 1987.

Appendix 4-2

ASK YOURSELF...

1. Do you lose time from work due to drinking?

2. Is drinking making your home life unhappy?

3. Do you drink because you are shy with other people?

4. Is drinking affecting your reputation?

5. Have you ever felt remorse after drinking?

6. Have you ever had financial troubles because of drinking?

7. Do you get the morning "shakes"?

8. Are you careless about your family welfare when drinking?

9. Has your ambition decreased...?

10. Do you crave a drink at a specific time each day?

11. Do you take a drink the next morning to "get going"?

12. Does drinking cause difficulty in sleeping?

13. Has your efficiency decreased...?

14. Is drinking jeopardizing your job?

15. Do you drink to escape from worries or troubles?

16. Do you drink alone?

17. Have you ever had a loss of memory due to drinking?

18. Has a doctor ever treated you for drinking?

19. Do you drink to build up your self-confidence?

20. Do others complain about your drinking behavior?

A total of three or more "yes" answers indicates that drinking is having a serious impact on your life.

Used with permission by Westcenter
Alcoholism Rehabilitation and Treatment Program

Appendix 4-3

Possible Effects on Sexual Function Caused by Prescription Drugs

In most cases, the effects incurred by ingestion of any of the pre-scription drugs listed below (the generic names are followed by the trade name in parentheses) disappear when treatment is dis-continued or the dose is decreased. The incidence of these side effects is low. Some of these drugs have similar effects on both men and women; others affect men and women differently. In sev-eral cases, no information is available on a drug's effect on women. This table is offered as a guide only. Any questions about medications need to be addressed to physicians or pharmacists.

ANTIHYPERTENSIVES

Generally, antihypertensives may cause decreased sexual desire, decreased vaginal lubrication, and delayed or inhibited orgasm in women. In men, decreased sexual desire, impotence, delayed or inhibited ejaculation, and inhibited orgasm may occur. Drug-induced priapism (persistent abnormal erection) is rare.

Bendroflumethiazide (Naturetin): impotence

Captopril (Capoten): impotence (slight)

252

Chlorothiazide (Diuril): delayed and inhibited ejaculation

Chlorthalidone (Hygroton): impotence

Clonidine (Catapres): erectile failure, decreased sexual desire, impotence

Guanadrel (Hylorel): impotence, ejaculatory disturbances and decreased sexual desire in men

Guanethidine (Ismelin): erectile and ejaculatory failure, decreased sexual desire in men and women

Hydrochlorothiazide (Hydrodiuril): decreased sexual desire in men and women

Indapamide (Lozol): impotence or reduced sexual desire

Labetalol (Normodyne): impotence and failure to ejaculate

Methyldopa (Aldomet): impotence, decreased sexual desire, erectile failure and ejaculation disturbances

Phenoxybenzamine (Dibenzyline): dry ejaculation

Reserpine (Serpasil): decreased sexual desire, erectile and ejaculatory failure

Spironolactone (Aldactone): impotence, decreased libido in men

Verapamil (Isoptin): slight chance of impotence

Most of the adrenergic inhibitors (atenolol, metoprolol, nadolol, pindolol, and timolol) cause a very low incidence of sexual dysfunction. Propranolol has been associated with impotence and with decreased sexual desire in both men and women. Among vasodilators, no significant effects have been noted.

PSYCHOTHERAPEUTIC AGENTS

Amitriptyline (Elavil): decreased sexual desire, impotence, and inhibited ejaculation

Amoxapine (Asendin): decreased sexual desire, impotence, and ejaculatory inhibition; lack of orgasm in women

Butaperazine (Repoise): interference with ejaculation

Chlorpromazine (Thorazine); failure to ejaculate; priapism

Desipramine (Norpramin): impotence, lack of sexual desire

Doxepin (Sinequan): ejaculatory dysfunction and decreased libido

Fluphenazine (Prolixin): difficulty in achieving and maintaining erection, decreased ability to orgasm in men and women

Imipramine (Tofranil): decreased sexual desire, impotence, ejaculatory failure; lack of orgasm in women

Isocarboxazid (Marplan): impotence and delayed ejaculation; lack of orgasm in women

Lithium (Eskalith): impotence and decreased sexual desire

Maprotiline (Ludiomil), nortriptyline (Aventyl), and trimipramine (Surmontil) rare cases of impotence, decreased sexual desire, ejaculatory dysfunction

Perphenazine (Trilafon): interference with emission and ejaculation

Phenelzine (Nardil): impotence, inhibited orgasm in men and women

Protriptyline (Vivactil): decreased sexual desire, impotence, interference with and pain on ejaculation

Thioridazine (Mellaril): dry orgasm in men; lack of orgasm in women

Thiothixene (Navane): impotence

Tranylcypromine (Parnate): impotence; lack of orgasm in women

Trazodone (Desyrel): priapism

Trifluoperazine (Stelazine): interference with emission and ejaculation

HORMONES

Estrogens: in women, decreased and increased sexual desire; generally decreased sexual desire in men

Methandienone (Dianabol): decreased sexual desire

CANCER CHEMOTHERAPY AGENTS

Procarbazine (Metulane), vinblastine (Velban), cytosine arabinoside (Cytosar), chlorambucil (Leukeran) cyclophosphamide (Cytoxan), busulphan (Myleran), and melphelan (Alkeran) have been associated with impotence, decreased sexual desire and infertility in men; decreased sexual desire, vaginal atrophy, amenorrhea, dyspareunia, and vaginal dryness have been seen in women.

MISCELLANEOUS

Aminocaproic acid (Amicar) dry ejaculation

Cimetidine (Tagamet): decreased sexual desire, erectile failure in men

Clofibrate (Atromid-S): impotence

Digoxin (Lanoxin): decreased sexual desire, impotence

Methazolamide (Neptazane): decreased sexual desire

-PROGRESSION-

EARLY STAGES

SOCIAL DRINKING

HEAVY SOCIAL DRINKING

3 OR MORE PER OCCASION -3 OR MORE TIMES PER WEEK

Drinking to calm nerves.
Increase in alcohol tolerance.
Desire to continue drinking when others stop.
Uncomfortable in situation where there is no alcohol.
Relief drinking commences.
Occasional memory lapses after heavy drinking.
Preoccupation with alcohol (thinking about next drink).
Secret irritation when your drinking is discussed.

MIDDLE STAGES

LOSS OF CONTROL PHASE-
RATIONALIZATION BEGINS

Lying about drinking.
Increasing frequency of relief drinking.
Hiding liquor; sneaking drinks.
Increasing dependence on alcohol.
Drinking bolstered with excuses.
Feeling guilty about drinking.
Increased memory blackouts.
Tremors and early morning drinks.
Promises and resolutions fail repeatedly.
Complete dishonesty.
Grandiose and aggressive behavior.
Loss of other interests / unable to discuss problems.
Family, work and money problems.
Neglect of food / controlled drinking fails.
Family and friends avoided; Drinking Alone - Secretly.
Possible Job Loss.

NOW THINKS: "RESPONSIBILITIES INTERFERE
WITH MY DRINKING."

LATE STAGES

HELP NEEDED

Radical Deterioration of family relationships.
Unreasonable resentments.
Physical and moral deterioration.
Loss of "will power" and onset of lengthy drunks.
Urgent need for morning drink.
Geographical escape attempted.
Persistent remorse.
Impaired thinking and memory loss.
Loss of family.
Decrease in alcohol tolerance.
Successive lengthy drunks.
Hospital / Sanitarium.
Indefinable fears.
Unable to initiate action; extreme indecisiveness.
Unable to work; obsession with drinking.
All alibis exhausted.
Complete abandonment: "I don't care."

Disease of
Alcoholism

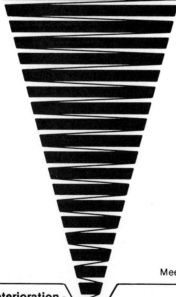

RECOVERY

LIFE IS BETTER

ACTION: is the magic word.
Recovery and sobriety continue/
Improved peace of mind.
A new appreciation of spiritual values.
Contentment in sobriety unfolds.
Return of vocational confidence and quality.
Activity with others increases.
Sense of financial responsibilities returns.

REBIRTH OF IDEALS.

new interests develop.
Increase in emotional stability/
Readjustment of needs to self and family.
Future is faced with new positive attitudes.
New circle of friends offer encouragement.

"Squirrel Cage" . . .
a vicious circle
Drinking to relieve hangovers.
Drinking with reckless abandon
Drinking to despair

with honest thinking.
A new set of values develops
Self-esteem starts to return.
notice change and growth.
You, family and friends
Diminishing fears and anxieties.
Thinking becomes more realistic.
Natural rest/sleep and appetite return.
Spiritual values develop.
Belief that a new life is possible.
and others grows.
Interest in group therapy

AWARENESS

DAWN OF NEW HOPE.

Spiritual needs examined.
Begins to get honest with self.
Pride in appearance is renewed.
Realizes alcoholism can be arrested.
other alcoholics/group therapy.
Starts to react to help from
Expresses desire for help.
alcoholism is a disease.
Medical help/drying out/learns
Meets recovering alcoholics; a ray of HOPE.

**DISCOVERY-
AN ATTITUDE CHANGE**

**Continued deterioration -
Insanity or Death**

CALLS FOR HELP

257

Appendix 5-1

The 21 Questions of Sex Addicts Anonymous

The following are some questions to ask yourself to determine if you may be sexually addicted and to evaluate your need for the SAA program.

1. Has your sexual behavior either caused you to seek help or made you feel scared or different—somehow alienated from other people?

2. Do you keep secrets about your sexual or romantic activities from those important to you? Do you lead a double life?

3. Have your needs driven you to have sex in places or situations or with people you would not normally choose?

4. Do you find yourself looking for sexually arousing articles or scenes in newspapers, magazines, or other media?

5. Do you find that romantic or sexual fantasies interfere with your relationships with others or are controlling you?

6. Do you frequently want to get away from a sex partner after having sex? Do you frequently feel remorse, shame, or guilt after a sexual encounter?

7. Do you feel uncomfortable or upset when masturbating or touching your body? Do you avoid touching your body because of feelings of shame?

8. Does each new relationship continue to have the same destructive patterns which prompted you to leave the last relationship?

9. Have you ever tried to leave a specific person or a destructive relationship and found yourself returning?

10. Have you ever tried to limit or stop masturbating because of your discomfort with the frequency, your fantasies, the props you use or the places you masturbate?

11. Do you obsess about sex or romance even when it interferes with your daily responsibilities or causes emotional discomfort?

12. Do you avoid sexual relationships altogether, or for long periods of time, because they are just too difficult or not worth the trouble?

13. Does the time you spend reading pornographic magazines or watching films interfere with your daily activities and relationships with people?

14. Do you sometimes wonder if you are asexual or fear that you have no sexual feelings?

15. Do you lose your sense of identity or meaning in life without sex or a love relationship?

16. Is it taking more variety and frequency of sexual and romantic activities than previously to bring the same levels of excitement and relief?

17. Have you been arrested or are you in danger of being arrested because of your practices of voyeurism, exhibitionism, prostitution, sex with minors, indecent phone calls, etc.?

18. Does your pursuit of sex or romantic relationships interfere with your spiritual development?

19. Do your sexual activities include the risk, threat, or reality of disease, pregnancy, coercion, or violence?

20. Do you seek or use sexual or romantic highs to avoid unpleasant realities in your life? Do you find your basic needs and relationships are neglected following a sexual or romantic encounter?

21. Has your sexual or romantic behavior ever left you feeling hopeless or suicidal?

Reprinted with permission from Sex Addicts Anonymous.

Appendix 5-2

Healthy Relationships

The prerequisites for intimacy are

- loving someone (being a lover)
- while staying with yourself and
- fully participating in your own life.

Intimacy is not static. It is always moving to a new level. It is an energy flow with no barriers. Intimacy cannot be controlled. Like a feeling, it cannot be held on to or reproduced at will. We notice intimacy. We do not produce it. Intimacy is

- knowing and being known by another
- sharing information openly
- stroking
- not necessarily romantic or sexual
- being alive and sharing that sense of aliveness
- being intimate with self first
- experiencing life together—developing a common history
- involving all the senses
- not brought about by techniques
- not confined to time and space—one can remain intimate without contact, allowing the other to go away when she or he needs to
- magical, beyond language, a hologram
- varied—one kind does not diminish another kind
- playful and fun—sharing mistakes and foolishness
- much talking, no analyzing
- a lot of paradoxes—requires being together, yet not having to be; it requires working at, yet cannot be worked at
- a gift.

Appendix 5-3

Addictive Relationships

The following are some of the skills used to form pseudo-(addictive) relationships. The ability to

- establish "instant intimacy"
- listen even when not interested or involved in what the other person is saying
- consistently lay aside your own needs for the sake of the relationship
- "take care of" the other person and quickly move in to meet his or her needs
- foster dependency and "attach" to the other in a dependent way
- "compromise" personal needs, values, ethics, or morality for the relationship (including family, children, and one's own work)
- quickly recognize a "cosmic mate" or a "special connection"
- instantly share secrets and pour out your life story
- have an instant physical or sexual attraction
- fit the other person into romantic fantasies and/or exotic situations having special songs, props, and symbols for the relationship even when such trappings really have little meaning except privately for the romantic person
- to form a "connection" and not know how to be friends
- establish an immediate intensity or "high" (being "in love") and allow that high to interfere with daily life
- feel as though the "relationship" has you in its grip, has taken over your life; ability to give yourself over to that feeling
- have the skills (imagined) and desire to "save" the other person from the life he or she has constructed

- be willing to use the other person to escape the life you have constructed for yourself
- define everything in one's existence in terms of the relationship and make the relationship "central" to your life
- ignore other facets of both lives for the sake of the relationship
- "make the other feel alive"
- attract others to you, that is, to emphasize physical appearance, like dressing and fixing oneself up to attract others
- ignore aspects of the person you do not trust or like, to ignore unshared values, hopes, and fears, and to see the other only through the eyes of illusion
- accept blame and fault for anything that goes wrong in the relationship
- "hang in there" much past the point of sanity
- shut off your feelings and awareness in the service of the relationship
- "enter into the other's world completely"
- use the "skills" of communication to form immediate relationships, the "skills" being much more important than being fully present to the other person
- use manipulation and impression management to try to be what the other wants in order to "hook" the other into the relationship
- "take on" and "feel" other's feelings
- accept jealousy as an indication of true love
- attach yourself to people who "like" you first
- use "honesty" as a "con"
- use your intuition to explain or "understand" the other
- develop the skills of seduction, flirtation, and titillation to a fine art
- look intimately involved while keeping safely hidden behind your wall

- interpret intensity as love and, therefore, to assume that intense feelings about someone is love

- lose your boundaries in the relationship

- suffer endlessly for the relationship

- gaze lovingly into the other's eyes with a look resembling a dying calf in a mudhole.

We have been taught that these skills lead to relationships when, in fact, they lead one into addictive pseudo-relationships.

Adapted from *Escape from Intimacy; The Pseudo-Relationship Addictions; Untangling the "Love" Addictions; Sex, Romance, Relationships,* by Anne W. Schaef (Harper and Row, 1986).

Appendix 5-4

Abstinence Contract

I, _____ agree to not participate in any
sexual behaviors for _____ days/months. These behaviors include trigger fantasies, suggestive remarks, inappropriate touching of myself or others, masturbation, inappropriate dressing,
going to locations or putting myself in situations that have in the
past been triggers for my disease.

I, _____ the partner, spouse, significant
other of the above will actively support his/her commitment to a
celibacy contract. I will honor his/her agreement and will not participate in any suggestive remarks, behaviors, or activities, or
manners of dress that will undermine this contract.

_____

Signed

_____

Dated

_____

Witnessed by

Appendix 6-1

Diagnostic Criteria for Codependency

1. Continued investment of self-esteem in the ability to control both oneself and others in the face of serious adverse consequences.

2. Assumption of responsibility for meeting others' needs to the exclusion of acknowledging one's own.

3. Anxiety and boundary distortions around intimacy and separation.

4. Enmeshment in relationships with personality disordered, chemically dependent, other codependent, and/or impulse disordered individuals.

5. Three or more of the following:

    a. Excessive reliance on denial

    b. Constriction of emotions (with or without dramatic outbursts)

    c. Depression

    d. Hypervigilance

    e. Compulsions

    f. Anxiety

    g. Substance abuse

    h. Has been (or is) the victim of recurrent physical or sexual abuse

    i. Stress-related medical illnesses

    j. Has remained in a primary relationship with an active substance abuser for at least two years without seeking outside help

Reprinted with permission from *Diagnosing and Treating Co-Dependence* by Timmen Cermak (Minneapolis: Johnson Institute, 1986), 11.

Appendix 6-2
Checklist to Help Identify Co-Sex Addicts

1. Do you have money problems because of someone else's sexual behavior?

2. Do you tell lies to cover up for someone else's sexual behavior?

3. Do you think that your loved one's behavior is caused by his or her companions?

4. Do you make threats, such as "If you don't stop, I'll leave you"?

5. Are you afraid to upset your partner for fear that he or she will leave you?

6. Have you been hurt or embarrassed by the addict's behavior?

7. Do you find yourself searching for hidden clues that might be related to the sexual behavior of a loved one?

8. Do you feel alone in your problem?

9. Have you ever gotten someone out of jail who was there as a result of the person's sexual behavior?

10. Does sex play an all-consuming role in your relationship?

11. Do you feel responsible for the addict's behavior?

12. Do you fantasize and obsess about the addict's problems?

13. Do you find yourself being sexual with the addict to prevent him or her from being sexual with others?

14. Do you find yourself engaging in self-defeating or degrading behavior?

15. Have you ever thought about or attempted suicide because of someone's sexual behavior?

Adapted from S-Anon "The Co-Addict's Checklist," Box 21075, Oklahoma City, OK 73156.

Appendix 7-1

Diagnostic Criteria for Anorexia Nervosa

A. Refusal to maintain body weight over a minimal normal weight for age and height, e.g. weight loss leading to maintenance of body weight 15% below that expected; or failure to make expected weight gain during period of growth, leading to body weight 15% below that expected.

B. Intense fear of gaining weight or becoming fat, even though underweight.

C. Disturbance in the way in which one's body weight, size, or shape is experienced, e.g., the person claims to "feel fat" even when emaciated, believes that one area of the body is "too fat" even when obviously underweight.

D. In females, absence of at least three consecutive menstrual cycles when otherwise expected to occur (primary or secondary amenorrhea). (A woman is considered to have amenorrhea if her periods occur only following hormone (estrogen) administration.)

Appendix 7-2

Diagnostic Criteria for Bulimia Nervosa

A. Recurrent episodes of binge eating (rapid consumption of a large amount of food in a discrete period of time).

B. A feeling of lack of control over eating behavior during the eating binges.

C. The person regularly engages in either self-induced vomiting, use of laxatives or diuretics, strict dieting or fasting, or vigorous exercise in order to prevent weight gain.

D. A minimum average of two binge eating episodes a week for at least three months.

E. Persistent overconcern with body shape and weight.

American Psychiatric Association, *Diagnostic and Statistical Manual of Mental Disorders*. Third Edition, Revised. Washington, D.C., American Psychiatric Association, 1987.

Appendix 7-3

Eating Disorders Questionnaire

Weight Issues

Are you still satisfied with your current weight?

If not, how many pounds would you like to lose?

Have you ever been satisfied with your weight?

Do you feel overweight even though you're at a reasonable weight according to height/weight tables?

How often do you weigh yourself?

Does the scale dictate your mood for the day?

Does the scale determine which social events you will attend?

Are you critical of other people's figures?

Exercise Issues

Do you exercise to maintain a certain scale weight?

Do you exercise every day?

How long are your workouts?

If you miss a workout, does it affect your mood?

Do you ever try to work off food indulgences with exercise?

Does your schedule revolve around your exercise?

Metabolic Rate Issues

Are you intolerant to cold?

Do you have dry skin or dry hair?

Is it difficult to get your heart rate up when you work out?

Is your sexual drive diminished?

Do you have problems with depression?

Has your "get up and go" got up and gone?

Do you have normal periods?

Food Issues

How do you feel about food?

Do you frequently eat alone?

Do you eat your meals with other people or in front of other people?

Do you prepare food for yourself?

Do you prepare food for everyone except yourself?

Do you connect food with your health?

Do you spend time procuring food?

Do you ever have a craving for something to eat and can't determine what it is?

Do you have any rituals concerning eating your food or preparation?

Do you feel food is the enemy?

Purging Issues

Have you ever taken diuretics in an effort to lose a few pounds?

Have you ever taken laxatives in an effort to lose a few pounds?

Have you ever induced vomiting as a means to control your weight?

Do you, on occasion, spontaneously throw up after you've eaten?

Do you drink more than five liters of water a day?

Do you eat 800-1000 calories a day to maintain your figure?

Do you eat large quantities of high fiber foods, such as salads, raw veggies, popcorn, bran cereals, and dried fruit?

Restrained Eating Issues

Do you allow yourself occasional desserts or treats?

Are you afraid of becoming overweight?

Are you afraid of losing control of your eating?

If you have a dessert or other "forbidden" food, do you tend to really overindulge in food, thinking you've already blown it?

Do you go to the store to get food once you've blown your diet?

Do you totally avoid fat?

Do you get hungry?

Do you have any food cravings?

Do you frequently skip meals or eat later in the day for fear once you start eating, you won't stop?

Do you feel excessive guilt when you eat a "forbidden" food?

Do you feel excessive guilt when you eat more than you feel you should?

PRE-DISEASE / EARLY SYMPTOMS

MIDDLE STAGE SYMPTOMS

CRUCIAL STAGE SYMPTOMS

- Low Self-Esteem
- Eat When Not Hungry
- Various Diets Undertaken
- Weight Loss Temporary
- Often Regain All of Weight Loss & Then Some
- Poor Impulse Control
- Mood Swings
- Embarrassment
- Plan Secret Binges Ahead of Time
- Paranoid Feelings
- Depression
- Self-Indulgent Behavior
- Unable to Discuss Problem
- Tiredness, Apathy, Irritability
- Elimination of Normal Activities
- Social Isolation/Distancing
- Family, Work and Money Problems
- Others Unhappy about Food Obsession
- Persistent Remorse
- Binging/High Carbohydrate Foods
- Weight Affects Way You Live Your Life
- General Ill Health/Constant Physical Problems
- Institutionalization or Death From Related Diseases
- Suicidal Tendencies/Attempts

- Occasional Binging to Relieve Anxiety
- Feeling of Guilt and Remorse after Overeating
- Feeling that Self-Worth is Dependent on Losing Weight
- Skips Meals - Often Breakfast and/or Lunch - Binges at Night
- Constant Concern with Weight and Body Image
- Increased Dependency on Binging
- Fear of Binging/Eating Getting Out of Control
- Constant Binging to Cope with Anxiety/Loneliness
- Efforts to Control Fail Repeatedly/ Loss of Ordinary Willpower
- Eats Alone - Hypertension
- Pre-Occupation with Eating and Food
- Gastrointestinal Disorders
- Fear of Going Out in Public
- Unreasonable Resentments
- Dishonesty, Lying
- Stealing Food/Money
- Feeling of Hopelessness
- Drug and Alcohol Abuse
- Edema
- Heart Disease, Diabetes, Arthritis

272

Compulsive Overeating

A Multidimensional Profile

ON-GOING SUPPORT

RECOVERY

- Calls for help/surrenders self-will
- Receives necessary medical help
- Meets other compulsive overeaters
- Learns C.O. is a disease
- Expresses desire for help
- Participation in group therapy/treatment
- Realizes C.O. can be arrested
- Learns about abstinence/starts practicing it
- Relief from guilt and depression
- Believes a new life is possible
- Starts to take pride in appearance
- Begins to consider spiritual needs
- Begins to get honest w/self
- Responds to help from others
- Thinking becomes more rational
- Mood swings decrease
- Natural sleep & appetite return
- Finds contentment in abstinence
- Outside interests in family, friends, hobbies start to return
- Fears and anxieties subside
- Friends and family notice positve changes
- Start making new friends
- Self-esteem starts to build
- Emotional stability returns
- Takes responsibility for actions
- New interests develop
- Deeper spiritual values develop
- Increasing serenity
- Accepts progress, not perfection, in recovery process
- Experiences joy in abstinence and recovery
- Helps other C.O. by sharing recovery

REHABILITATION

RECOGNITION OF NEED FOR HELP

273

PRE-DISEASE / EARLY SYMPTOMS

BULIMIA

- Low Self-Esteem
- Feel That Self-Worth is Dependent On Low Weight
- Dependent on Opposite For Approval
- Normal Weight
- Constant Concern With Weight & Body Image
- Experimentation With Vomiting Laxatives & Diuretics
- Poor Impulse Control
- Fear of Binging/Eating Getting Out of Control
- Embarrassment
- Anxiety
- Depression
- Self-Indulgent Behavior
- Eats Alone
- Preoccupation With Eating & Food
- Tiredness, Apathy, Irritability
- Gastrointestinal Disorders
- Elimination of Normal Activities
- Anemia
- Social Isolation/Distancing Friends & Family
- Dishonesty-Lying
- Stealing Food/Money
- Tooth Damage (Gum Disease)
- Binging/High Carbohydrate Foods
- Drug & Alcohol Abuse
- Laxative & Diuretic Abuse
- Mood Swings
- Chronic Sore Throat
- Difficulties in Breathing/Swallowing
- Hypokalemia (Abnormally Low Potassium Concentration)
- Electrolyte Imbalance
- General Ill Health/Constant Physical Problems
- Possible Rupture of Heart Or Esophagus/Peritonitis
- Dehydration
- Irregular Heart Rhythms
- Suicidal Tendencies Attempts

ANOREXIA

- Low Self-Esteem
- Misperception of Hunger, Satiety & Other Bodily Sensations
- Feelings of Lack of Control In Life
- Distorted Body Image
- Over-Achiever
- Compliant
- Anxiety
- Menstrual Cycle Stops (Amenorrhea)
- Progressive Preoccupation With Food & Eating
- Isolates Self From Family & Friends
- Perfectionistic Behavior
- Compulsive Exercise
- Eats Alone
- Fights With Family
- Overeating (May Begin to Cook & Control Family's Eating)
- Fatigue
- Increased Facial & Body Hair (Lanugo)
- Decreased Scalp Hair
- Thin, Dry Scalp
- Emaciated Appearance (At Least 25% Loss of Total Body Weight)
- Feelings of Control Over Body
- Rigid
- Depression
- Apathy
- Fear of Food & Gaining Weight
- Malnutrition
- Mood Swings (Tyranical)
- Diminished Capacity to Think
- Sensitivity to Cold
- Electrolyte Imbalance (Weakness)
- Lassitude Cardia Arrest
- Denial of Problem (See Self as Fat)
- Joint Pain (Difficulty Walking & Sitting)
- Sleep Disturbance
- Fear of Food & Gaining Weight

MIDDLE STAGE SYMPTOMS

CRUCIAL STAGE SYMPTOMS

274

Anorexia Nervosa–Bulimia

A Multidimensional Profile

ON-GOING SUPPORT

RECOVERY

- Trust/Openness
  - Understanding of Personal Needs
- Honesty
  - Increased Assertiveness
- Improved Self-Image
  - Developing Optimism
  - Respect of Family & Friends
  - More Understanding of Family
  - Full Awareness & At Ease With Life
  - Appreciation of Spiritual Values
  - Enjoyment of Eating Food Without Guilt
  - Acceptance of Personal Limitations
  - Return of Regular Menstrual Cycles
- New Interest
- New Friends
  - Achievement of Personal Goals
  in a Wide Range of Activities
  - Self-Approval (Not Dependent on Weight)
  - Relief From Guilt & Depression
- Diminished Fears
  - Resumption of Normal Eating
  - Resumption of Normal Self-Control
- Begin to Relax
- Acceptance of Illness
- Participation in a Treatment Program
- Acceptance of a Psychiatric Treatment Plan

REHABILITATION

The progression of symptoms and recovery signs are based on the most repeated experiences of those with Anorexia and Bulimia. When a patient with Anorexia becomes bulimic, she will experience symptoms characteristic of both eating disorders. While every symptom in the chart does not occur in every case or in any specific sequence, it does portray an average progression pattern. The goals and resultant behavior changes in the recovery process are similar for both eating disorders.

RECOGNITION OF NEED FOR HELP

Appendix 8-1

Some General Characteristics of Adult Children of Alcoholics and Other Dysfunctional Families

- Fear commitment
- Find it difficult to have fun and play
- Try to be perfect
- Constantly seek the approval of others
- Act impulsively
- Take themselves very seriously
- Are afraid of failure, but sabotage their success
- Fear intimacy
- Have trouble forming loving relationships
- Make excuses for others' weaknesses
- Isolate themselves and are afraid of authority figures
- Judge themselves harshly
- Have low self-esteem
- Don't know their own needs and are unable to ask for what they want or need
- Have not developed the ability to trust themselves or others
- Tend to see things as black or white, right or wrong
- Feel they are different from other people
- Remain loyal even when their loyalty is undeserved
- Tend to repeat relationship patterns and are attracted to other obsessive compulsive individuals
- Often give in to others
- Feel guilty when they stand up for themselves

Appendix 9-1

Diagnostic Criteria for Post-Traumatic Stress Disorder

A. The person has experienced an event that is ouside the range of usual human experience and that would be markedly distressing to almost anyone, e.g., serious threat to one's life or physical integrity; serious threat or harm to one's children, spouse, or other close relatives and friends; sudden destruction of one's home or community; or seeing another person who has recently been or is being, seriously injured or killed as the result of an accident or physical violence.

B. The traumatic event is persistently reexperienced in at least one of the following ways:

   1. recurrent and intrusive distressing recollections of the event (in young children, repetitive play in which themes or aspects of the trauma are expressed)

   2. recurrent distressing dreams of the event

   3. sudden acting or feeling as if the traumatic event were recurring (includes a sense of reliving the experience, illusions, hallucinations, and dissociative [flashback] episodes, even those that occur upon awakening or when intoxicated)

   4. intense psychological distress at exposure to events that symbolize or resemble an aspect of the traumatic event, including anniversaries of the trauma

C. Persistent avoidance of stimuli associated with the trauma or numbing of general responsiveness (not present before the trauma), as indicated by at least three of the following:

   1. efforts to avoid thoughts or feelings associated with the trauma

   2. efforts to avoid activities or situations that arouse recollections of the trauma

3. inability to recall important aspect of the trauma (psychogenic amnesia)

4. markedly diminished interest in significant activities (in young children, loss of recently acquired developmental skills such as toilet training or language skills)

5. feeling of detachment or estrangement from others

6. restricted range of affect, e.g., unable to have loving feelings

7. sense of a foreshortened future, e.g., does not expect to have a career, marriage, or children, or a long life

D. Persistent symptoms of increased arousal (not present before the trauma), as indicated by at least two of the following:

1. difficulty falling or staying asleep

2. irritability or outbursts of anger

3. difficulty concentrating

4. hypervigilance

5. exaggerated startle response

6. physiologic reactivity upon exposure to events that symbolize or resemble an aspect of the traumatic event (e.g., a woman who was raped in an elevator breaks out in a sweat when entering any elevator)

E. Duration of the disturbance and symptoms for a period of one month.

Reprinted with permission, American Psychiatric Association: *Diagnostic and Statistical Manual of Mental Disorders*. Third Edition, Revised. Washington, DC, American Psychiatric Association, 1987.

Appendix 9-2

How to Identify an Incest Survivor

Therapists look for various signs and symptoms when assessing possible incest survivors. These signals include behaviors and cues that usually show up in a pattern that reveals covert or overt incest. This list is a guide. The number of signs and symptoms seen in individuals varies, but few persons have most or all of them. These signs and symptoms may appear in children and adults. The order of the items in no way reflects their importance in the evaluation process.

1. Eating disorders: stuffing, starving, skipping

2. Alcohol or other chemical addiction

3. Attempted suicide

4. Self-harming behaviors, such as cutting themselves with objects, burning the skin with cigarettes, pulling out hair, hitting themselves with sticks, chains, or other objects

5. Running away from home, repeatedly skipping school or work

6. Withdrawing from friends, peers, and other social settings

7. Trouble relating to friends, peers, family

8. Verbal or physical indications by children that they know much more about sexual matters than seems appropriate for their age

9. Being turned off, disgusted, or very fearful of sexual involvement; lack of sexual desire; an aversion to being touched or touching others

10. Acting out in sexually inappropriate ways, such as compulsive masturbation, cruising, going to prostitutes; manipulating their sex partners; engaging in prostitution, pornography, or sexually oriented offenses, such as child molestation, incest, or rape

11. Excessive shame about their bodies and attempts to hide themselves with clothing or to alter themselves with makeup, wigs, padding, or surgery

12. Shame or disgust with their sexual identity and attempts to hide or change it, including cutting or harming sexual body parts and dressing to disguise their sexual identity

13. Acting like a martyr; generally behaving in a passive manner that allows them to be victims or to be taken advantage of by others

14. Repeatedly getting into abusive relationships

15. Fear of becoming vulnerable or being unable to trust in relationships

16. Attempting to be perfect: the perfect lover, wife, husband, mother, father

17. Assuming the role of their parents and taking responsibility or rationalizing their actions and feelings

18. Low self-esteem, self-hatred, or feelings of worthlessness

19. Feelings of shame or guilt

20. Difficulty in defining boundaries and getting a sense of their identity as sexual men and women

21. Sleep disturbances: afraid to fall asleep, recurring nightmares, sleep walking, irregular, interrupted sleep patterns

22. Frequent episodes of lower abdominal pain, infections, pain with intercourse, menstrual difficulties, colitis, ulcer pain

23. Visual or auditory hallucinations that are not drug induced

24. Dramatic mood and personality changes

25. Repeated difficulty in focusing or concentrating; feeling that they do not have a firm grasp on being present in the world

26. Chronic depression and/or anxiety

Some questions asked of potential incest survivors include these about the behavior of their family members. Do you remember any family member ever doing the following?

1. Trying to touch you or your friends in ways that made you and them feel uncomfortable?

2. Repeatedly making remarks about your body that made you feel ashamed of it in any way?

3. Insisting on sleeping with you or bathing with you, which made you feel uncomfortable?

4. Refusing to respect your need for privacy, especially when dressing, bathing, or using the bathroom?

5. Insisting that wearing sleeping or swimming attire was inappropriate, making you feel uncomfortable with your body?

6. Accusing you of engaging in "dirty" behaviors that you did not do?

7. Forcing you to strip as punishment or before being punished?

8. Exposing you to pornography, dirty jokes, or pornographic movies?

9. Performing sexual acts in front of you?

Appendix 12-1

External Female Sex Organs

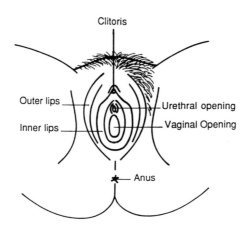

Clitoris

Outer lips

Inner lips

Urethral opening

Vaginal Opening

Anus

Appendix 12-2

Internal Female Sex Organs Side View

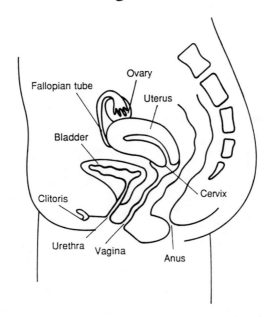

Fallopian tube

Ovary

Uterus

Bladder

Clitoris

Cervix

Urethra

Vagina

Anus

Appendix 12-3

Male Sex Organs Side View

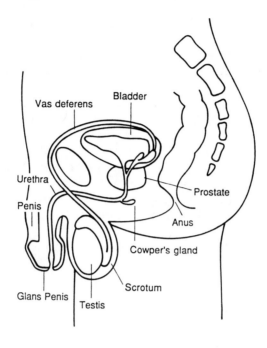

Appendix 12-4
Method to Cure Premature Ejaculation

After initial sensual explorations, the steps include:

1. The man masturbates with a dry hand until he can last fifteen minutes. He also focuses on his arousal process.

2. He masturbates with a lubricated hand until he can last fifteen minutes.

3. The woman strokes his penis with a dry hand until he can last fifteen minutes. The lovers should also feel free to engage in nongenital sensual touching so that neither one, particularly the woman, feels bored during steps three through eight.

4. She uses a lubricated hand or her mouth until he can last fifteen minutes.

5. The man lies on his back and breathes deeply. She slides his penis into her lubricated vagina or mouth and remains still, simply holding the penis inside her. He moves just enough to maintain his erection for fifteen minutes.

6. Begin as in #5 above, only this time, he remains still and she moves just enough to maintain his erection for fifteen minutes.

7. Begin as in #5 above; he moves more energetically while she stays relatively still until he can last for fifteen minutes.

8. Begin as in #5 above, but both move as they please until he can last fifteen minutes or as long as they like.

Reprinted by permission from *Sexual Solutions*, by Michael Castleman (Simon and Schuster, 1980) p. 94.

Appendix 12-5

Signs That You May Be Suffering from Depression

A. Are you bothered by feeling sad, depressed, blue, hopeless, down in the dumps? Are you feeling that you just don't care much about things anymore? And have these feelings persisted for at least two weeks? Or have you been having very low, sad days which seem to alternate with days when you feel elated and exuberant?

B. If you would agree that the above description fits you—say, that you're feeling sad, down, and blue, and as though nothing much in life really matters to you—then examine the following list of the common symptoms of depression, and formulate your own individual set of answers:

1. Have your eating habits changed recently? Although persistent or progressive appetite loss is the more commonly encountered depressive symptom, one sometimes does see the opposite: accelerating food intake, followed by weight gain. This appears to be part of a self-perpetuating obesity-depression cycle: the depressed person stuffs herself, without experiencing increased hunger.

2. Have you been having trouble with sleep? Are you snapping awake in the middle of the night, or in the early hours of the morning? Or have you been having trouble falling asleep? Are you sleeping unusually much or long?

3. Are you feeling fatigued, tired, run-down, and without your usual energy? The depressed person's complaints about feeling "exhausted, for no reason" are frequent, although the reasons for his profound energy loss are not clear.

4. Are you less interested in sex, and do you find sex less pleasurable? Loss of libido is common in states of depression, as is a diminished capacity for

orgasm, in the female (and a diminished ability to maintain an erection, in the male). Some depressed people do, however, seek more and more diverse sexual experiences.

5. Are you having trouble thinking, concentrating, or making decisions?

6. Have you been unable to sit still, to the point where it's necessary to be moving about constantly? Or, on the contrary, are you feeling unusually slowed down—as if it's too much trouble to move about and as if there's nothing much worth doing anyhow?

   The first instance suggests the possibility of an agitated or hyperactive depression, characterized by restlessness, pacing, pressured and repetitive speech. The second instance raises the question of a retarded, or generally slowed-down depressive state, affecting not only one's abilities to think, talk, and move about, but even one's capacity to recall recent events. A person afflicted by this form of depression often speaks in sentences that are slow and halting; facial expression tends to be flat, fixed, and unchanging.

7. Have you been preoccupied by thoughts of taking your own life—or by wishing that you were dead?

8. Are you more prone to anger, more irritable, more easily annoyed and resentful than is usual for you?

9. Are you feeling extremely discouraged and pessimistic about most things?

10. Are you feeling guilty, worthless, or down on yourself?

11. Have you been brooding about unpleasant things that happened in the past?

12. Have you been feeling inadequate and self-critical, as though you've recently realized that you're much less attractive or competent than you thought you were?

13. Are you crying more than usual?

14. Have you been feeling needier than at other times? Desperately in need of help or reassurance from somebody?

15. Have you been suffering from physical complaints lately, such as gastrointestinal problems (constipation is common) or severe headache or backache, for which no medical explanation or cause can be found?

16. Does your mouth often feel dry? Do you have a persistent bad taste in your mouth?

If you answered A in the affirmative, and two or more of the questions under B in the affirmative, perhaps you ought to consider the possibility that you are depressed.

Appendix 13-1

Anger Dos and Don'ts

Here is a review of some basic dos and don'ts to keep in mind when you are feeling angry:

1. **Do speak up when an issue is important to you**. Obviously, we do not have to address personally every injustice and irritation that comes along. To simply let something go can be an act of maturity. But it is a mistake to stay silent if the cost is to feel bitter, resentful, or unhappy. We de-self ourselves when we fail to take a stand on issues that matter to us.

2. **Don't strike while the iron is hot**. A good fight will clear the air in some relationships, but if your goal is to change an entrenched pattern, the worst time to speak up may be when you are feeling angry or intense. If your fires start rising in the middle of a conversation, you can always say, "I need a little time to sort out my thoughts. Let's set up another time to talk about it more." Seeking *temporary* distance is not the same as cold withdrawal or an emotional cutoff.

3. **Do take time out to think about the problem and to clarify your position.** Before you speak out, ask yourself the following questions: "What is it about the situation that makes me angry?" "What is the real issue here?" "Where do I stand?" "What do I want to accomplish?" "Who is responsible for what?" "What, specifically, do I want to change?" "What are the things I will and will not do?"

4. **Don't use "below-the-belt" tactics.** These include: blaming, interpreting, diagnosing, labeling, analyzing, preaching, moralizing, ordering, warning, interrogating, ridiculing, and lecturing.

5. **Do speak in "I" language.** Learn to say, "I think..." "I feel..." "I fear..." "I want..." A true "I" statement says something about the self without criticizing or blaming the other person and without holding the other person responsible for our feelings or reactions. Watch out for disguised "you" statements or pseudo—"I" statements. ("I think *you* are controlling and self-centered.")

6. **Don't make vague requests.** ("I want you to be more sensitive to my needs.") Let the other person know specifically what you want. ("The best way that you can help me now is simply to listen. I really don't want advice at this time.") Don't expect people to anticipate your needs or do things that you have not requested. Even those who love you can't read your mind.

7. **Do try to appreciate the fact that people are different**. We move away from fused relationships when we recognize that there are as many ways of seeing the world as there are people in it. If you're fighting about who has the "truth," you may be missing the point. Different perspectives and ways of reacting do not necessarily mean that one person is "right" and the other is "wrong."

8. **Don't tell another person what she or he thinks or feels or "should" think or feel**. If other persons get angry in reaction to a change you make, don't criticize their feelings or tell them they have no right to be

288

angry. Better to say, "I understand that you're angry, and if I were in your shoes, perhaps I'd be angry, too. But I've thought it over, and this is my decision." Remember that one person's right to be angry does not mean that the other person is to blame.

9. **Do recognize that each person is responsible for his or her own behavior.** Don't blame your dad's new wife because she "won't let him" be close to you. If you are angry about the distance between you and your dad, it is *your* responsibility to find a new way to approach the situation. Your dad's behavior is *his* responsibility, not his wife's.

10. **Don't participate in intellectual arguments that go nowhere.** Don't spin your wheels trying to convince another of the "rightness" of your position. If the other person is not hearing you, simply say, "Well, it may sound crazy to you, but this is how I feel." Or, "I understand that you disagree, but I guess we see the problem differently."

11. **Do try to avoid speaking through a third party.** If you are angry with your brother's behavior, don't say, "I think my daughter felt terrible when you didn't find the time to come to her school play." Instead, try, "I was upset when you didn't come. You're important to me, and I really wanted you to be there."

12. **Don't expect change to come about from hit-and-run confrontations.** Change occurs slowly in close relationships. If you make even a small change, you will be tested many times to see if you "really mean it." Don't get discouraged if you fall on your face several times as you try to put theory into practice. You may find that you start out fine but then blow it when things heat up. Getting derailed is just part of the process, so be patient with yourself. You will have many opportunities to get back on track...and try again.

Adapted from *The Dance of Anger: A Woman's Guide to Changing the Patterns of Intimate Relationships*, by Harriet Goldhor Lerner (Harper and Row, 1985).

Appendix 14-1

Affirmations: The Power of Positive Thinking

1. I am a sexual man (or woman) who deserves a healthy sex life.

2. Who I am as a sexual woman (or man) is a gift from my higher power.

3. I deserve to nurture myself.

4. I accept my body as it is today, with any imperfections it may have.

5. I change those things that I want to change.

6. I deserve unconditional love and affection.

7. I live one day at a time.

8. I am capable of experiencing a wide range of sexual activities.

9. I forgive myself for any past sexual misbehavior.

10. I have the right to accept and refuse sexual advances from others.

11. I am capable of achieving a sexual balance in my life.

12. I deserve to experience the joy, warmth, and love of a sexual relationship.

13. I have a right to my own sexual moral values.

14. Sexual expression is a positive part of my life.

Appendix 14-2

Recovery Checklist

_____ Maintaining appropriate daily routine

_____ Setting and achieving daily and long-term goals

_____ Personal care

_____ Setting and sticking to limits with children and others

_____ Constructive planning

_____ Appropriate decision-making and problem-solving efforts

_____ Choosing behaviors

_____ Resting well

_____ Resentment-free

_____ Accepting (versus denying)

_____ Neither controlling others nor feeling controlled by them

_____ Open to appropriate criticism and feedback

_____ Free of excessive criticism of self and others

_____ Gratitude versus self-pity and deprivation

_____ Responsible financial decisions (not over- or underspending)

_____ Not escaping or avoiding through work or sex

_____ Self-responsibility (versus scapegoating and blaming)

_____ Valuing wants and needs

_____ Free of victim self-image

_____ Free of fear and anxiety

_____ Free of guilt and shame

_____ Free of worry and obsession

_____ Not feeling excessively responsible for others

_____ Faith in higher power

_____ Trusting and valuing self

_____ Making appropriate decisions about trusting others

_____ Maintaining recovery routine (attending support groups and other helpful activities)

_____ Mind clear and peaceful; logical thinking; free of confusion

_____ Feeling and dealing appropriately with feelings, including anger
_____ Appropriately disclosing
_____ Reasonable expectations of self and others
_____ Needing people versus NEEDING them
_____ Feeling secure with self; self-affirming
_____ Communicating clearly, directly, and honestly
_____ Balanced mood
_____ Maintaining contact with friends
_____ Feeling connected and close to people versus lonely and isolated
_____ Healthy perspective; life looks worth living
_____ Not using alcohol and medication to cope
_____ Having fun, relaxing during leisure activities
_____ Enjoying daily routine
_____ Giving appropriate positive feedback to self and others
_____ Getting and allowing self to believe—positive feedback

Adapted from *Beyond Codependency,* by Melody Beattie (Hazelden, 1987).

Appendix 17-1

Sex History

Clients do a personal sex history to help them determine which events in their past influenced their current attitudes and feelings about sex. The example below is an abbreviated version of a longer history.

Childhood Experiences and Memories

1. Was sex discussed openly in your family? Were you allowed to ask questions about sex? How were your questions answered?

2. Were your parents affectionate toward each other? How did they display their affection for one another?

3. Were your parents affectionate toward you? Toward your siblings?

4. Did you play games that involved exploring your body or the bodies of your friends or siblings, such as "doctor"?

5. Did you talk about sex with your friends or siblings? Do you remember what you talked about and how you felt about what you discussed?

6. Did you attend church or Sunday school or a school in which religion was taught? What messages about sex do you remember from your religious background?

7. How old were you the first time you masturbated?

8. Did anyone ever "catch" you masturbating? How did they react? How did you feel?

9. What do you remember about your first wet dream? Did anyone explain wet dreams to you?

10. How old were you when you first menstruated? Did anyone explain menstruation to you before your first period? Did you talk about menstruation with your friends?

11. How did you feel about yourself after menstruation began? Did you have any difficulties with menstruation? Were you ever ashamed or made to feel ashamed about your period?

12. When did you learn how babies are conceived? How did you feel about it?

Dating and Sexual Experiences

13. At what age did you begin dating?

14. At what age did you begin petting? How did it make you feel? Did you feel pressured by your partner to be sexual?

15. What kind of petting behavior did you engage in? What activities did you like or dislike?

16. Did you have premarital intercourse? At what age did you first have intercourse?

17. How did you feel after your first sexual experience? Were you sexually excited, scared, worried about getting pregnant?

18. Did anyone ever discuss birth control with you? Did you use contraception?

19. Have you ever had a venereal disease? Have you ever had painful intercourse or unusual bleeding?

20. Has anyone ever forced you to have sex? Has anyone ever threatened to hurt you or been violent during sex?

21. Have you ever had sexual experiences with a person of the same sex? The opposite sex? Have you thought about what such experiences would be like?

22. Did you experience orgasm? Did you ever lie to your partner about how you felt during your sexual encounters?

Current Sexual Attitudes and Beliefs

23. What kinds of sexual behaviors have you engaged in?

24. What kinds of sexual behaviors do you enjoy? What do you find uncomfortable or embarrassing?

25. How do you feel about masturbation? How often do you masturbate? How do you feel about masturbating in front of your partner?

26. What kind of sexual fantasies do you have? How often do you have them? Have you ever shared your fantasies with your partner?

27. How do you feel about oral sex? Anal sex?

28. Have you ever used erotic literature or pornography to enhance your sexual encounters?

29. How do you feel about your body? Your partner's body?

30. How important is foreplay to you? What do you like and dislike?

31. Are you sometimes totally uninterested in sex? Do you give in to your partner's sexual advances because you feel you "should"?

32. What is your attitude toward sex in general?

Bibliography

Part I

Bancroft, John. *Human Sexuality and Its Problems*. New York: Churchill Livingstone, 1989.

Boston Women's Health Book Collective. *The New Our Bodies, Ourselves: A Book by and for Women*. New York: Simon and Schuster, 1984.

Berger, Richard and Deborah Berger. *Biopotency: A Guide to Sexual Success*. New York: Rodale Press, 1987.

Bullard, David, and Susan Knight. *Sex and Physical Disability. Personal Perspectives*. St. Louis: C.V. Mosby, 1981.

Bullough, Vern and Bonnie Bullough. *Contraception: A Guide to Birth Control Methods*. Buffalo, NY: Prometheus Books, 1990.

Burns, D. D. *Feeling Good: The New Mood Therapy*. New York: Signet, 1980.

Covington, Timothy R. *Sex Care: The Complete Guide to Safe and Healthy Sex*. New York: Pocket Books/Simon and Schuster, 1987.

Everett, Jane, and Walter Glanze. *The Condom Book: The Essential Guide for Men and Women*. New York: Signet, 1987.

Goldblum, Delaney and Peter Goldblum. *Strategies for Survival: A Gay Men's Health Manual for the Age of AIDS*. New York: St. Martin's Press, 1987.

Goldman, D., and T. Bennett-Goleman. *The Relaxed Body Book*. Garden City, NY: Doubleday, 1986.

Hite, Shere. *The Hite Report: A Nationwide Study of Female Sexuality*. New York: Bantam, 1981.

Kaplan, Helen Singer. *Sexual Aversion, Sexual Phobias, and Panic Disorders*. New York: Brunner/Mazel Inc., 1987.

———. *The New Sex Therapy*. New York: Brunner/Mazel, 1974.

Katchadourian, Herant A., and Donald T. Lunde. *Fundamentals of Human Sexuality*. New York: Holt Rinehart and Winston, 1989.

Kilby, Donald. *Manual of Safe Sex*. St. Louis: C.V. Mosby, 1986.

Kinsey, Alfred C., Wardell B. Pomeroy, and Clyde E. Martin. *Sexual Behavior in the Human Male*. Philadelphia: W.B. Saunders, 1984.

————. *Sexual Behavior in the Human Female*. Philadelphia: W.B. Saunders, 1966.

Lumiere, Richard, and Stephani Cook. *Healthy Sex and Keeping It That Way*. New York: Simon and Schuster, 1983.

McCary, Stephen and James Leslie McCary. *Human Sexuality*. Bellmont, Calif.: Wattsworth Publishers, 1984.

Oakley, Ray. *Drugs, Society, and Human Behavior*. St. Louis: C.V. Mosby, 1983.

Rosen, Raymond C. and Gayle J. Beck. *Patterns of Sexual Arousal: Psychophysiological Processes and Clinical Application*. New York: Guilford Press, 1988.

Sarrell, Phillip and Lorna Sarrell. *Sexual Turning Point: The Seven Stages of Adult Sexuality*. New York: McNorm Publishers, 1984.

Starr, B.D., and M.B. Weiner. *Sex and Sexuality in the Mature Years*. New York: Stein and Day, 1981.

Part II

Allen, Charlotte Vail. *Daddy's Girl*. New York: Berkeley Books, 1980.

Armstrong, Louise. *Kiss Daddy Goodnight, A Speakout on Incest*. New York: Pocket Books, 1978.

Bass, Ellen, and Laura Davis. *The Courage to Heal: A Guide for Women Survivors of Child Sexual Abuse*. New York: Harper and Row, 1988.

Beattie, Melody. *Codependent No More*. Center City, Minn.: Hazelden Foundation, 1987.

Bill B. *Compulsive Overeater*. Minneapolis: CompCare, 1981.

Birnbaum, Jean. *Men Who Rape: The Psychology of the Offender*. New York: Plenum Press, 1979.

Black, Claudia. *It Will Never Happen to Me*. Denver, Colo.: Medical Administration Co., 1982.

Bowlby, John. *Loss, Sadness, and Depression*. New York: Basic Books, 1980.

Bradshaw, John. *Homecoming: Reclaiming and Championing Your Inner Child*. New York: Bantam, 1990.

————. *Bradshaw On: The Family*. Deerfield Beach, Fla.:

Health Communications, 1988.

———. *Healing the Shame That Binds You*. Deerfield Beach, Fla.: Health Communications, 1988.

Brownmiller, Susan. *Against Their Will: Men, Women, and Rape*. Toronto: Bantam, 1975.

Califia, Pat. *Sapphistry. The Book of Lesbian Sexuality*. Tallahassee, Fla.: Naiad Press, 1988.

Carnes, Patrick. *Don't Call It Love: Recovery from Sexual Addiction*. New York: Bantam, 1991.

———. *Contrary to Love: Helping the Sexual Addict*. Minneapolis: CompCare, 1983.

———. *A Gentle Path through the Twelve Steps*. Minneapolis: CompCare, 1989.

———. *Counseling the Sexual Addict*. Minneapolis: Golden Valley Health Center, 1986.

———. *Out of the Shadows: Understanding Sexual Addiction*. Minneapolis: CompCare, 1983.

Carter, Steven, and Julia Sokol. *Men Who Can't Love. When A Man's Fear Makes Him Run from Commitment*. New York: Doubleday, 1987.

Caruso, Beverly. *The Impact of Incest*. (Pamphlet) Center City, Minn.: Hazelden Foundation, 1987.

Cermak, Timmen L. *Diagnosing and Treating Co-Dependency*. Minneapolis: Johnson Institute, 1986.

Covington, Stephanie, and Liana Beckett. *Leaving the Enchanted Forest: The Path from Relationship Addiction to Intimacy*. San Francisco: Harper and Row, 1988.

Cutler, W.B., C.R. Garcia, and D.A. Edward. *Menopause: A Guide for Women and Men Who Love Them*. New York: W.W. Norton, 1983.

Davis, Laura. *The Courage to Heal Workbook: For Women and Men Survivors of Child Sexual Abuse*. New York: Harper and Row, 1990.

Dobson, James. *Love Must Be Tough. New Hope for Families in Crisis*. Waco, Tex.: Worldbook, 1983.

Drew, Toby Rice. *Sex and the Sober Alcoholic*. Baltimore: Recovery Communications, 1988.

Earle, Ralph, and Gregory Crow. *Lonely All the Time: Recognizing, Understanding and Overcoming Sexual Addiction for Addicts and Co-Dependents*. New York: Pocket Books, 1989.

Eichenbaum, Louise and Susie Orbach. *Between Women.* New York: Penguin Books, 1987.

———. *What Do Women Want? Exploding the Myth of Dependency.* New York: Berkeley Books, 1983.

Forward, Susan. *Betrayal of Innocence.* New York: Penguin Books, 1988.

———. *Toxic Parents: Overcoming Their Hurtful Legacy and Reclaiming Your Life.* New York: Bantam, 1989.

Halpern, Howard. *How to Break Your Addiction to Another Person.* New York: Bantam Books/McGraw-Hill, 1982.

Hope and Recovery: A Twelve Step Guide for Healing from Compulsive Sexual Behavior. Minneapolis: CompCare, 1987.

Hunter, Mic. *Abused Boys: The Neglected Victims of Sexual Abuse.* Lexington, Mass.: Lexington Books, 1990.

Kaplan, Helen Singer. *Disorders of Sexual Desire and Other New Concepts and Techniques in Sex Therapy.* New York: Brunner/Mazel, 1979.

———. *Disorders of Sexual Desire.* New York: Brunner/Mazel, 1979.

———. *Sexual Aversion, Sexual Phobias and Panic Disorders.* New York: Brunner/Mazel, 1987.

Kasl, Charlotte. *Women, Sex and Addiction.* New York: Harper and Row, 1990.

Kritsberg, Wayne. *The Adult Children of Alcoholics Syndrome: From Discovery to Recovery.* Pompano Beach, Fla.: Health Communications, 1985.

Leiblum, Sandra R. and Raymond C. Rosen. *Sexual Desire Disorders.* New York: Guilford Press, 1988.

Leonard, Linda Schierse. *The Wounded Woman: Healing the Father/Daughter Relationship.* Boulder, Colo.: Shambhala, 1982.

Lew, Mike. *Victims No Longer: Men Recovering from Incest and Other Sexual Child Abuse.* New York: Harper and Row, 1989.

Maltz, W., and B. Holman. *Incest and Sexuality: A Guide to Understanding and Healing.* Lexington, Mass.: D.C. Heath, 1987.

Middleton-Moz, Jan and Lorie Dwinell. *After the Tears, Reclaiming the Personal Loses of Childhood.* Pompano Beach, Fla.: Health Communications, 1986.

Milkman, Harvey B., and Stanley G. Sunderwirth. *Craving for Ecstacy: The Consciousness and Chemistry of Escape.* Lexington, Mass.: Lexington Books, 1987.

Morris, Michelle. *If I Could Die Before I Wake*. Los Angeles: Jeremy Tarcher, 1982.

Norwood, Robin, *Women Who Love Too Much*. New York: Pocket Books, 1985.

Orbach, Susie. *Hunger Strike: The Anorexic Struggle as a Metaphor for Our Age*. New York: W.W. Norton, 1986.

Peele, Stanton. *Love and Addiction*. New York: Signet, 1976.

Powell, David J., ed. *Alcoholism and Sexual Dysfunction*. Binghamton, N.Y. Haworth Press, 1984.

Recovery Publications. *The Twelve Steps for Adult Children*. San Diego: 1987.

Russinoff, Penelope. *Why Do I Think I Am Nothing without a Man?* Toronto: Bantam, 1982.

Sandmaier, Marilyn. *The Invisible Alcoholics: Women and Alcohol Abuse in America*. New York: McGraw-Hill, 1981.

Schaef, Anne Wilson. *When Society Becomes an Addict*. San Francisco: Harper and Row, 1987.

Schneider, Jennifer. *Back from Betrayal: Recovery from His Affairs*. San Francisco: Harper/Hazelden Books, 1988.

Sex and Love Addicts Anonymous. *The Basic Text for the Augustine Fellowship*. Boston: Sex and Love Addicts Anonymous, Fellowship-Wide Services, 1986.

Sexaholics Anonymous. Essay Literature, P.O. Box 300, Simi Valley, Calif. 93062, 1984.

SLAA, Sex and Love Addicts Anonymous. Van Nuys, Calif.: World Service Office, 1982.

Shaffer, Brenda. *Is It Love or Is It Addiction?* New York: Harper/Hazelden, 1987.

Subby, Robert. *Lost in the Shuffle, The Co-dependent Reality*. Pompano Beach, Fla.: Health Communications, 1987.

What Everyone Needs to Know about Sex Addiction. Anonymous. Minneapolis: CompCare, 1989.

Whitfield, Charles L. *Healing the Child Within*. Pompano Beach, Fla.: Health Communications, 1987.

Wills-Brandon, Carla. *Eat Like a Lady: Guide for Overcoming Bulimia*. Deerfield Beach, Fla.: Health Communications, 1989.

———. *Is It Love or Is It Sex?* Deerfield Beach, Fla.: Health Communications, 1989.

Wineburg, Martin and Collen Williams. *Male Homosexuals*,

Their Problems, and the Adaptations. New York: Oxford University Press, 1974.

Woititz, Janet Geringer. *Adult Children of Alcoholics.* Hollywood, Fla.: Health Communications, 1983.

———. *Healing Your Sexual Self.* Hollywood, Fla.: Health Communications, 1989.

Part III

Bach, G.R. and P. Wyden. *The Intimate Enemy: How to Fight Fair in Love and Marriage.* New York: Avon Books, 1981.

Barbach, Lonnie. *Erotic Interludes, Tales Told by Women.* New York: Doubleday, 1986.

———. *For Each Other.* New York: New American Library, 1982.

———. *For Yourself: The Fulfillment of Female Sexuality.* New York: Anchor Press, 1975.

Carrera, Michael. *Sexual Health for Men: Your A to Z Guide.* New York: Friedman Group Book, 1990.

Sexual Health for Women: Your A to Z Guide. New York: Friedman Group Book, 1990.

Brecher, Edward M. *Love, Sex, and Aging.* Boston: Little, Brown, 1984.

Castleman, Michael. *Sexual Solutions.* New York: Simon and Schuster, 1980.

Chia, Mantak and Maneewan. *Healing Love through the Tao—Cultivating Female Sexual Energy.* Huntington, N.Y.: Healing Tao Books, 1984.

Clark, Keith. *An Experience of Celibacy, A Creative Reflection on Intimacy, Loneliness, Sexuality, and Commitment.* Notre Dame, Ind.: Ave Maria Press, 1982.

Comfort, A. *The Joy of Sex.* New York: Crown, 1972.

———. *More Joy.* New York: Crown, 1974.

Downing, G. *The Massage Book.* New York: Random House, 1972.

Ferguson, Marilyn. *The Aquarian Conspiracy.* Los Angeles: Jeremy Tarcher, 1980.

Franklin, Steven and Jacqueline Franklin. *The Ultimate Kiss.* Los Angeles: Media Publications, 1982.

Friday, Nancy. *Forbidden Flowers, More Womens' Sexual Fantasies.* New York: Pocket Books, 1975.

————. *My Secret Garden*. New York: Pocket Books, 1973.

Garrison, Omar. *Tantra: The Yoga of Sex*. New York: Julian Press, 1964.

Harris, A. *Sexual Exercises for Women*. New York: Carroll and Graf Publishers, 1988.

Hartman, William and Marilyn Fithian. *Any Man Can: The Multiple Orgasmic Technique for Every Loving Man*. New York: St. Martin's Press, 1984.

Heiman, Julia R. and Joseph LoPiccolo. *Becoming Orgasmic*. New York: Prentice Hall, 1988.

Henderson, Julia. *The Lover Within: Opening to Sexual Energy*. Barrytown, N.Y.: Station Hill Press, 1986.

Kennedy, Adele P. and Susan Dean. *Touching for Pleasure: A Twelve Step Program for Sexual Enhancement*. Chatsworth, Calif.: Chatsworth Press, 1988.

Kitzinger, Sheila. *Woman's Experience of Sex: The Facts and Feelings of Female Sexuality at Every Stage of Life*. New York: Penguin Books, 1985.

Kline-Graber, Georgia, and Benjamin Graber. *A Guide to Sexual Satisfaction. Woman's Orgasm*. New York: Warner Books, 1975.

LeBoyer, Frederick. *Loving Hands*. New York: Alfred A. Knopf, 1979.

Lerner, Rokelle. *Affirmations for the Inner Child*. Hollywood, Fla.: Health Communications, 1990.

McCarthy, Barry. *Male Sexual Awareness: Increasing Sexual Satisfaction*. New York: Carroll and Graf, 1988.

McCarthy B., and E. McCarthy. *Couple Sexual Awareness: Building Sexual Happiness*. New York: Carroll and Graf, 1990.

————. *Sexual Awareness: Enhancing Sexual Pleasure*. New York: Carroll and Graf, 1984.

Mason, Terry, and Valerie G. Norman. *Making Love Again: Renewing Intimacy and Helping Your Man Overcome Impotency*. Chicago: Contemporary Books, 1988.

Masters, William H., and Virginia E. Johnson. *Human Sexual Inadequacy*. Boston: Little, Brown, 1982.

————. *Human Sexual Response*. Boston: Little, Brown, 1966.

————. "The Sexual Response Cycle of the Human Female. III. The Clitoris: Anatomic and Clinical Considerations." *Western*

Journal of Surgery, Obstetrics, and Gynecology 70, 1962.: 248-257.

Maxwell-Hudson, Clare. *The Complete Book of Massage*. New York: Random House, 1988.

Montagu, Ashley. *Touching*. New York: Harper and Row, 1971.

Nugent, Christopher. *Masks of Satan*. Atlanta: Christian Classics, 1989.

Rosenberg, Jack L. *Total Orgasm*. New York: Random House, 1973.

Rossi, William A. *The Sex Life of the Foot and Shoe*. New York: Ballantine Books, 1976.

Sex Information and Education Council of the U.S., Inc. (SIECUS). *SIECUS Report 18* (2), December 1989/January 1990.

Slattery, William J. *The Erotic Imagination: Sexual Fantasies of the Adult Male*. New York: Bantam, 1976.

Stewart, Jessica. *The Complete Manual of Sexual Positions*. Chatsworth, Calif.: Media Press, 1983.

Terry, Maury. *The Ultimate Evil*. New York: Bantam, 1989.

Wegscheider-Cruse, Sharon. *Choice Making: For Co-Dependents, Adult Children and Spirituality Seekers*. Pompano Beach, Fla.: Health Communications, 1987.

———. *Learning To Love Yourself. Finding Your Self Worth*. Pompano Beach, FL: Health Communications, 1987.

Woititz, Janet Geringer. *Struggle for Intimacy*. Pompano Beach, Fla.: Health Communications, 1985.

Yaffe, Maurice, and Elizabeth Fenwick. *Sexual Happiness for Men: A Practical Approach*. New York: Henry Holt and Co., 1988.

———. *Sexual Happiness for Women: A Practical Approach*. New York: Henry Holt and Co., 1988.

Young, C. *Self-Massage*. New York: Bantam, 1973.

Zilbergeld, Bernie. *Male Sexuality*. New York: Bantam, 1978.

General

Brecher, Edward M. *Love, Sex and Aging: A Consumer's Union Report*. Boston: Little, Brown, 1984.

Clark, Don. *The New Loving Someone Gay*. Berkeley, Calif.: Celestial Arts, 1987.

Dowling, Collette. *The Cinderella Complex: Woman's Hid-*

den Fear of Independence. New York: Pocket Books, 1981.

Goldberg, Herb. *The New Male/Female Relationship*. New York: William Morrow, 1983.

Kilmann, P.R., and Mills, K.H. *All about Sex Therapy*. New York: Plenum Press, 1983.

Kline, Nathan S. *From Sad to Glad*. New York: Ballantine: 1975.

Lerner, Harriet Goldhor. *The Dance of Anger: A Woman's Guide to Changing the Patterns of Intimate Relationships*. New York: Harper and Row, 1985.

Levine, Linda and Lonnie Barbach. *The Intimate Male: Candid Discussions about Women, Sex, and Relationships*. New York: Signet Books, 1983.

McNaught, Bryan. *On Being Gay—Thoughts of Family, Faith and Love*. New York: St. Martin's Press, 1988.

McWhirter, David P., and Mattison, Andrew M. *The Male Couple: How Relationships Develop*. Englewood Cliff, N.J. Prentice-Hall, 1984.

Miller, Alice. *Thou Shall Not Be Aware. Society's Betrayal of a Child*. New York: Meridian Books, 1986.

Oakley, Ray. *Drugs, Society, and Human Behavior*. St. Louis: C.V. Mosby, 1983.

Phelps, Stanlee, and Nancy Austin. *The Assertive Woman*. Fredricksburg, Va.: Books Crafter, 1975.

Rosellini, Gayle, and Mark Worden. *Barriers to Intimacy: For People Torn by Addiction and Compulsive Behavior*. New York: Ballantine/Recovery, 1989.

Ruben, Lillian. *Intimate Strangers: Men and Women Together*. New York: Harper and Row, 1983.

Silverstein, Charles. *Man to Man: Gay Couples in America*. New York: Simon and Schuster, 1981.

INDEX

A

AA *See* Alcoholics Anonymous; Twelve Steps
Abandonment, fear of and intimacy, 152
Abortion, 49
  scars and painful intercourse, 28
  shame, 9
Abstinence in recovery, purpose of, 68
  contract, 212-213, 264
  and sexuality, 148
Abuse *See also* Eating disorders
  child, 1, 15, 49, 84
  childhood, as root of sex addiction, 54
  childhood sexual, 54-55, 89--90
  childhood sexual, in sexual addiction, 59-60
  containment, 117
  emotional, 115
  ritual, 1, 84
  ritual and trauma response, 127-129
  sexual, covert and overt, 89
  and sexualization, 107-108
  unresolved, 28, 46
  verbal, 78
ACoA (Adult Children of Alcoholics, the organization). *See also* Adult children of alcoholics (individuals), 10
Addict. *See also* Sex; Alcohol; Cocaine
  romance, 36, 53-70
Addiction
  combination of, 2
  Consulting Corporation, 89
  and isolation, 69-70
  and isolation, cycle of, 61-62
  multiple is normative, 62-63
  object of, 54
  romance (defined), 53-54
  sex, 3, 6, 53-54 (defined)
  and sex, 4
  and sexual issues, 5
  versus healthy sexuality, 154-155
Addictive
  behaviors and sexual trouble, connection between, 3
  relationships, characteristics of, 261-263
  sexual behaviors, 31-34
Adolescence and same sex feelings, 35-36
Adult children of alcoholics (individuals). *See* ACoA, 1, 10, 13, 78
  abuse and sexualization, 107-108
  and aversion to sex, 103-104
  classic traits of, 101-107
  co-sex addiction, 108
  and excessive loyalty, 102
  and gender identity, 109-110
  and impotence, 106-107
  and incest, 108-109
  and intimacy disorders, 102
  and intimate relationships, 99
  and lack of sexual desire, 103
  and other issues, 8

and retarded ejaculation, 30
and sexual addiction, 107-110
and survival mechanisms and sexual development, 100
and taking blame, 102
and vaginismus, 104-105
and virginity, primary and secondary, 104
Affairs, 12
  extramarital, and sex addiction, 56-57
Affection, 213
Affirmations, 184
  and power of positive thinking, 290
AIDS, 131-132, 169-170. *See also* Sexually transmitted diseases
  and anal intercourse, 159
  Hot Line, 170
Al-Anon, 10, 81
Alcohol and women's mortality, 48
Alcohol, 8, 12, 26
  and contraceptives, 48
  dependency and cross dressing, 44-45
  and emotional issues, 48-50
  and gynecological problems, 48
  hormones and sexual functioning, 167
  impairment from, 42
  and menses, 48
  metabolizing by women, 48
  physiological effects of on women, 48
  and sexual activity, 41-42
  women's tolerance of, 48
Alcoholic, 1, 10
  and gay, 133-134
  gay women, 136
Alcoholism, 5, 11
  disease of (chart), 256-257
  and impotence, 29
  and premature ejaculation, 29
  and romance addiction, 67
Altered state of chemical dependency, 40
Amphetamines, 26, 43
Amyl nitrite, 44
Anal intercourse, 159
Anger, 26, 28, 47, 101, 132. *See also* Feelings; Rageaholic
  dos and don'ts, 287-289
Anorexia Nervosa, 78, 87, 88, 92, 167, 274-275 (chart)
  diagnostic criteria for, 267
  and romance addiction, 66
Antihypertensives, 252-253
Anus, manual stimulation of, 232-233
Apathy, 43
Aphorisms, inadequacy of, 8
Ask Yourself questionnaire, 251-252
Assertion skills, lack of, 29

B

Balanced life, importance of, 184-185
Barbiturates. *See* Depressants

Becoming Orgasmic, J. Heiman and J. LoPiccolo, 240
Behavior
  addictive, 8
  addictive, revealing combination of, 9
  insane, 244
  therapy, 4
Beliefs, rigid, 15
Benzopyrene in marijuana, 43
Bestiality, 32-33
  and sex addiction, 59
Biological
  issues, sexual function and sexuality, 165-167
  mood disorder, 48
Birth
  control, 170-172
  defects, 43, 44
Blackouts, 11
Blood pressure
  high, and impotence, 29
  and inhalants, 44
Body
  chemical high (romance addict), 36
  distortions, 44, 141
  image exercises, 196-197
  as temple, 187
Bondage and sex addiction, 59
Bonds, healthy, 1
Boundaries, 214
  and eating disorders, 89
  and self-awareness, 194-195
  in sex and romance addiction, 69
Bradshaw, John, 75
Brain chemicals and sexual functioning, 43
Bulimia, 3, 80, 88, 92
  diagnostic criteria for, 268

C

Callaway Diet, C, The, W. Callaway, 88
Cancer chemotherapy agents, 255
Caretakers in codependency, 75
Carnes, Patrick, 55-61
Cervix, 158-159
Chemical dependency, 6, 9, 13
  diagnostic criteria for, 250
  as dissociative state, 15
  as intimacy disorder, 15
Child molestation. *See also* Abuse, child; Incest; Molestation, child
  characteristics of, 276
  and trauma response, 119-120
Chromosome damage and hallucinogens, 44
Cirrhosis and impotence, 29
Clitoris, 158
Cocaine, 1, 2, 5, 6, 26, 42-43, 62-63
  addiction, 246
  and brain chemicals, 43
  and sex, 2
  and sexual dysfunction, 40
Codependency, 1, 3, 6, 9-11, 13
  abandonment, fear of, 73
  action/reaction in, 73-74
  as ancient condition, 71-72
  characteristics of, 72-74